The Campus History Series

THE ART INSTITUTE OF FORT LAUDERDALE

1968–2008

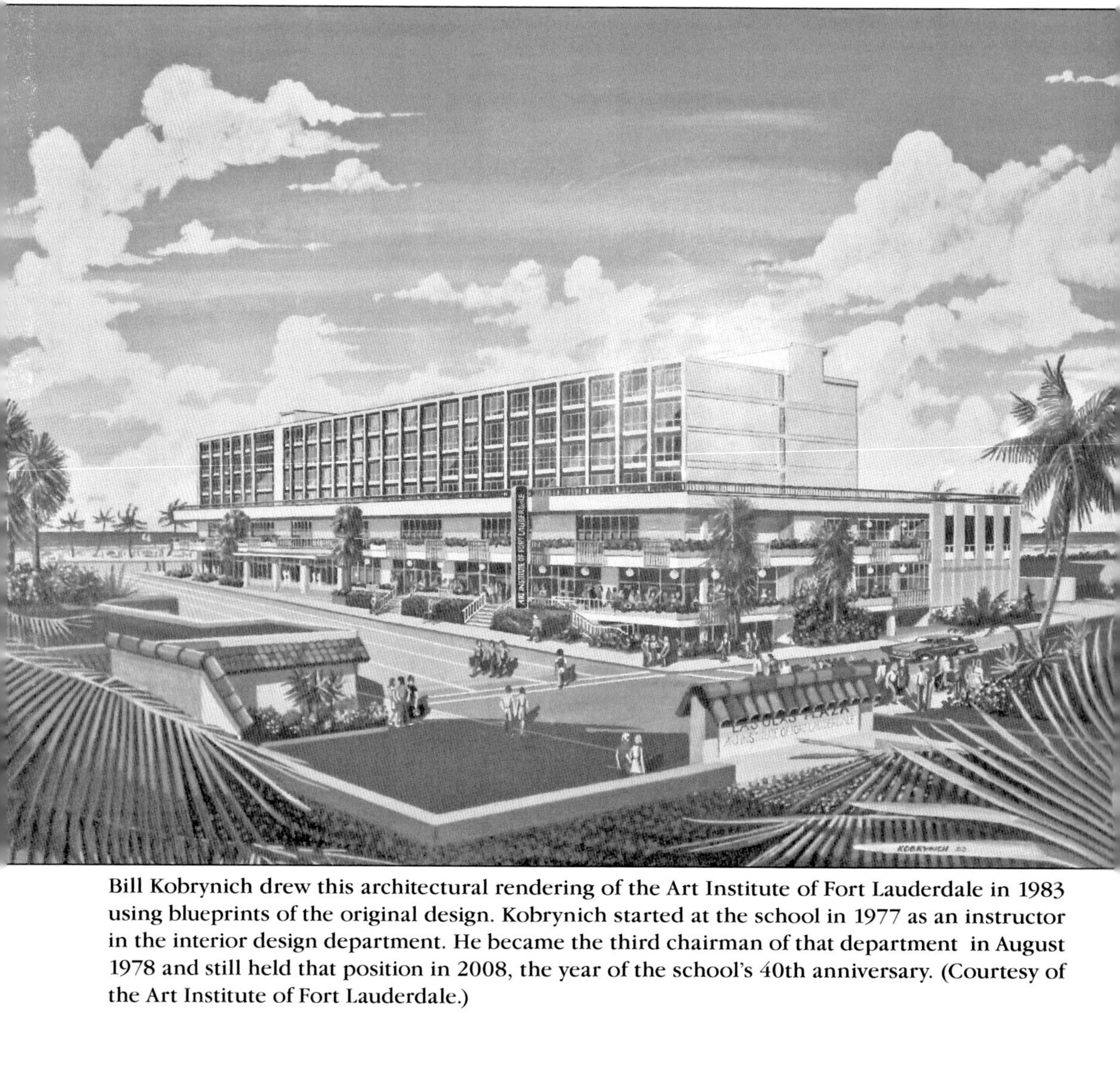

Bill Kobrynich drew this architectural rendering of the Art Institute of Fort Lauderdale in 1983 using blueprints of the original design. Kobrynich started at the school in 1977 as an instructor in the interior design department. He became the third chairman of that department in August 1978 and still held that position in 2008, the year of the school's 40th anniversary. (Courtesy of the Art Institute of Fort Lauderdale.)

On the Cover: The Art Institute of Fort Lauderdale opened on September 16, 1968. Located at 3000 East Las Olas Boulevard, the school was just west of the Atlantic Ocean. Originally, the Art Institute of Fort Lauderdale occupied 5,000 square feet in the northwest section of the Oceanside Holiday Inn. (Courtesy of the Art Institute of Fort Lauderdale.)

The Campus History Series

THE ART INSTITUTE OF FORT LAUDERDALE 1968–2008

DAVID WALCZAK, PH.D., AND MONIKA REUTER, PH.D.

ARCADIA PUBLISHING

ISBN 978-0-7385-5442-6

Published by Arcadia Publishing
Charleston SC, Chicago IL, Portsmouth NH, San Francisco CA

Printed in the United States of America

Library of Congress Catalog Card Number: 2008924878

For all general information contact Arcadia Publishing at:
Telephone 843-853-2070
Fax 843-853-0044
E-mail sales@arcadiapublishing.com
For customer service and orders:
Toll-Free 1-888-313-2665

Visit us on the Internet at www.arcadiapublishing.com

To those who built a school: the faculty, staff, and graduates

CONTENTS

ACKNOWLEDGMENTS

We would like to offer a very special thank you to communications director Arlene Wites, who allowed us to look through nearly 10 years of photographs taken by her and her staff. This book would not have been possible otherwise.

Bill Kobrynich, Jodi Berkshire, and Kathy Colussy not only supplied photographs, but also made the school's history come alive for us. Gary Tepper and Ms. V. also helped us understand the history of this school.

Merrilyn C. Rathbun, research director at the Fort Lauderdale Historical Society's Hoch Heritage Center, specifically its Gene Hyde Collection, provided important historical photographs, as did researchers at the Florida Memory Project and curator Denyse Cunningham at the Broward County Historical Commission.

The skill, talent, and creativity of Artemis student Marinés Espinoza and the knowledge and experience of Artemis director and instructor Paul Kane combined to reproduce the high quality images provided to Arcadia Publishing. Thanks for making it possible for us to spend most of our time gathering and analyzing pictures, and for making the technical process easy, fun, and enjoyable.

We are indebted to both Dr. Kristin Berkey-Abbott and Shefali Choksi for their outstanding editing skills.

Thank you to the following people who also helped make this book a reality: RoxeAnne Apperson, Norma Ayee, Peter Babcock, Brett Baker, Marnie Betz, Andy Bing, Lauren Bobier, Rick Boggs, Mimi Botscheller, Denise and Paolo Caliari, Michael Carnegie, Edward Cayia, Kate Crawford, Luke Cunningham, Joe Del Sordo, Rachel Feinleib, Sheila Getman, Rosita Hurtado, Vicky Izlar, Michael Kain, Kate Kellett, Spencer Kerrigan, Dorothy Kurki, Barbara Lang, Melanie Levi, Winston Menish, Suzanne Morrison-Williams, Alicia Nestor, Lorraine Nitabach, Susan Pawela, Heather Payne, Dr. Amy Phillips, Peter Primak, Suean Minahan, Sandra Robinson, Debbie Rose Myers, Felicia Raia Blanksi, Richard Rostron, LuWin Sanchez, Rex Shaw, Brenda Sneathen-Mattox, Daniela Stolk, Gary Tepper, Donna Thomas, Lorena Thurman, Ms. V., Val Vigil, Jane Vigna, Brad Waterman, Laura Waterman, Stacy Wolfe, Brian Wood, Dan Wood, and Catherine Ziegler.

None of this would have been possible without school president Chuck Nagele and the support of the executive committee members: Lisa Whitelock, Eileen Northrop, Maria Barron, Ed Galizia, Wendy Wagner, and Kathy Deaner.

Unless otherwise noted, the pictures included in this book appear courtesy of the Art Institute of Fort Lauderdale.

INTRODUCTION

Both Morocco's University of Al-Karaouine, founded in 856 AD, and Al-Azhar University in Cairo, where the first lecture was given in 975 AD, claim to be the oldest institution of higher learning in the world. The University of Bologna in Italy, established in 1088, is said to be Europe's oldest, while Harvard dates back to 1636. By comparison, the Art Institute of Fort Lauderdale is in its infancy, but it certainly has grown quickly in just 40 years.

The Art Institute of Fort Lauderdale opened its doors to 55 students on September 16, 1968. The school offered diplomas that could be earned in 24 months in commercial art, interior design, and fashion illustration. It was founded as a subsidiary of the Art Institute of Pittsburgh, with Mark K. Wheeler as the school's first president. The new institution of higher learning was originally housed in the now-defunct Oceanside Holiday Inn, where Las Olas Boulevard meets the Atlantic Ocean, in a city referred to as the "Venice of America." Like the colors blending together on the palette of an artist, the combination of an exotic location; warm, sunny days; palm tree–lined beaches; soft sand; the inspiration, creativity, and talent of local, career-oriented residents; and, of course, the 1960s made 3000 East Las Olas Boulevard the perfect location for a commercial art and design school.

The school's mission was, and remains, to educate students interested in pursuing art and design-related careers. Taglines found in the school's catalogs over the years include "education that builds careers" and "what we teach works," illustrating this focus. As the 40th anniversary logo proudly states: "40 years of creative careers."

By 2008, the definition of creative careers has changed substantially. Students can enroll in 17 different programs awarding bachelor's and associate's degrees, as well as diplomas. The original commercial art program has broadened into three separate programs: illustration, graphic design, and advertising. The original fashion illustration program has split into fashion design and fashion merchandising. The interior design program has grown to become the largest department on campus today. During the past 40 years, the following additional programs have been added: animation, broadcasting, culinary arts, digital filmmaking and video production, game art and design, industrial design, interactive media design, photography, video production, visual effects and motion graphics, and yacht and marine design.

In all of these programs, the student-centered curriculum is competency based and guided by market forces. Practical, hands-on, real-life work experience is an essential part of each major. The school measures excellence in education by employment outcomes. Quarterly statistics show that since the mid-1990s, more than 90 percent of the school's graduates work in their field within six months of graduating. Students are the school's most important resource and its greatest achievement.

This book is divided into four chapters, each covering one decade, with competency-based, career-focused education as the major theme. Throughout the book, readers will find many illustrations of the successful translation of classroom instruction into real-life applications. One example is the annual fashion show, which has blossomed into one of south Florida's most popular events. Competency-based education also manifests itself through the many art and design competitions in which students participate. For example, student culinary teams compete and triumph with assured regularity, winning top honors in cooking competitions around the country. Another way students develop the skill sets necessary to succeed in their chosen career is through working on events in the community and for benevolent organizations. Graphic design students have created numerous posters for many special community events, including the Las Olas Wine and Food Festival, benefiting the American Lung Association of Florida; the Palm Beach Opera, on behalf of the Bonnet House; and the May 11, 2004, grand-opening celebration of the Ronald McDonald House in Fort Lauderdale. Students have also designed posters for the Fort Lauderdale Museum, the United Way, and the annual Winterfest Boat Parade.

When we first started to look for images that could tell the story of the early years of the Art Institute of Fort Lauderdale, it seemed that the school was not the subject of photographs because of the popularity of the surrounding sites, or it was the vantage point from which pictures of other popular attractions were taken. For example, we found pictures of the Elbo Room, many of which were taken from the school's original Oceanside Holiday Inn location across Las Olas Boulevard. The same is true for pictures taken of beautiful Fort Lauderdale Beach, either with or without students on spring break. When the school moved to its new location on Seventeenth Street, we found plenty of pictures of Ocean World, Pier 66, Port Everglades, and the beautiful homes and luxurious yachts on the many miles of interconnecting waterways that characterize Fort Lauderdale but none of the school.

There are many pictures of the school that have been published in local newspapers and magazines, but their quality did not satisfy the specifications for this book. We looked at literally thousands of pictures and still came away with only a partial history of the school. This book is not the definitive photo history of the Art Institute of Fort Lauderdale; rather it is a sample collection of reproducible images we have been able to assemble. We take full responsibility for all errors.

We hope this book lives up to the expectations of all who have been associated with the Art Institute of Fort Lauderdale during its short yet stellar maturation. We look forward to the next 40 years.

One

Beginnings

This chapter is about firsts: the Art Institute of Fort Lauderdale's first president, first location, first catalog, first curriculum, first instructors, first staff, first graduates, first facilities, and first decade. During the first 10 years, the school witnessed tremendous growth, from 55 students on the day it opened its doors to 800 students a decade later.

The school's original location was in the Oceanside Holiday Inn, located across the street from the beach. Mimi Botscheller, a graphic design and illustration instructor, started her 34-year career at the school running the student store. In an interview for the first issue of the alumni newsletter in 2001, Botscheller said, "It was very exciting to be part of such a revolutionary type of education where creativity flowed and the pioneering spirit of the school's creators, the Wheeler brothers, took the concept of preparing artists for the commercial work art force and made it a reality. Times were different then. Students and faculty could not escape the beach's spring break atmosphere. Students wore their bathing suits under their clothes to catch some quick rays between classes. There was no need for a clock back then. You could always tell it was 3:00 p.m. by the vibrating floor that pulsated with the daily wet T-shirt contest held in one of the hotel's three bars." My, how things have changed.

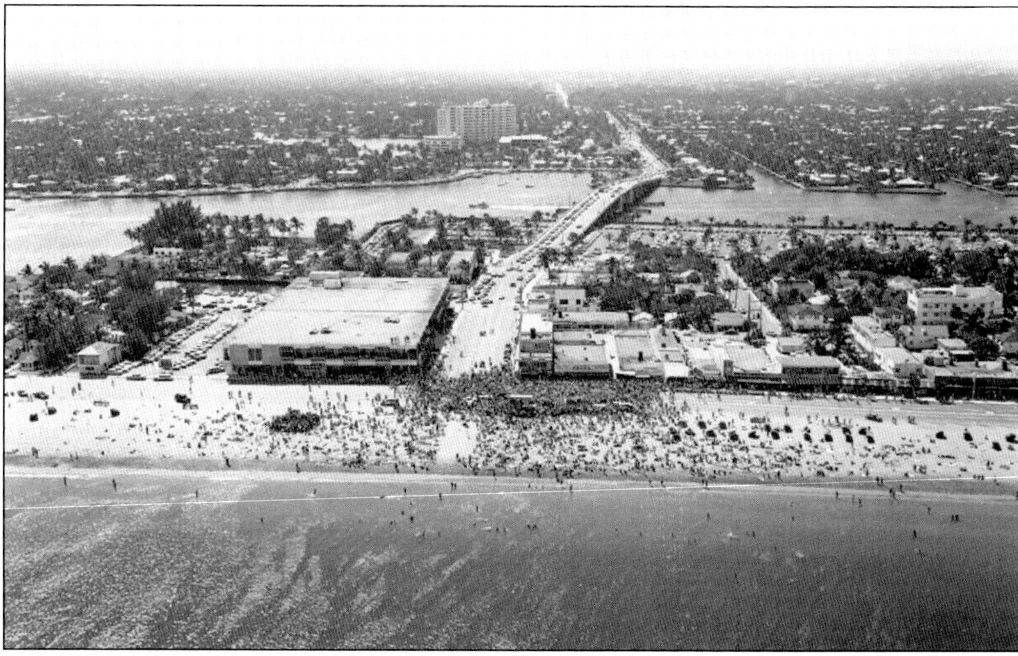

The Las Olas Plaza Shopping Center was built in the mid-1950s at the corner of Atlantic Boulevard (now A1A) and Las Olas Boulevard. The Franklin Simon department store, the Forum restaurant, Stephanie's Incorporated Women's Clothing, Casual-Aire Men's Apparel, and the Button Lounge were originally located in the shopping center. (Courtesy of the Fort Lauderdale Historical Society.)

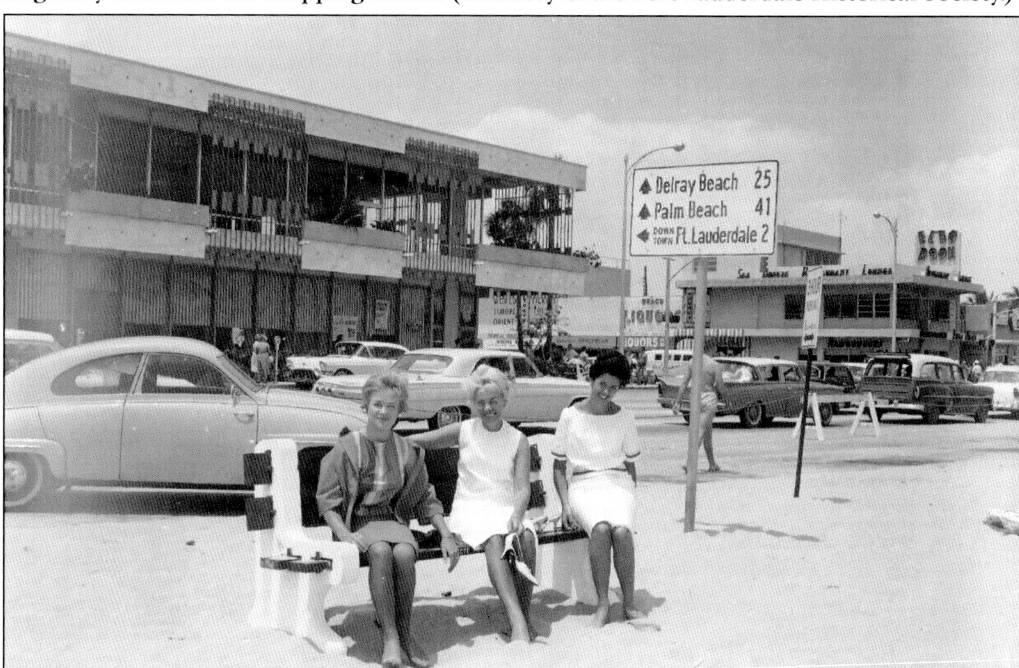

This 1962 photograph of three women on a bench shows the northeast corner of the Las Olas Plaza Shopping Center. The Elbo Room is in the background. (Courtesy of the Florida Memory Project.)

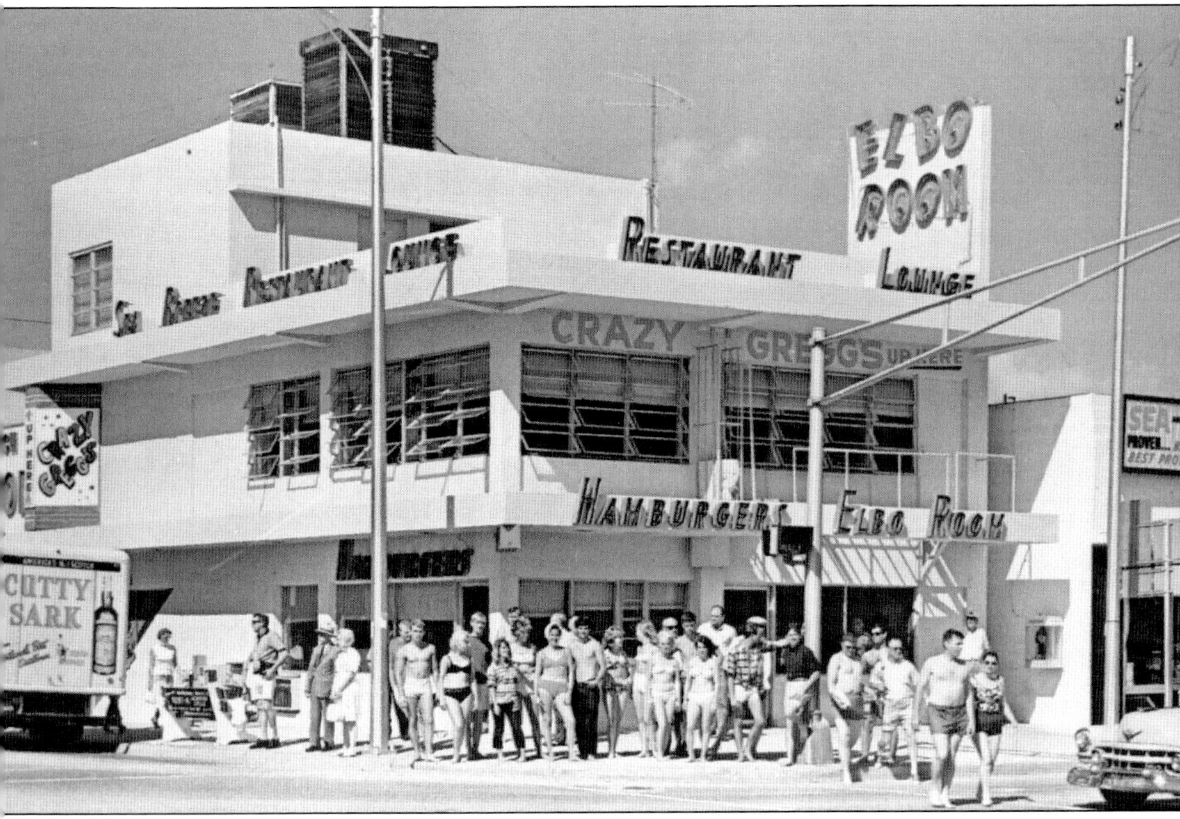

The Elbo Room restaurant and lounge was the destination of many students during spring break. The location was made famous by the 1963 movie *Where the Boys Are*, starring Connie Francis, Frank Gorshin, George Hamilton, Dolores Hart, Jim Hutton, Yvette Mimieux, Barbara Nichols, and Paula Prentiss. The Elbo Room was still at that same location in 2008. (Courtesy of the Fort Lauderdale Historical Society.)

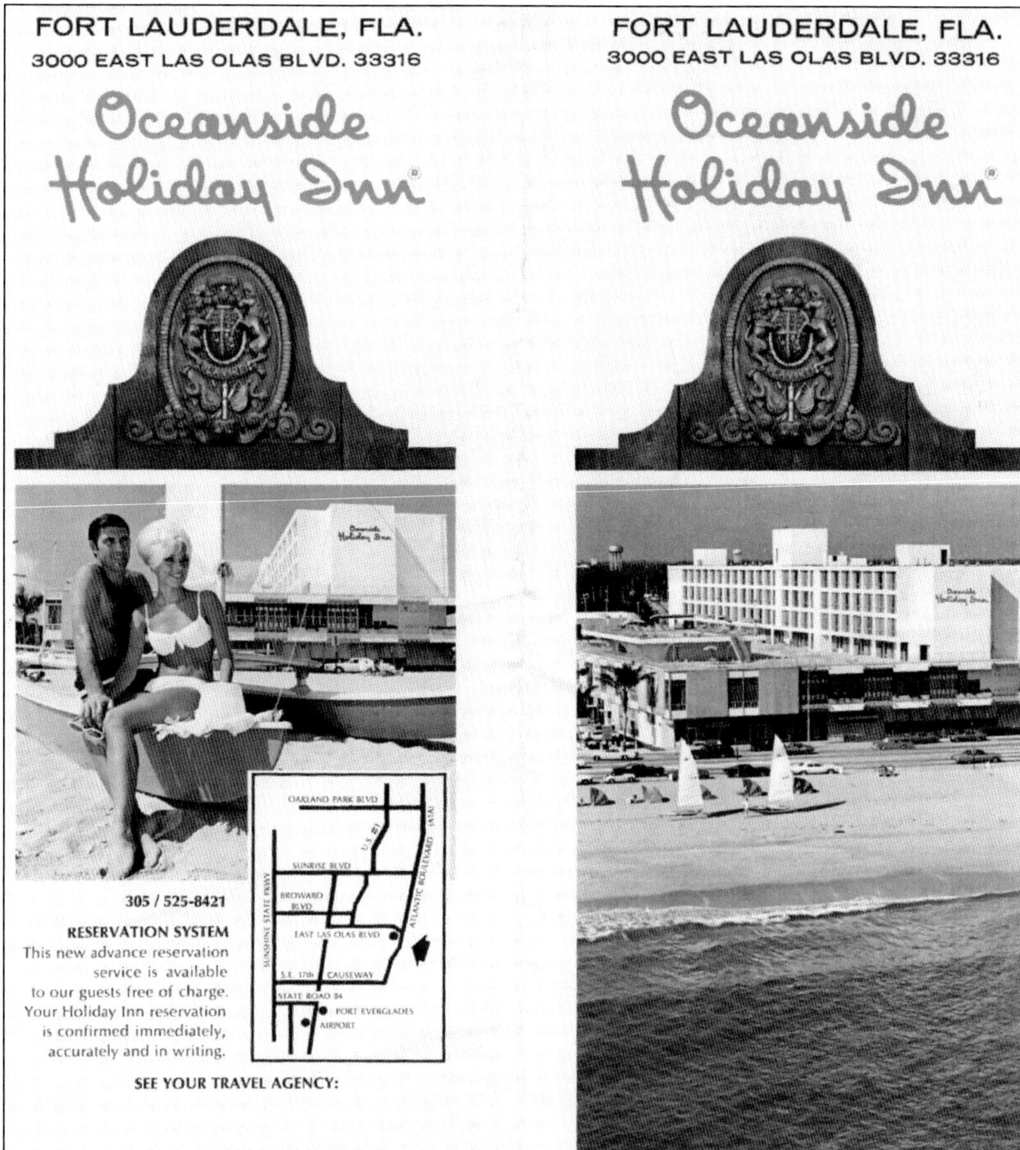

In the mid-1960s, a Holiday Inn was built on top of the Las Olas Plaza Shopping Center. Pictured here are the front and back covers of a brochure for the Oceanside Holiday Inn. The hotel provided 243 rooms, protected parking, screened sundecks, a rooftop pool, and 45,000 square feet of wind-screened terrace with food and lounge facilities. (Courtesy of the Fort Lauderdale Historical Society.)

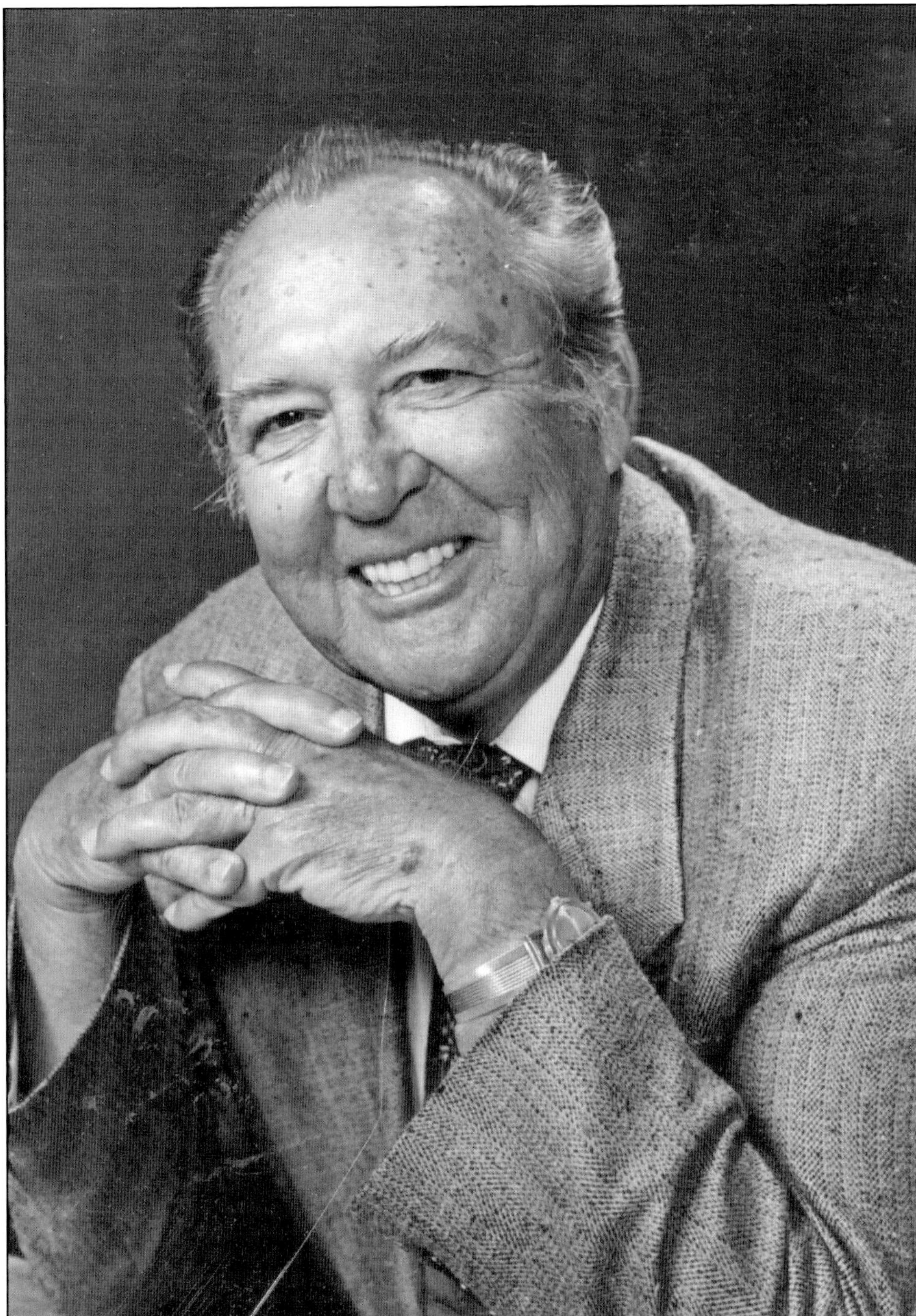

Here is a portrait of Mark K. Wheeler, the school's first president. Wheeler presided over the Fashion Institute of Pittsburgh. Mark's older brother, Earl, served as the president of the Art Institute of Pittsburgh. In the mid-1960s, Earl bought a small art guild on Las Olas Boulevard called the "Fashion Institute." Mark ran this school, which ultimately became the Art Institute of Fort Lauderdale.

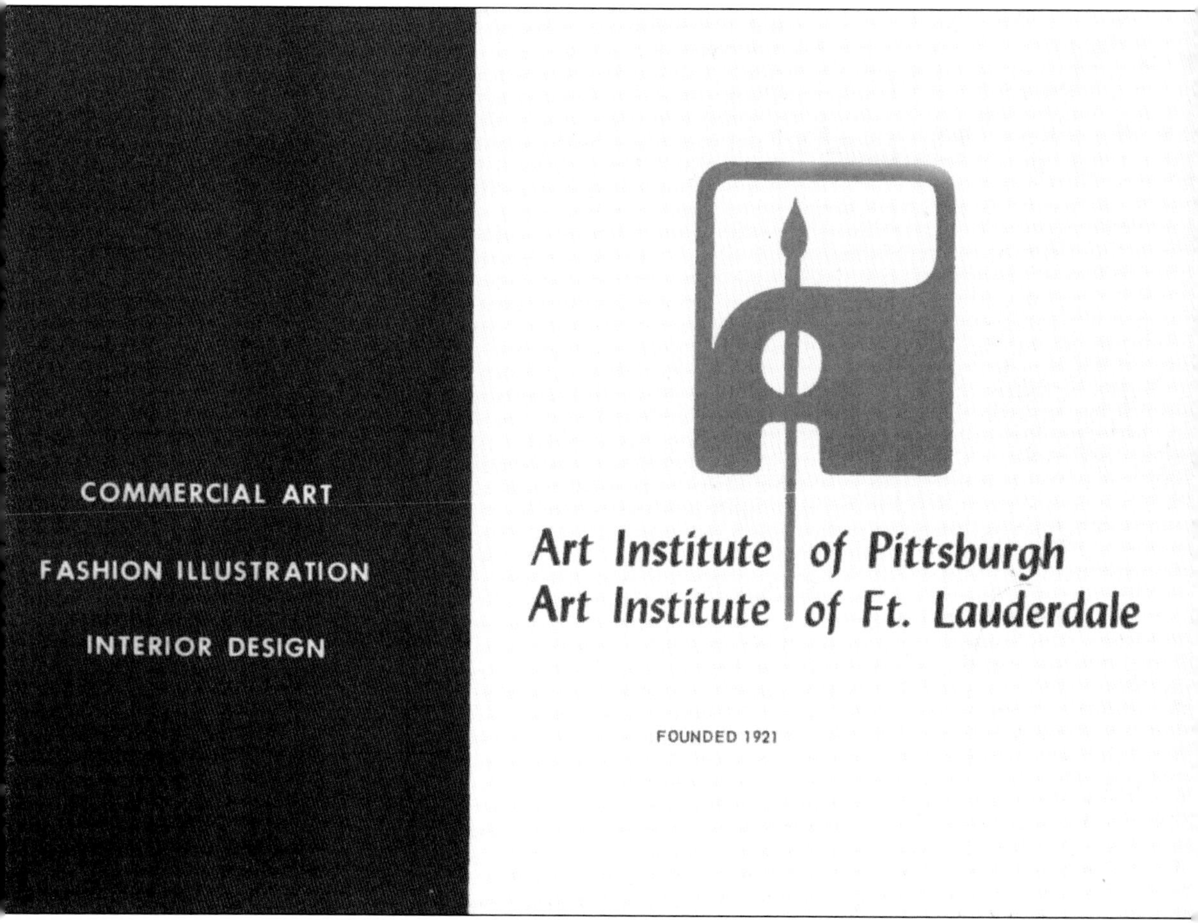

The first catalog of the Art Institute of Fort Lauderdale was the same as the Art Institute of Pittsburgh's catalog in 1968.

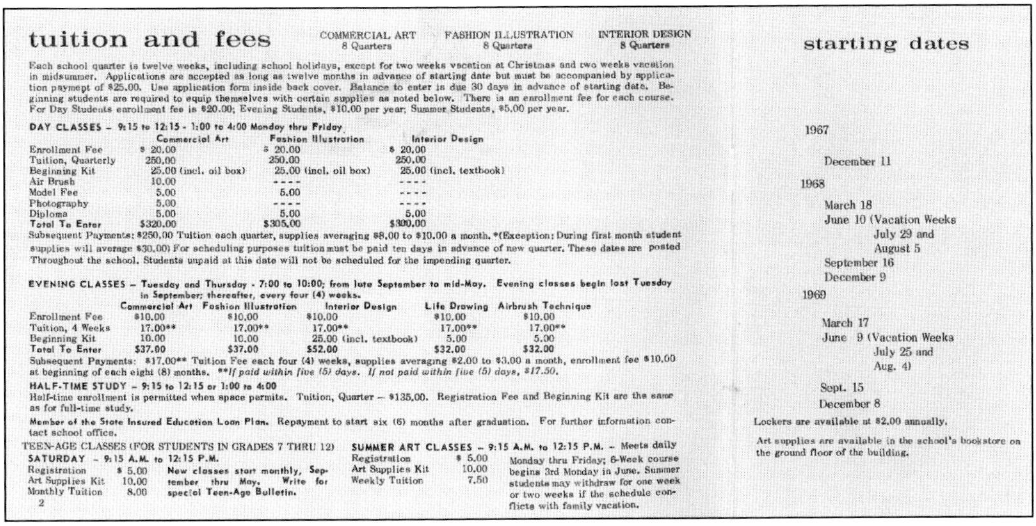

tuition and fees

COMMERCIAL ART 8 Quarters — FASHION ILLUSTRATION 8 Quarters — INTERIOR DESIGN 8 Quarters

Each school quarter is twelve weeks, including school holidays, except for two weeks vacation at Christmas and two weeks vacation in midsummer. Applications are accepted as long as twelve months in advance of starting date but must be accompanied by application paymept of $25.00. Use application form inside back cover. Balance to enter is due 30 days in advance of starting date. Beginning students are required to equip themselves with certain supplies as noted below. There is an enrollment fee for each course. For Day Students enrollment fee is $20.00; Evening Students, $10.00 per year; Summer Students, $5.00 per year.

DAY CLASSES – 9:15 to 12:15 - 1:00 to 4:00 Monday thru Friday

	Commercial Art	Fashion Illustration	Interior Design
Enrollment Fee	$ 20.00	$ 20.00	$ 20.00
Tuition, Quarterly	250.00	250.00	250.00
Beginning Kit	25.00 (incl. oil box)	25.00 (incl. oil box)	25.00 (incl. textbook)
Air Brush	10.00	----	----
Model Fee	5.00	5.00	----
Photography	5.00	----	----
Diploma	5.00	5.00	5.00
Total To Enter	$320.00	$305.00	$300.00

Subsequent Payments: $250.00 Tuition each quarter, supplies averaging $8.00 to $10.00 a month. *(Exception: During first month student supplies will average $30.00) For scheduling purposes tuition must be paid ten days in advance of new quarter. These dates are posted Throughout the school. Students unpaid at this date will not be scheduled for the impending quarter.

EVENING CLASSES – Tuesday and Thursday - 7:00 to 10:00; from late September to mid-May. Evening classes begin last Tuesday in September; thereafter, every four (4) weeks.

	Commercial Art	Fashion Illustration	Interior Design	Life Drawing	Airbrush Technique
Enrollment Fee	$10.00	$10.00	$10.00	$10.00	$10.00
Tuition, 4 Weeks	17.00**	17.00**	17.00**	17.00**	17.00**
Beginning Kit	10.00	10.00	25.00 (incl. textbook)	5.00	5.00
Total To Enter	$37.00	$37.00	$52.00	$32.00	$32.00

Subsequent Payments: $17.00** Tuition Fee each four (4) weeks, supplies averaging $2.00 to $3.00 a month, enrollment fee $10.00 at beginning of each eight (8) months. ***If paid within five (5) days. If not paid within five (5) days, $17.50.*

HALF-TIME STUDY – 9:15 to 12:15 or 1:00 to 4:00
Half-time enrollment is permitted when space permits. Tuition, Quarter — $135.00. Registration Fee and Beginning Kit are the same as for full-time study.

Member of the State Insured Education Loan Plan. Repayment to start six (6) months after graduation. For further information contact school office.

TEEN-AGE CLASSES (FOR STUDENTS IN GRADES 7 THRU 12)
SATURDAY – 9:15 A.M. to 12:15 P.M.

Registration	$ 5.00
Art Supplies Kit	10.00
Monthly Tuition	8.00

New classes start monthly, September thru May. Write for special Teen-Age Bulletin.

2

SUMMER ART CLASSES – 9:15 A.M. to 12:15 P.M. – Meets daily

Registration	$ 5.00
Art Supplies Kit	10.00
Weekly Tuition	7.50

Monday thru Friday; 6-Week course begins 3rd Monday in June. Summer students may withdraw for one week or two weeks if the schedule conflicts with family vacation.

starting dates

1967
December 11
1968
March 18
June 10 (Vacation Weeks
July 29 and
August 5
September 16
December 9
1969
March 17
June 9 (Vacation Weeks
July 25 and
Aug. 4)
Sept. 15
December 8

Lockers are available at $2.00 annually.

Art supplies are available in the school's bookstore on the ground floor of the building.

Tuition, fees, and starting dates are announced in the first catalog.

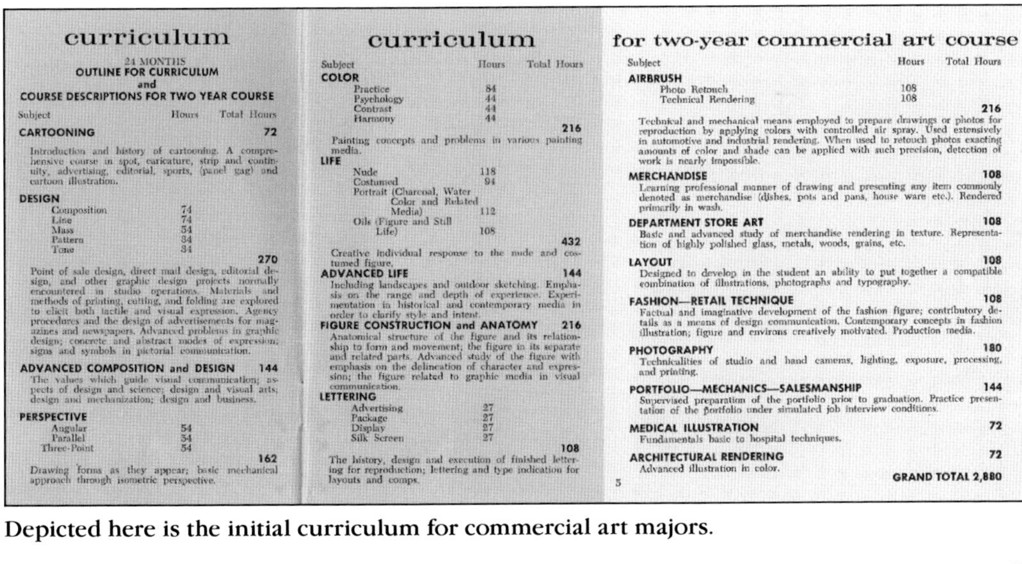

curriculum

24 MONTHS
OUTLINE FOR CURRICULUM and COURSE DESCRIPTIONS FOR TWO YEAR COURSE

Subject	Hours	Total Hours
CARTOONING		**72**

Introduction and history of cartooning. A comprehensive course in spot, caricature, strip and continuity, advertising, editorial, sports, (panel gag) and cartoon illustration.

Subject	Hours	Total Hours
DESIGN		
Composition	74	
Line	74	
Mass	54	
Pattern	34	
Tone	34	
		270

Point of sale design, direct mail design, editorial design, and other graphic design projects normally encountered in studio operations. Materials and methods of printing, cutting, and folding are explored to elicit both tactile and visual expression. Agency procedures and the design of advertisements for magazines and newspapers. Advanced problems in graphic design; concrete and abstract modes of expression; signs and symbols in pictorial communication.

ADVANCED COMPOSITION and DESIGN **144**
The values which guide visual communication; aspects of design and science; design and visual arts; design and mechanization; design and business.

Subject	Hours	Total Hours
PERSPECTIVE		
Angular	54	
Parallel	54	
Three-Point	54	
		162

Drawing forms as they appear; basic mechanical approach through isometric perspective.

curriculum

Subject	Hours	Total Hours
COLOR		
Practice	84	
Psychology	44	
Contrast	44	
Harmony	44	
		216

Painting concepts and problems in various painting media.

Subject	Hours	Total Hours
LIFE		
Nude	118	
Costumed	94	
Portrait (Charcoal, Water Color and Related Media)	112	
Oils (Figure and Still Life)	108	
		432

Creative individual response to the nude and costumed figure.

ADVANCED LIFE **144**
Including landscapes and outdoor sketching. Emphasis on the range and depth of experience. Experimentation in historical and contemporary media in order to clarify style and intent.

FIGURE CONSTRUCTION and ANATOMY **216**
Anatomical structure of the figure and its relationship to form and movement; the figure in its separate and related parts. Advanced study of the figure with emphasis on the delineation of character and expression; the figure related to graphic media in visual communication.

Subject	Hours	Total Hours
LETTERING		
Advertising	27	
Package	27	
Display	27	
Silk Screen	27	
		108

The history, design and execution of finished lettering for reproduction; lettering and type indication for layouts and comps.

for two-year commercial art course

Subject	Hours	Total Hours
AIRBRUSH		
Photo Retouch	108	
Technical Rendering	108	
		216

Technical and mechanical means employed to prepare drawings or photos for reproduction by applying colors with controlled air spray. Used extensively in automotive and industrial rendering. When used to retouch photos exacting amounts of color and shade can be applied with such precision, detection of work is nearly impossible.

MERCHANDISE **108**
Learning professional manner of drawing and presenting any item commonly denoted as merchandise (dishes, pots and pans, house ware etc.). Rendered primarily in wash.

DEPARTMENT STORE ART **108**
Basic and advanced study of merchandise rendering in texture. Representation of highly polished glass, metals, woods, grains, etc.

LAYOUT **108**
Designed to develop in the student an ability to put together a compatible combination of illustrations, photographs and typography.

FASHION—RETAIL TECHNIQUE **108**
Factual and imaginative development of the fashion figure; contributory details as a means of design communication. Contemporary concepts in fashion illustration; figure and environs creatively motivated. Production media.

PHOTOGRAPHY **180**
Technicalities of studio and hand cameras, lighting, exposure, processing, and printing.

PORTFOLIO—MECHANICS—SALESMANSHIP **144**
Supervised preparation of the portfolio prior to graduation. Practice presentation of the portfolio under simulated job interview conditions.

MEDICAL ILLUSTRATION **72**
Fundamentals basic to hospital techniques.

ARCHITECTURAL RENDERING **72**
Advanced illustration in color.

5

GRAND TOTAL 2,880

Depicted here is the initial curriculum for commercial art majors.

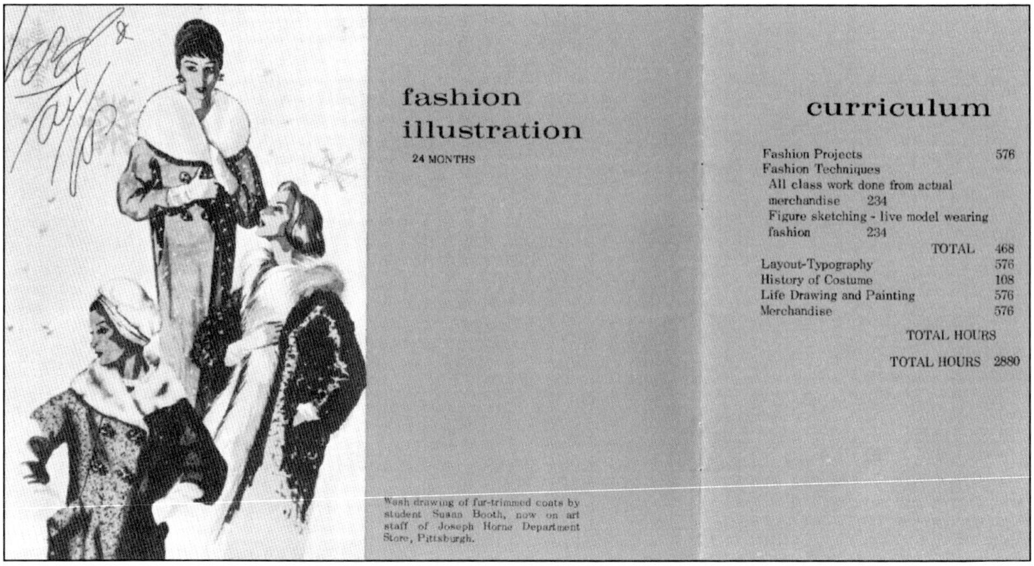

fashion illustration

24 MONTHS

Wash drawing of fur-trimmed coats by student Susan Booth, now on art staff of Joseph Horne Department Store, Pittsburgh.

curriculum

Fashion Projects	576
Fashion Techniques	
All class work done from actual merchandise 234	
Figure sketching - live model wearing fashion 234	
TOTAL	468
Layout-Typography	576
History of Costume	108
Life Drawing and Painting	576
Merchandise	576
TOTAL HOURS	
TOTAL HOURS	2880

The original curriculum for the fashion illustration degree shows some of the fashion styles at that time.

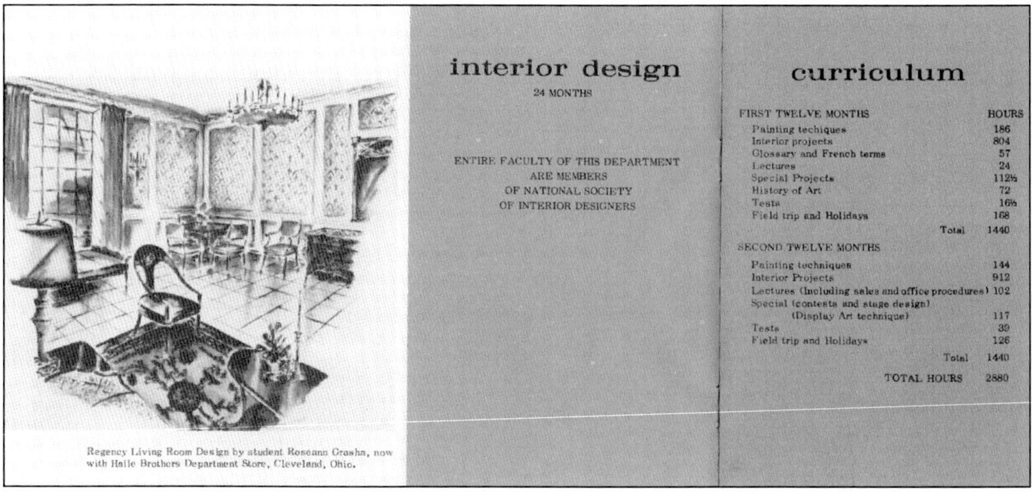

interior design

24 MONTHS

ENTIRE FACULTY OF THIS DEPARTMENT ARE MEMBERS OF NATIONAL SOCIETY OF INTERIOR DESIGNERS

Regency Living Room Design by student Roseann Grasha, now with Halle Brothers Department Store, Cleveland, Ohio.

curriculum

FIRST TWELVE MONTHS	HOURS
Painting techiques	186
Interior projects	804
Glossary and French terms	57
Lectures	24
Special Projects	112½
History of Art	72
Tests	16½
Field trip and Holidays	168
Total	1440
SECOND TWELVE MONTHS	
Painting techniques	144
Interior Projects	912
Lectures (Including sales and office procedures)	102
Special (contests and stage design) (Display Art technique)	117
Tests	39
Field trip and Holidays	126
Total	1440
TOTAL HOURS	2880

The first interior design curriculum breaks down course requirements for the two-year degree.

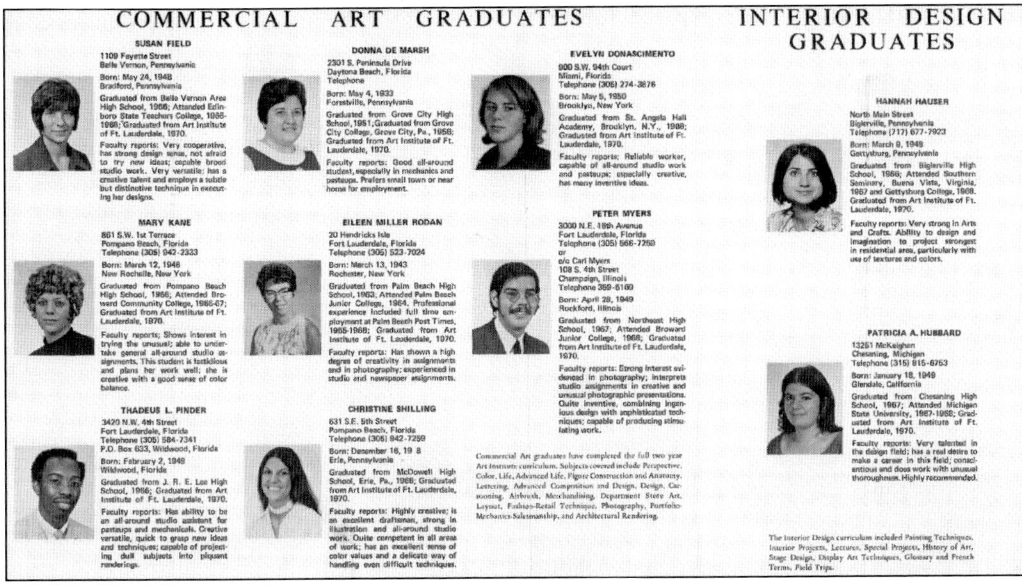

COMMERCIAL ART GRADUATES

SUSAN FIELD
1109 Fayette Street
Belle Vernon, Pennsylvania
Born: May 24, 1948
Bradford, Pennsylvania
Graduated from Belle Vernon Area High School, 1966; Attended Edinboro State Teachers College, 1966-1968; Graduated from Art Institute of Ft. Lauderdale, 1970.
Faculty reports: Very cooperative, has strong design sense, not afraid to try new ideas; capable broad studio work. Very versatile; has a creative talent and employs a subtle but distinctive technique in executing her designs.

MARY KANE
861 S.W. 1st Terrace
Pompano Beach, Florida
Telephone (305) 942-2333
Born: March 12, 1948
New Rochelle, New York
Graduated from Pompano Beach High School, 1966; Attended Broward Community College, 1966-67; Graduated from Art Institute of Ft. Lauderdale, 1970.
Faculty reports; Shows interest in trying the unusual; able to undertake general all-around studio assignments. This student is fastidious and plans her work well; she is creative with a good sense of color balance.

THADEUS L. PINDER
3420 N.W. 4th Street
Fort Lauderdale, Florida
Telephone (305) 584-7341
P.O. Box 633, Wildwood, Florida
Born: February 2, 1949
Wildwood, Florida
Graduated from J. R. E. Lee High School, 1966; Graduated from Art Institute of Ft. Lauderdale, 1970.
Faculty reports: Has ability to be an all-around studio assistant for pasteups and mechanicals. Creative versatile, quick to grasp new ideas and techniques; capable of projecting dull subjects into piquant renderings.

DONNA DE MARSH
2301 S. Peninsula Drive
Daytona Beach, Florida
Telephone
Born: May 4, 1933
Forestville, Pennsylvania
Graduated from Grove City High School, 1951; Graduated from Grove City College, Grove City, Pa., 1956; Graduated from Art Institute of Ft. Lauderdale, 1970.
Faculty reports: Good all-around student, especially in mechanics and pasteups. Prefers small town or near home for employment.

EILEEN MILLER RODAN
20 Hendricks Isle
Fort Lauderdale, Florida
Telephone (305) 523-7024
Born: March 13, 1943
Rochester, New York
Graduated from Palm Beach High School, 1963; Attended Palm Beach Junior College, 1964. Professional experience included full time employment at Palm Beach Post Times, 1965-1968; Graduated from Art Institute of Ft. Lauderdale, 1970.
Faculty reports: Has shown a high degree of creativity in assignments and in photography; experienced in studio and newspaper assignments.

CHRISTINE SHILLING
631 S.E. 5th Street
Pompano Beach, Florida
Telephone (305) 942-7259
Born: December 16, 19 8
Erie, Pennsylvania
Graduated from McDowell High School, Erie, Pa., 1966; Graduated from Art Institute of Ft. Lauderdale, 1970.
Faculty reports: Highly creative; is an excellent draftsman, strong in illustration and all-around studio work. Quite competent in all areas of work; has an excellent sense of color values and a delicate way of handling even difficult techniques.

EVELYN DONASCIMENTO
900 S.W. 94th Court
Miami, Florida
Telephone (305) 274-3876
Born: May 5, 1950
Brooklyn, New York
Graduated from St. Angela Hall Academy, Brooklyn, N.Y., 1968; Graduated from Art Institute of Ft. Lauderdale, 1970.
Faculty reports; Reliable worker, capable of all-around studio work and pasteups; especially creative, has many inventive ideas.

PETER MYERS
3000 N.E. 18th Avenue
Fort Lauderdale, Florida
Telephone (305) 566-7259
or
c/o Carl Myers
108 S. 4th Street
Champaign, Illinois
Telephone 359-6169
Born: April 28, 1949
Rockford, Illinois
Graduated from Northeast High School, 1967; Attended Broward Junior College, 1968; Graduated from Art Institute of Ft. Lauderdale, 1970.
Faculty reports: Strong interest evidenced in photography; interprets studio assignments in creative and unusual photographic presentations. Quite inventive, combining ingenious design with sophisticated techniques; capable of producing stimulating work.

Commercial Art graduates have completed the full two year Art Institute curriculum. Subjects covered include Perspective, Color, Life, Advanced Life, Figure Construction and Anatomy, Lettering, Advanced Composition and Design, Design, Cartooning, Airbrush, Merchandising, Department Store Art, Layout, Fashion-Retail Technique, Photography, Portfolio-Mechanics-Salesmanship, and Architectural Rendering.

INTERIOR DESIGN GRADUATES

HANNAH HAUSER
North Main Street
Biglerville, Pennsylvania
Telephone (717) 677-7923
Born: March 9, 1948
Gettysburg, Pennsylvania
Graduated from Biglerville High School, 1966; Attended Southern Seminary, Buena Vista, Virginia, 1967 and Gettysburg College, 1968. Graduated from Art Institute of Ft. Lauderdale, 1970.
Faculty reports: Very strong in Arts and Crafts. Ability to design and imagination to project strongest in residential area, particularly with use of textures and colors.

PATRICIA A. HUBBARD
13251 McKeighan
Chesaning, Michigan
Telephone (315) 815-6753
Born: January 18, 1949
Glendale, California
Graduated from Chesaning High School, 1967; Attended Michigan State University, 1967-1968; Graduated from Art Institute of Ft. Lauderdale, 1970.
Faculty reports: Very talented in the design field; has a real desire to make a career in this field; conscientious and does work with unusual thoroughness. Highly recommended.

The Interior Design curriculum included Painting Techniques, Interior Projects, Lectures, Special Projects, History of Art, Stage Design, Display Art Techniques, Glossary and French Terms, Field Trips.

The date of December 1, 1970, marked the first graduating class in commercial art, interior design, and fashion illustration. Commercial art graduate Peter Myers became a faculty member at the school in advertising design several years later.

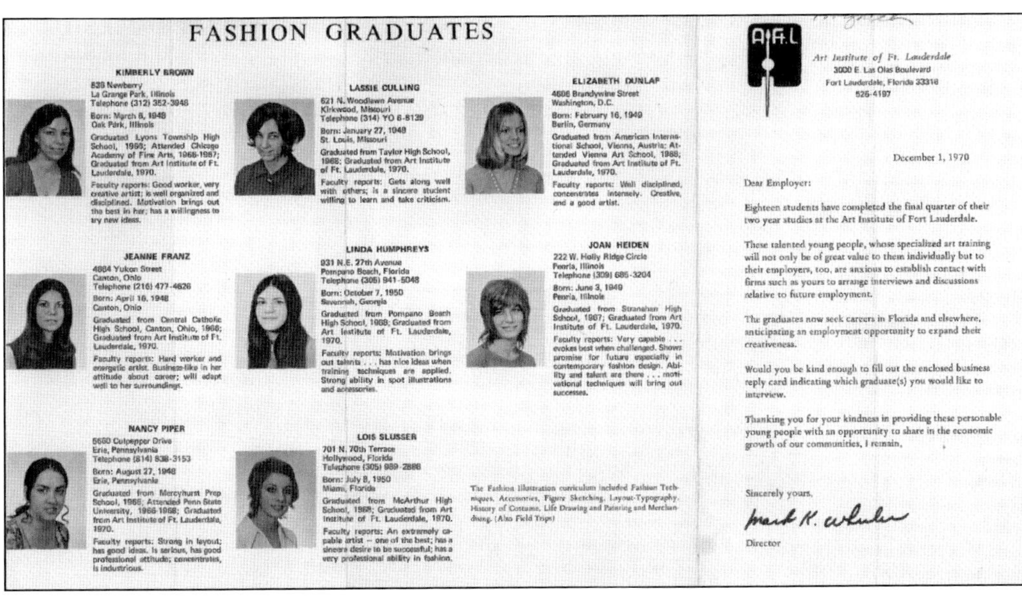

FASHION GRADUATES

KIMBERLY BROWN
836 Newberry
La Grange Park, Illinois
Telephone (312) 352-3948
Born: March 6, 1948
Oak Park, Illinois
Graduated Lyons Township High School, 1966; Attended Chicago Academy of Fine Arts, 1966-1967; Graduated from Art Institute of Ft. Lauderdale, 1970.
Faculty reports: Good worker, very creative artist; is well organized and disciplined. Motivation brings out the best in her; has a willingness to try new ideas.

JEANNE FRANZ
4884 Yukon Street
Canton, Ohio
Telephone (216) 477-4626
Born: April 16, 1948
Canton, Ohio
Graduated from Central Catholic High School, Canton, Ohio, 1966; Graduated from Art Institute of Ft. Lauderdale, 1970.
Faculty reports: Hard worker and energetic artist. Business-like in her attitude about career; will adapt well to her surroundings.

NANCY PIPER
5660 Culpepper Drive
Erie, Pennsylvania
Telephone (814) 838-3153
Born: August 27, 1948
Erie, Pennsylvania
Graduated from Mercyhurst Prep School, 1966; Attended Penn State University, 1966-1968; Graduated from Art Institute of Ft. Lauderdale, 1970.
Faculty reports: Strong in layout; has good ideas. Is serious, has good professional attitude; concentrates, is industrious.

LASSIE CULLING
621 N. Woodlawn Avenue
Kirkwood, Missouri
Telephone (314) YO 6-8139
Born: January 27, 1948
St. Louis, Missouri
Graduated from Taylor High School, 1966; Graduated from Art Institute of Ft. Lauderdale, 1970.
Faculty reports: Gets along well with others; is a sincere student willing to learn and take criticism.

LINDA HUMPHREYS
931 N.E. 27th Avenue
Pompano Beach, Florida
Telephone (305) 941-5048
Born: October 7, 1950
Savannah, Georgia
Graduated from Pompano Beach High School, 1968; Graduated from Art Institute of Ft. Lauderdale, 1970.
Faculty reports: Motivation brings out talents . . . has nice ideas when training techniques are applied. Strong ability in spot illustrations and accessories.

LOIS SLUSSER
701 N. 70th Terrace
Hollywood, Florida
Telephone (305) 989-2886
Born: July 8, 1950
Miami, Florida
Graduated from McArthur High School, 1968; Graduated from Art Institute of Ft. Lauderdale, 1970.
Faculty reports: An extremely capable artist — one of the best; has a sincere desire to be successful; has a very professional ability in fashion.

ELIZABETH DUNLAP
4606 Brandywine Street
Washington, D.C.
Born: February 16, 1949
Berlin, Germany
Graduated from American International School, Vienna, Austria; Attended Vienna Art School, 1968; Graduated from Art Institute of Ft. Lauderdale, 1970.
Faculty reports: Well disciplined, concentrates intensely. Creative, and a good artist.

JOAN HEIDEN
222 W. Holly Ridge Circle
Peoria, Illinois
Telephone (309) 685-3204
Born: June 3, 1949
Peoria, Illinois
Graduated from Stranahan High School, 1967; Graduated from Art Institute of Ft. Lauderdale, 1970.
Faculty reports: Very capable . . . evokes best when challenged. Shows promise for future especially in contemporary fashion design. Ability and talent are there . . . motivational techniques will bring out successes.

The Fashion Illustration curriculum included Fashion Techniques, Accessories, Figure Sketching, Layout-Typography, History of Costume, Life Drawing and Painting and Merchandising. (Also Field Trips)

AIFtL
Art Institute of Ft. Lauderdale
3000 E. Las Olas Boulevard
Fort Lauderdale, Florida 33316
525-4197

December 1, 1970

Dear Employer:

Eighteen students have completed the final quarter of their two year studies at the Art Institute of Fort Lauderdale.

These talented young people, whose specialized art training will not only be of great value to them individually but to their employers, too, are anxious to establish contact with firms such as yours to arrange interviews and discussions relative to future employment.

The graduates now seek careers in Florida and elsewhere, anticipating an employment opportunity to expand their creativeness.

Would you be kind enough to fill out the enclosed business reply card indicating which graduate(s) you would like to interview.

Thanking you for your kindness in providing these personable young people with an opportunity to share in the economic growth of our communities, I remain,

Sincerely yours,

Mark K. Wheeler

Director

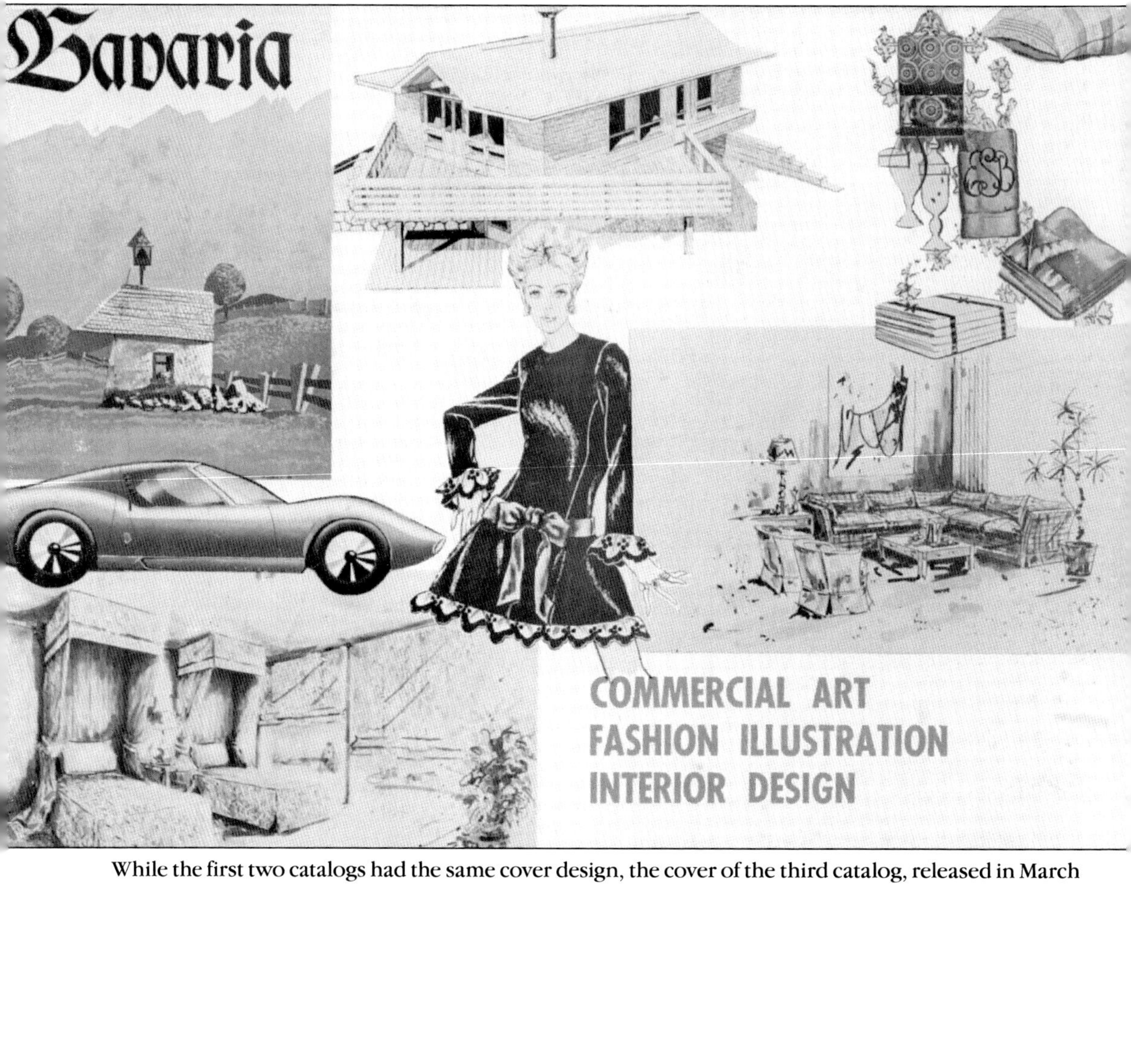

While the first two catalogs had the same cover design, the cover of the third catalog, released in March

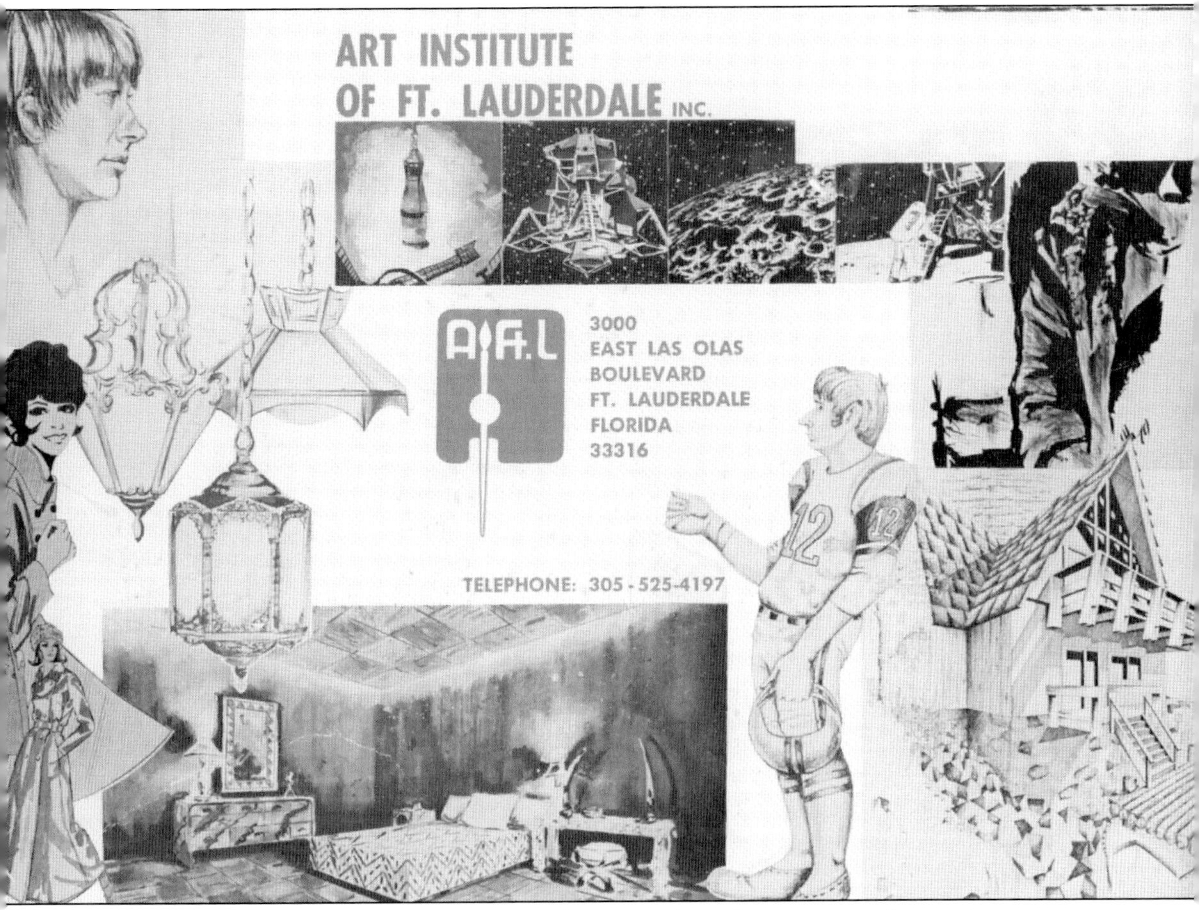

1971, uses art to illustrate the programs offered. The catalog's front cover is shown above.

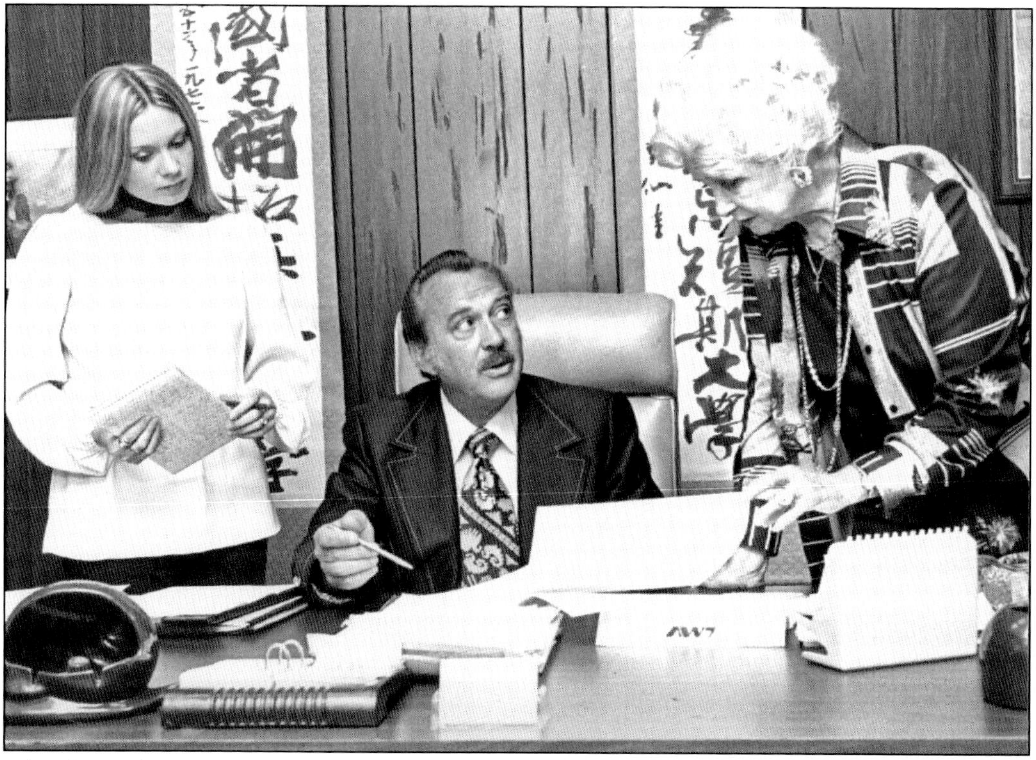

School president Mark K. Wheeler (center) discusses business with receptionist Linda Steele (left) and placement director Erlaine Pitts.

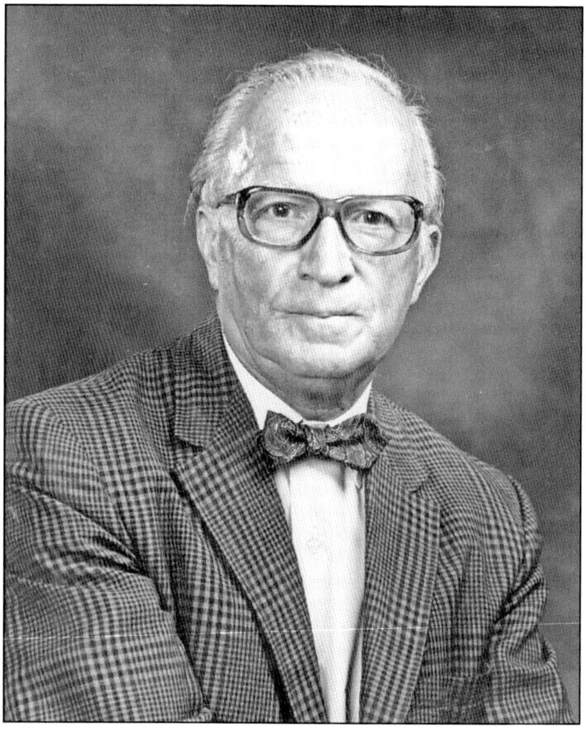

This is a portrait of Michael Angelo DiVincenzo, who was one of the first Art Institute of Fort Lauderdale teachers. A member of the faculty of the Art Institute of Pittsburgh since 1947, DiVincenzo taught life drawing and figure sketching classes at the Art Institute of Fort Lauderdale. (Photograph by Rex Shaw.)

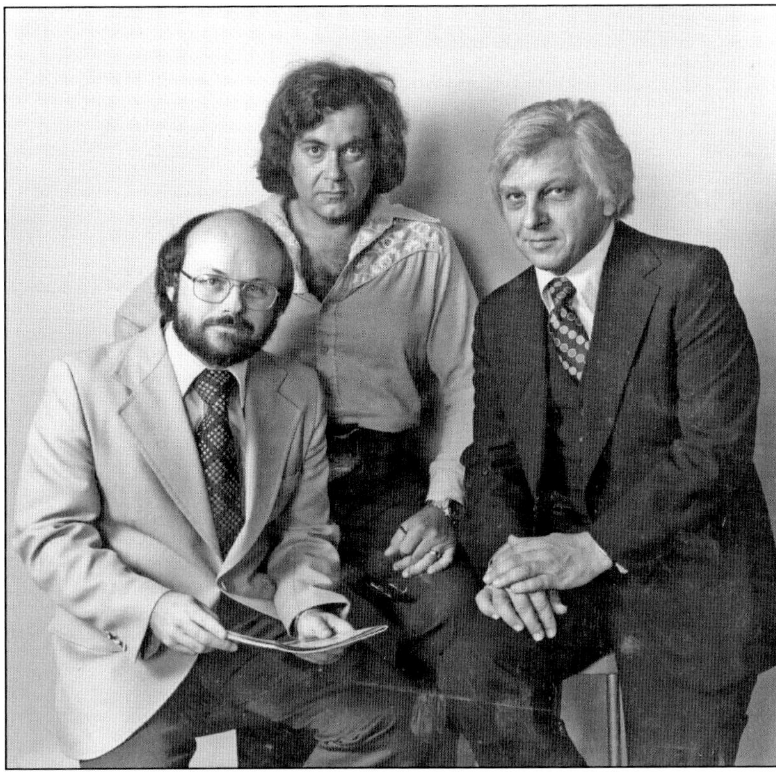

This is a portrait of three early instructors. From left to right are Jim Boyd, the director of the photography department; unidentified; and Hank Balamut. (Courtesy of Felicia Raia Blanski.)

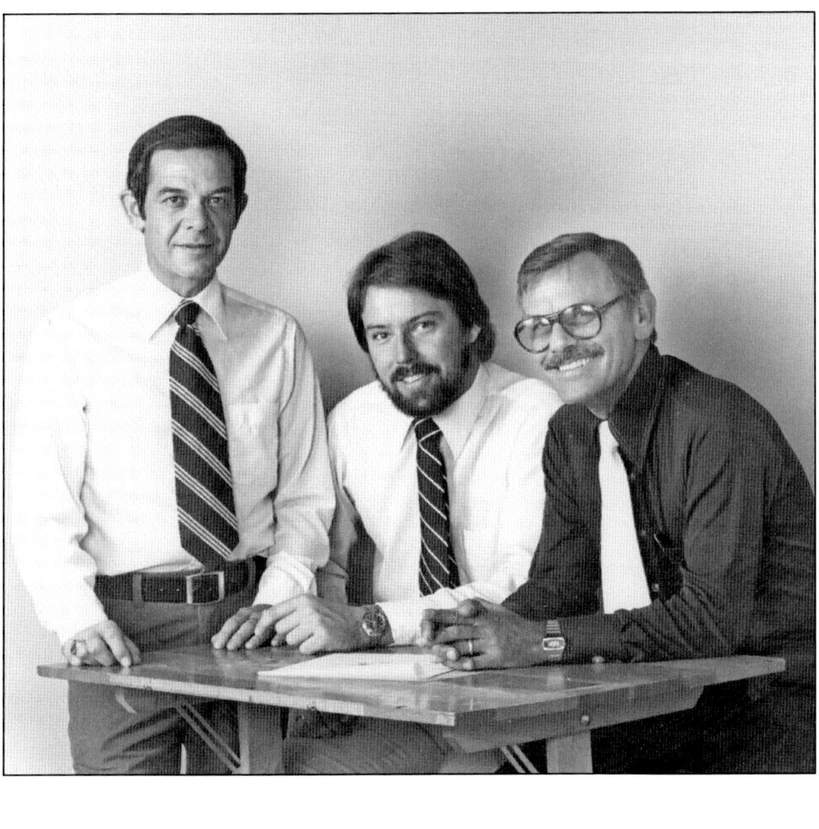

Three more early instructors are depicted in this picture. From left to right are Nevin Meinhardt, Dennis Harkins and Chuck Ax. (Courtesy of Felicia Raia Blanski.)

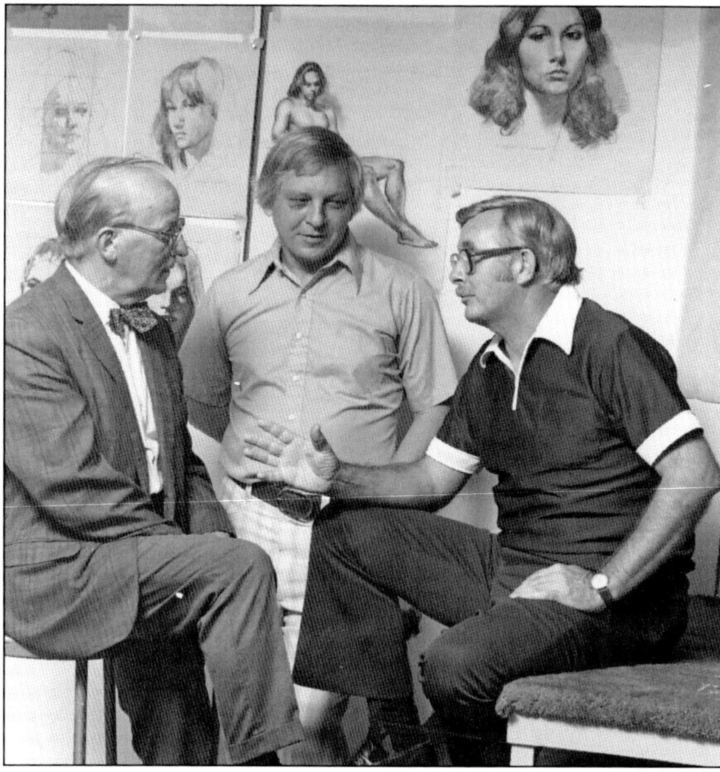

From left to right, painter and sculptor Angelo DiVincenzo, advertising design faculty member Henry Balamut, and photography instructor Homer Karnes discuss art in 1979. (Courtesy of Felicia Raia Blanski.)

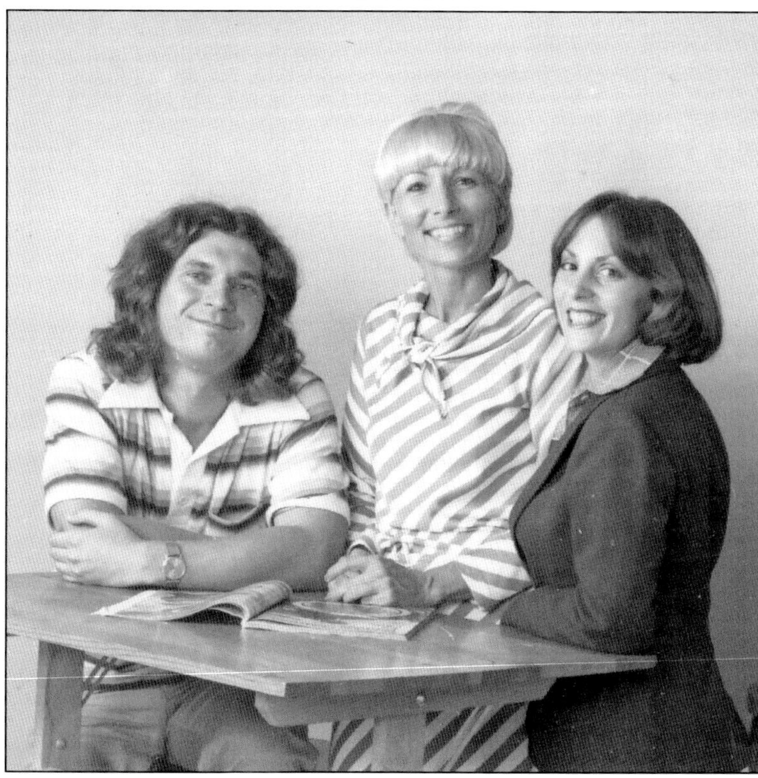

From left to right, instructors Peter Primak, Pat Richards, and Jody Berkshire are seen in this photograph from the late 1970s or early 1980s. (Courtesy of Felicia Raia Blanski.)

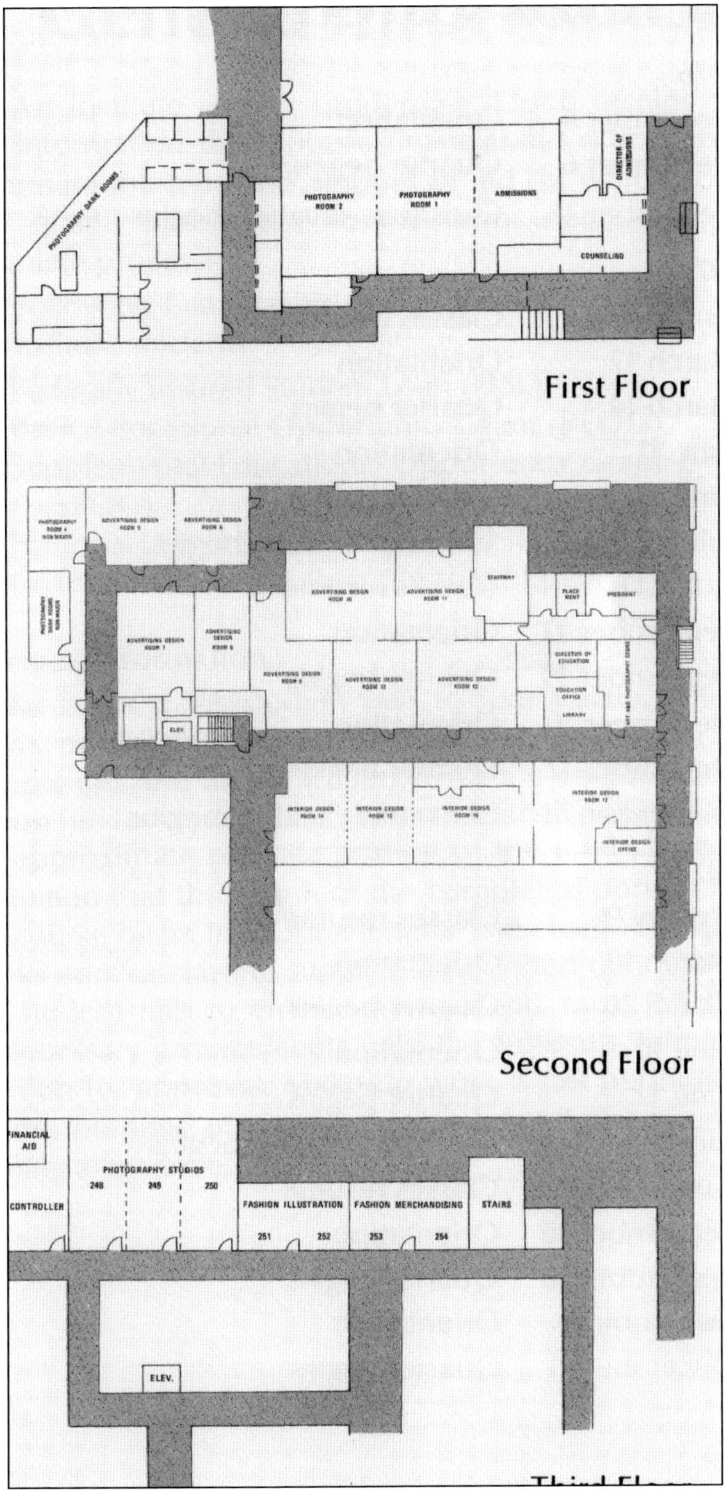

Floor plans depict the layout of the school's rooms over three floors at the Oceanside Holiday Inn.

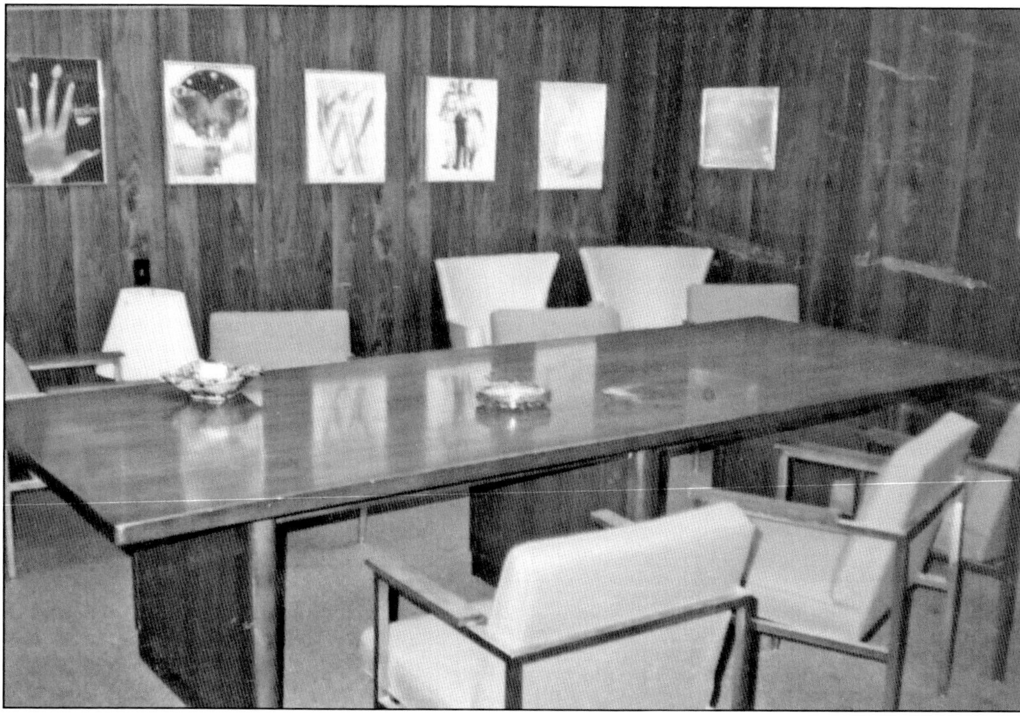

The executive conference room at the Oceanside Holiday Inn location displays posters on the wall from other Art Institute locations in the United States. (Courtesy of Jodi Berkshire.)

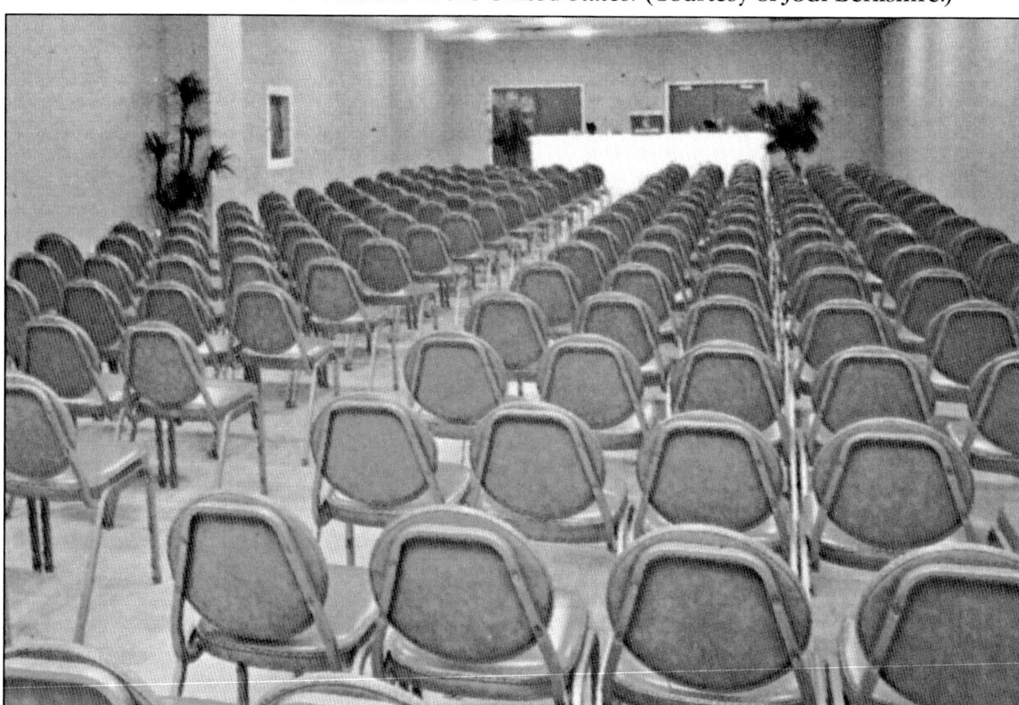

Depicted here is the ballroom of the hotel. (Courtesy of the Fort Lauderdale Historical Society.)

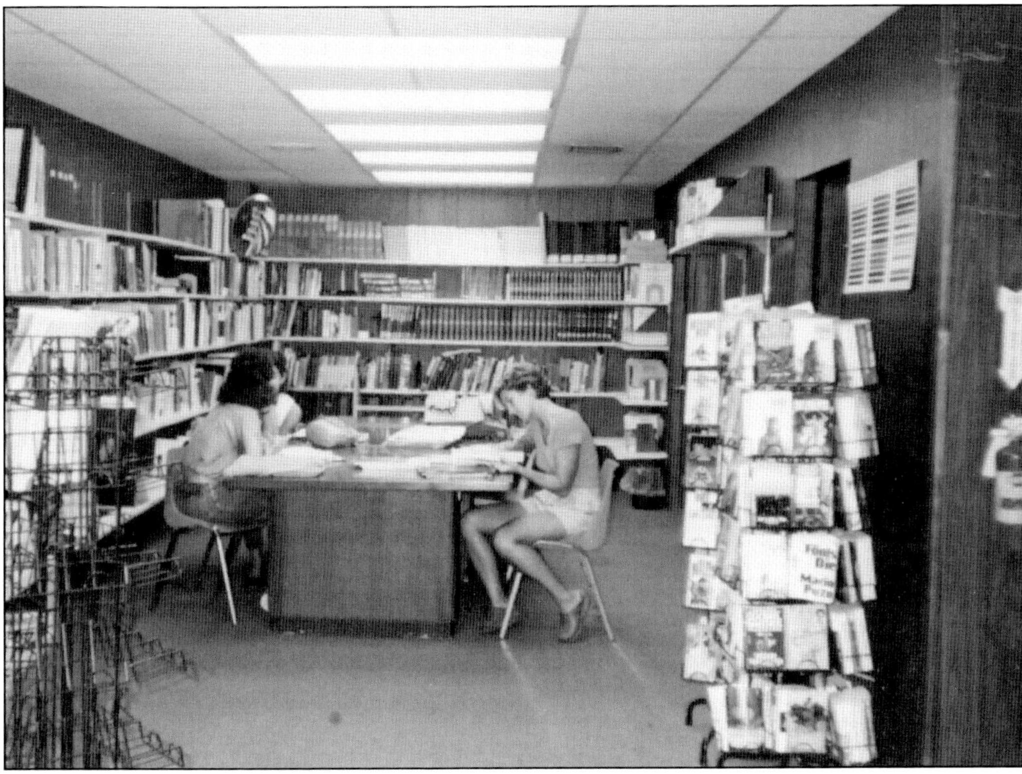

The library provided space for students to work. (Courtesy of Jodi Berkshire.)

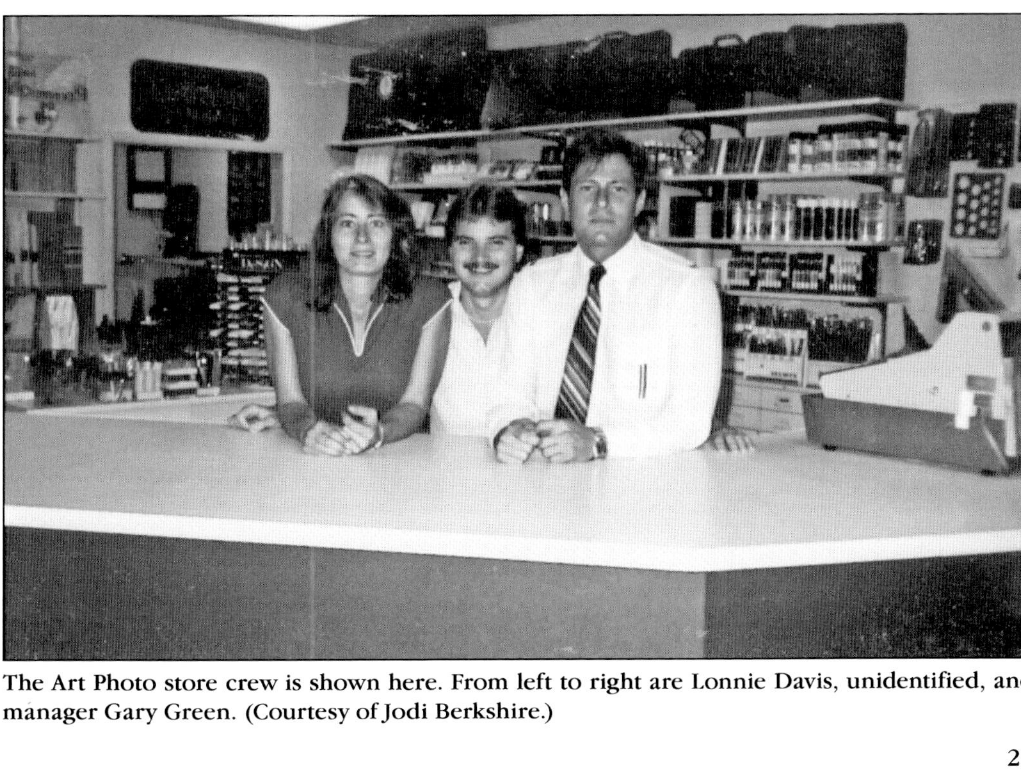

The Art Photo store crew is shown here. From left to right are Lonnie Davis, unidentified, and manager Gary Green. (Courtesy of Jodi Berkshire.)

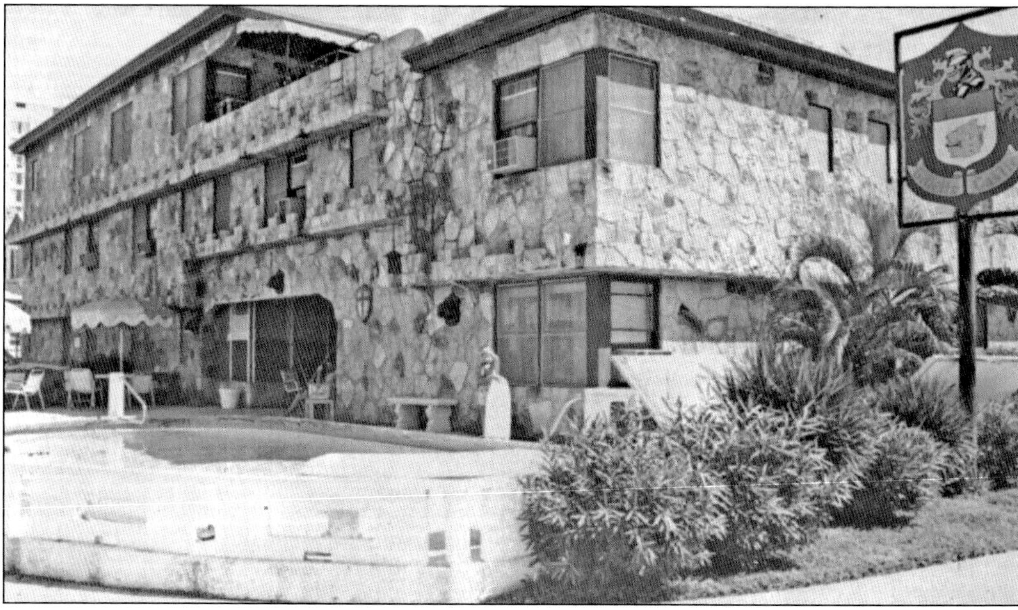

Granada Hall, also known as the "Castle," was the school's first dormitory. The catalog described it as, "a housemother-supervised private dormitory exclusively for female students." Its 25 apartments served as homes for students from 1968 to 1977. It featured a private swimming pool and sundeck for students, who shared air-conditioned apartments with fully equipped kitchens. The dorm was one block south of the school on Atlantic Boulevard.

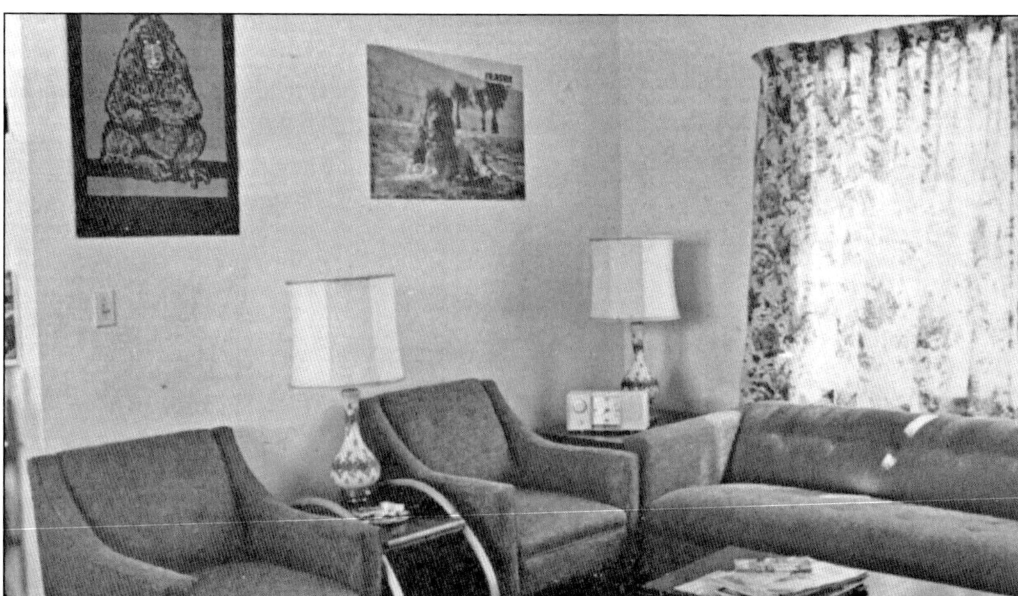

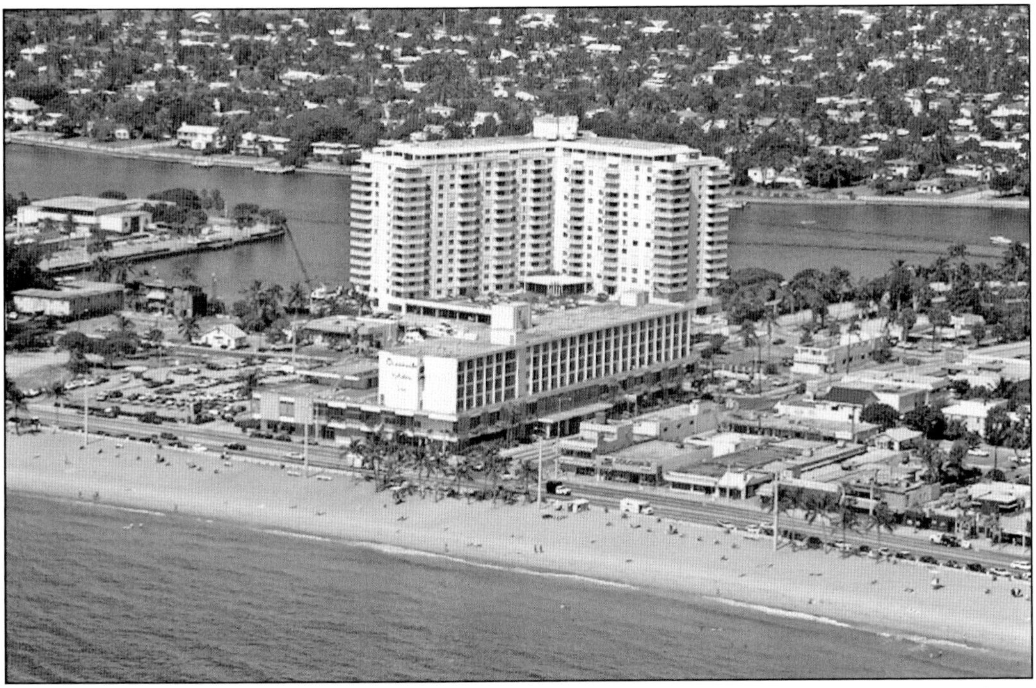

This aerial view of the school's location was photographed by alumnus Scott Atkins in 1976.

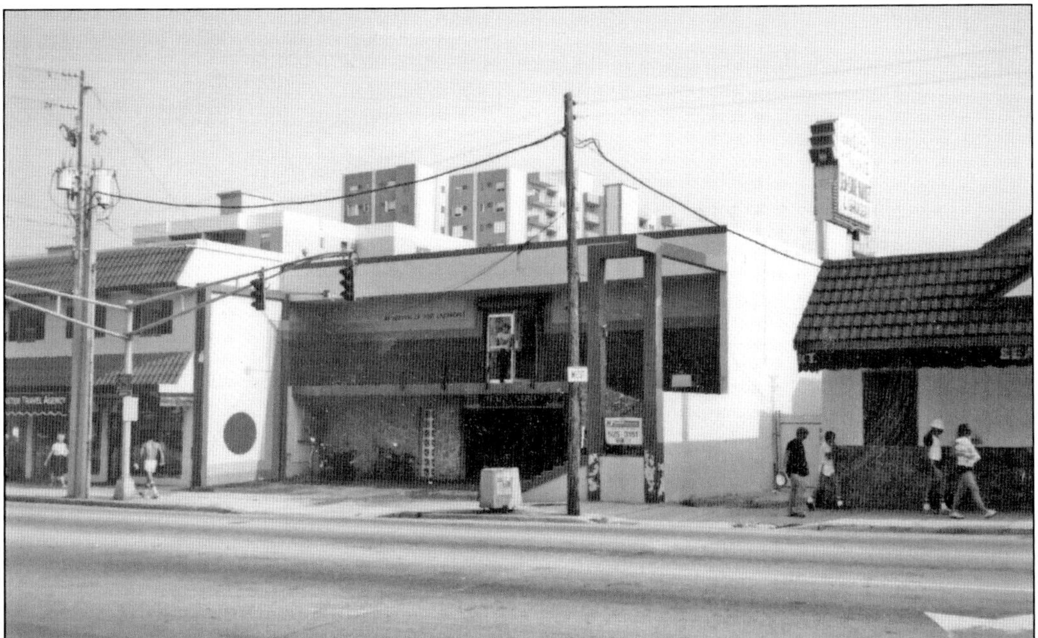

By 1976, the school took up 25,000 square feet of space at the Oceanside Holiday Inn. In 1977, it reached a record enrollment of 800 students. To accommodate the growing student body, the school rented two buildings across Las Olas Boulevard. They were called Annex I, pictured here, and Annex II. (Courtesy of Jodi Berkshire.)

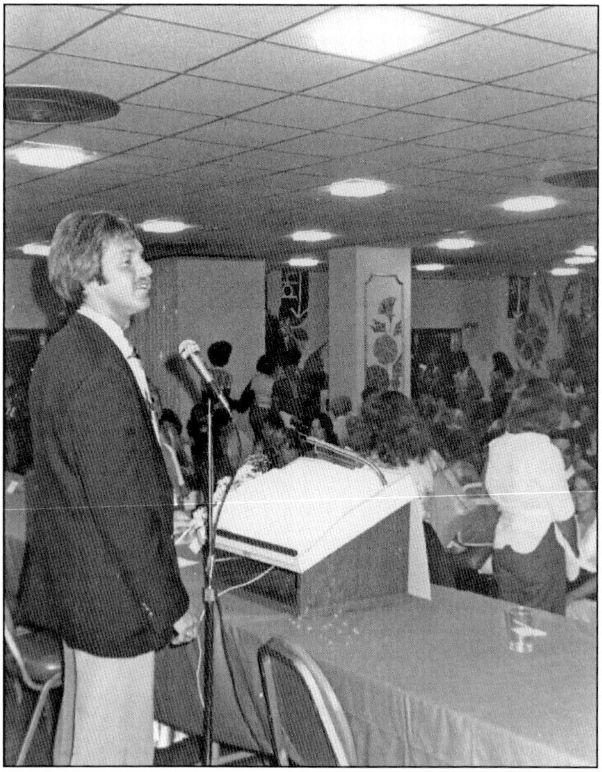

This photograph shows vice president and director of admissions Robert Peterson at the podium in the ballroom in 1978. (Courtesy of Felicia Raia Blanski.)

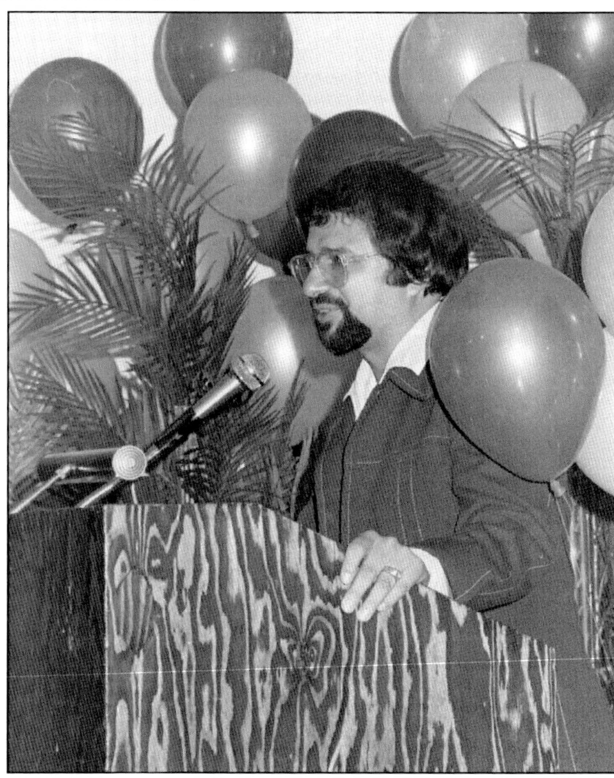

Vice president and director of education Frank Raia stands at the podium during an early "Viddy" awards ceremony. "Viddies" were annual video awards given to students for professional excellence in television graphics. (Courtesy of Felicia Raia Blanski.)

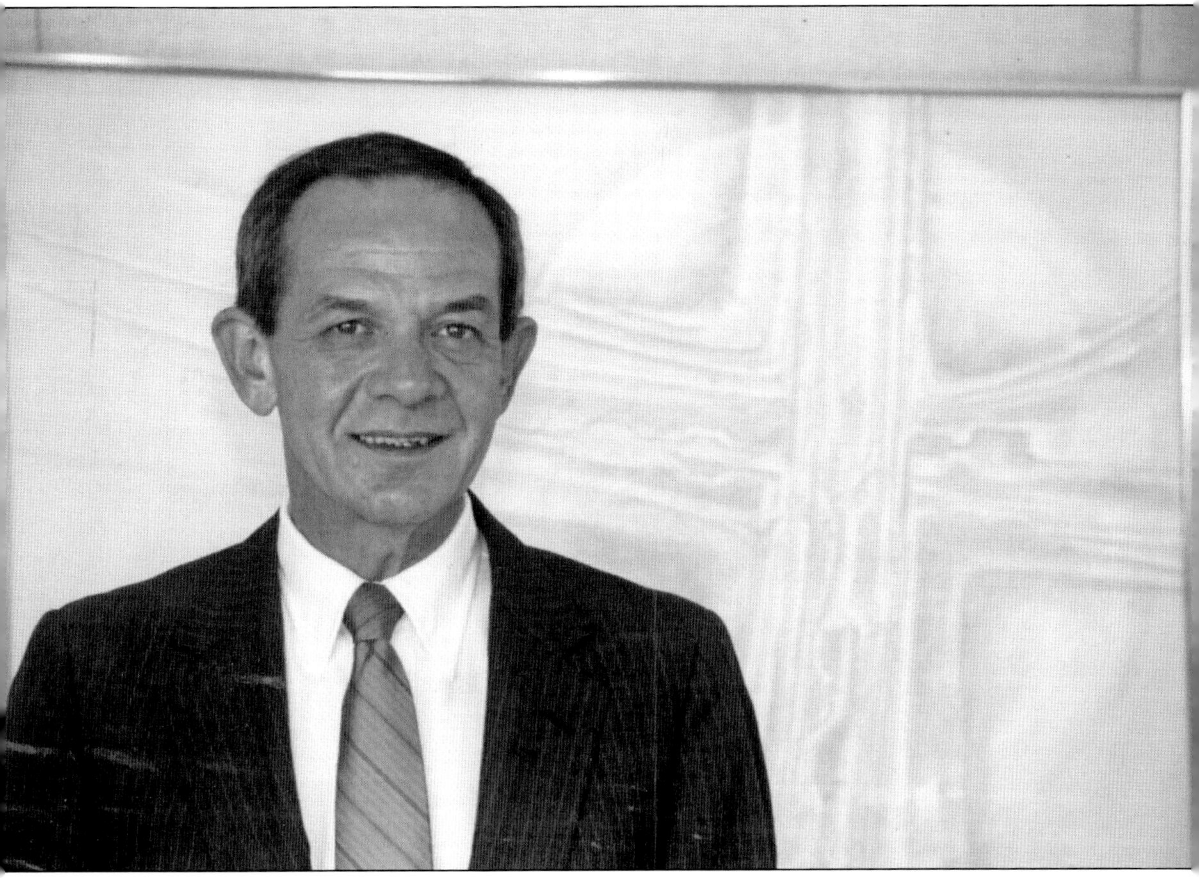

Nevin C. Meinhardt was a long-time faculty member and academic director. The school's library is named after him.

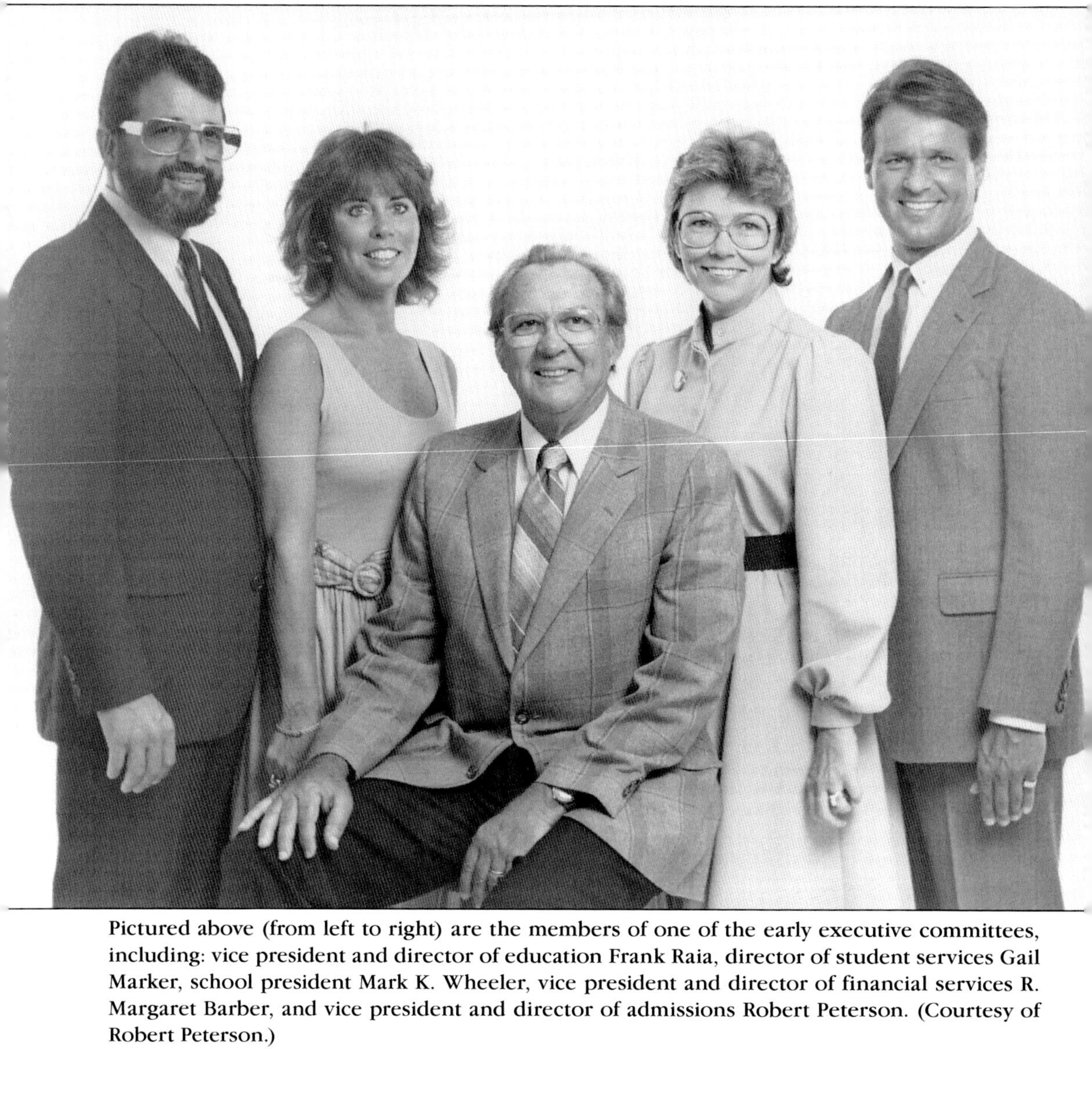

Pictured above (from left to right) are the members of one of the early executive committees, including: vice president and director of education Frank Raia, director of student services Gail Marker, school president Mark K. Wheeler, vice president and director of financial services R. Margaret Barber, and vice president and director of admissions Robert Peterson. (Courtesy of Robert Peterson.)

Two

EXPANSION

During this decade, the Art Institute of Fort Lauderdale continued to grow. By 1985, there were 1,000 students enrolled in classes. Annex I, Annex II, and 25,000 square feet at the original location were not enough to accommodate the growth. In May 1986, the school moved to its current location at 1799 South East Seventeenth Street. The four-story, 75,000-square-foot facility won an award in recognition for outstanding achievement for urban environmental design from the City of Fort Lauderdale.

As the number of students grew, industry professionals were added to the faculty, and many are still with the school today. By the time the Art Institute of Fort Lauderdale celebrated its 20th anniversary, students found an expanded curriculum, which included classes in photography, fashion marketing, music and video business, travel and tourism, and fashion design. In 1987 and 1988, the State Board of Independent Colleges and Universities approved the conferring of Bachelor of Science degrees.

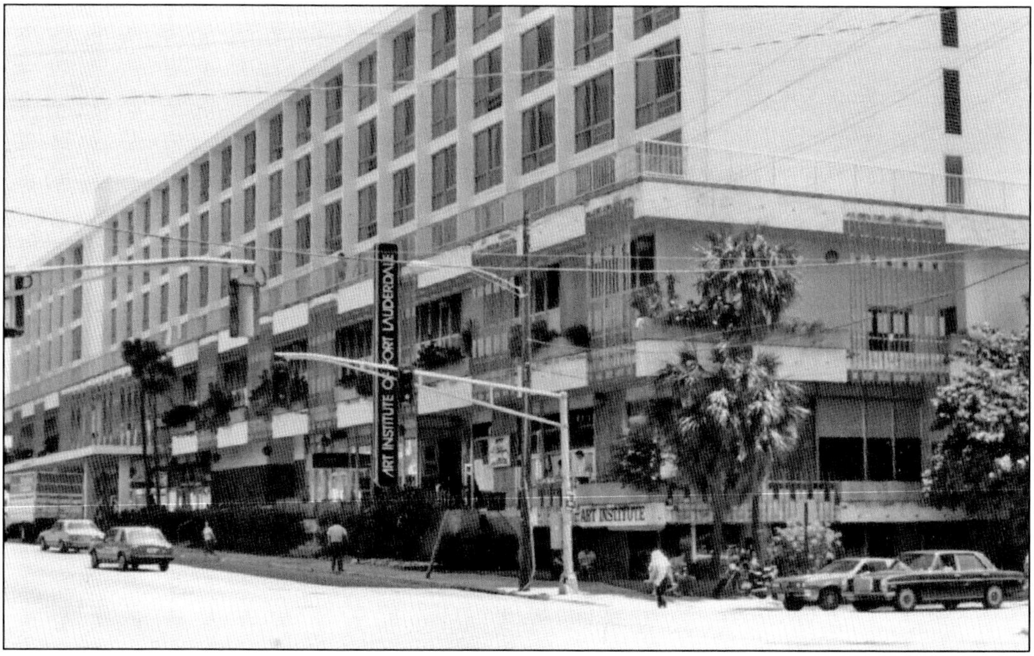

Brenda Sneathen-Mattox took this photograph on the day of her arrival in Fort Lauderdale in 1980. (Courtesy of Brenda Sneathen-Mattox.)

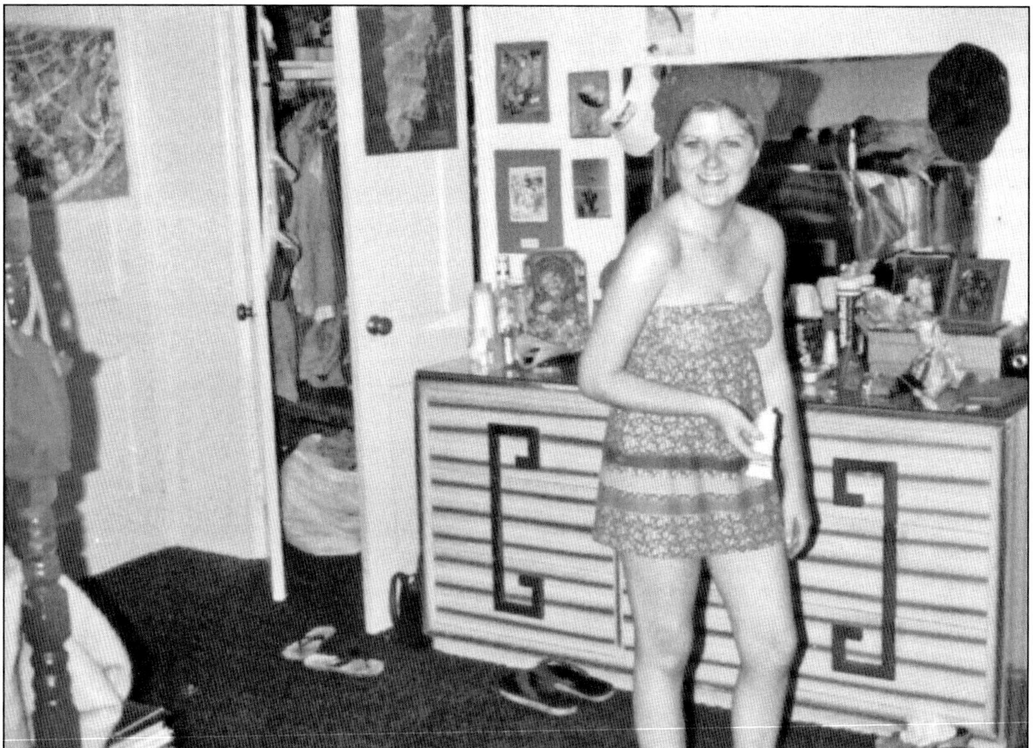

Brenda Sneathen-Mattox applies suntan lotion in her dorm room at Grenada Hall in March 1980. The dorm mom at the time was a Mrs. Horvath. (Courtesy of Brenda Sneathen-Mattox.)

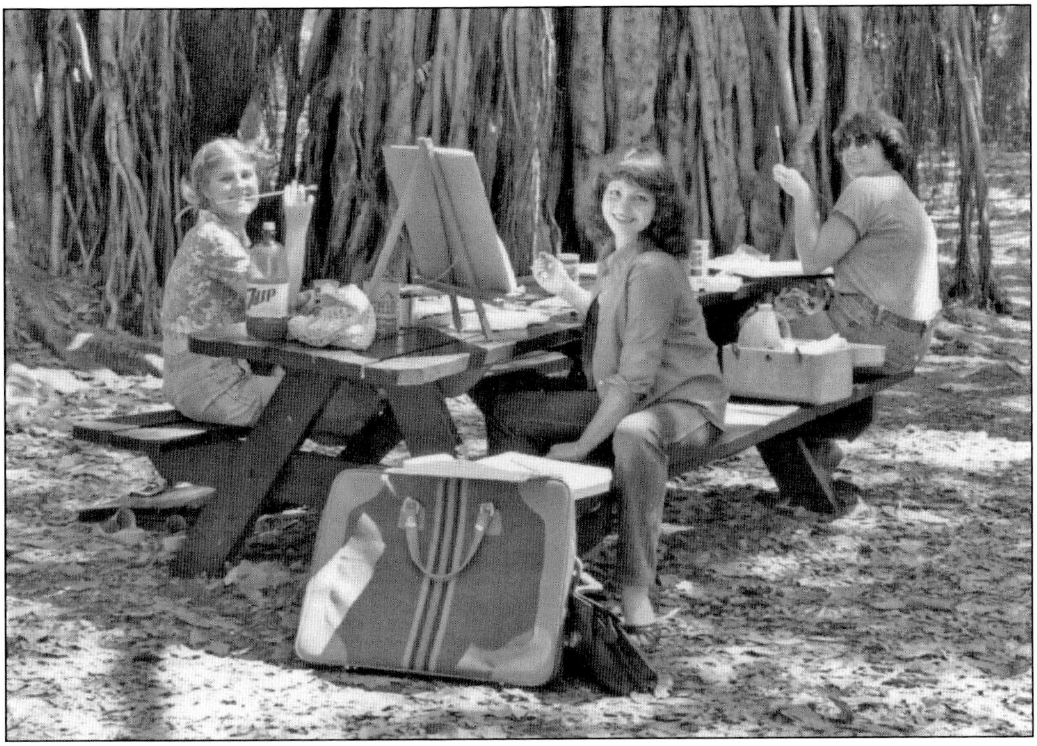

From left to right, Brenda Sneathen-Mattox and her friends Violet Hernandez and Carol "Phred" Frederick use watercolors to paint while at Birch State Park in 1981. (Courtesy of Brenda Sneathen-Mattox.)

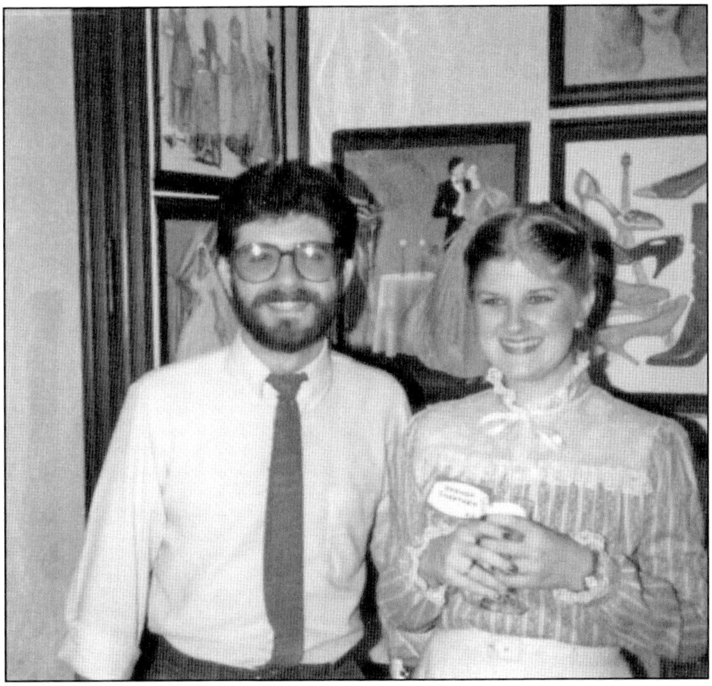

This is Brenda Sneathen-Mattox with John Miele in March 1982, during portfolio review. Miele began his career at the school as an instructor, teaching fashion illustration in 1976. He served as the director of fashion illustration from 1988 to 1990. Sneathen-Mattox became a creator of paper dolls, and Dover Press has published several of her books. (Courtesy of Brenda Sneathen-Mattox.)

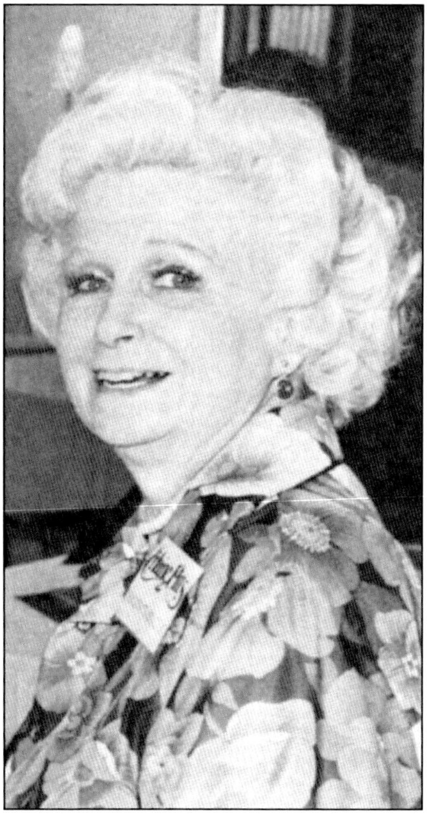

This is a portrait of Erlaine Pitts, the director of career services. She built close ties with students and was instrumental in keeping the school going on a daily basis.

From left to right, school president Mark K. Wheeler; Lauren Schuman, the first winner of the Erlaine Pitts scholarship award; and vice president Frank Raia are pictured on September 11, 1980.

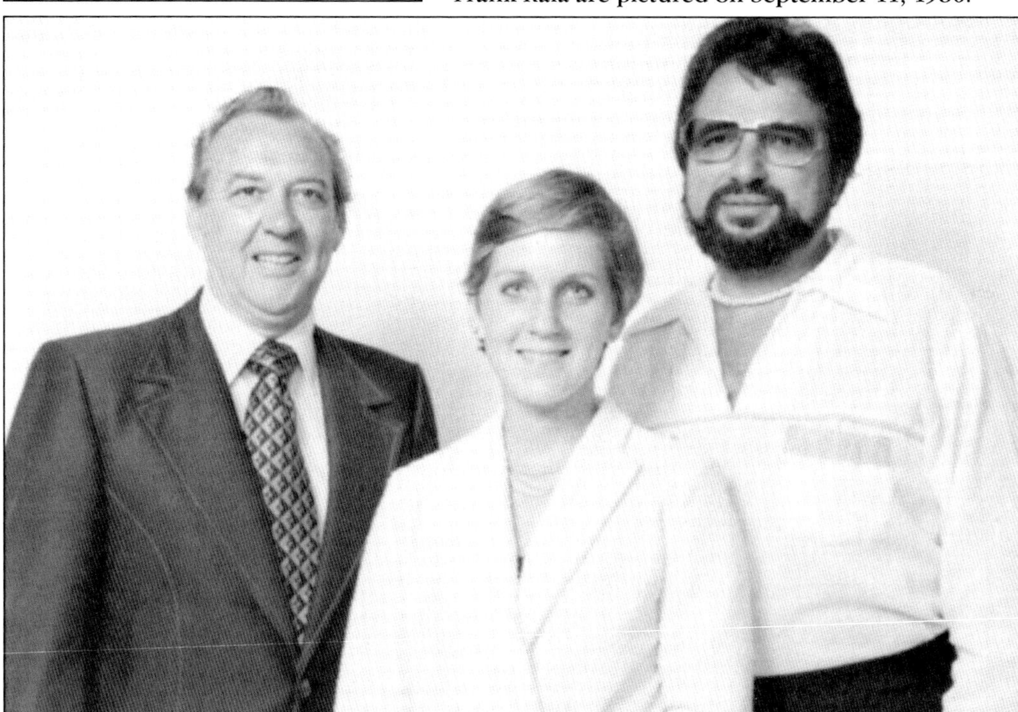

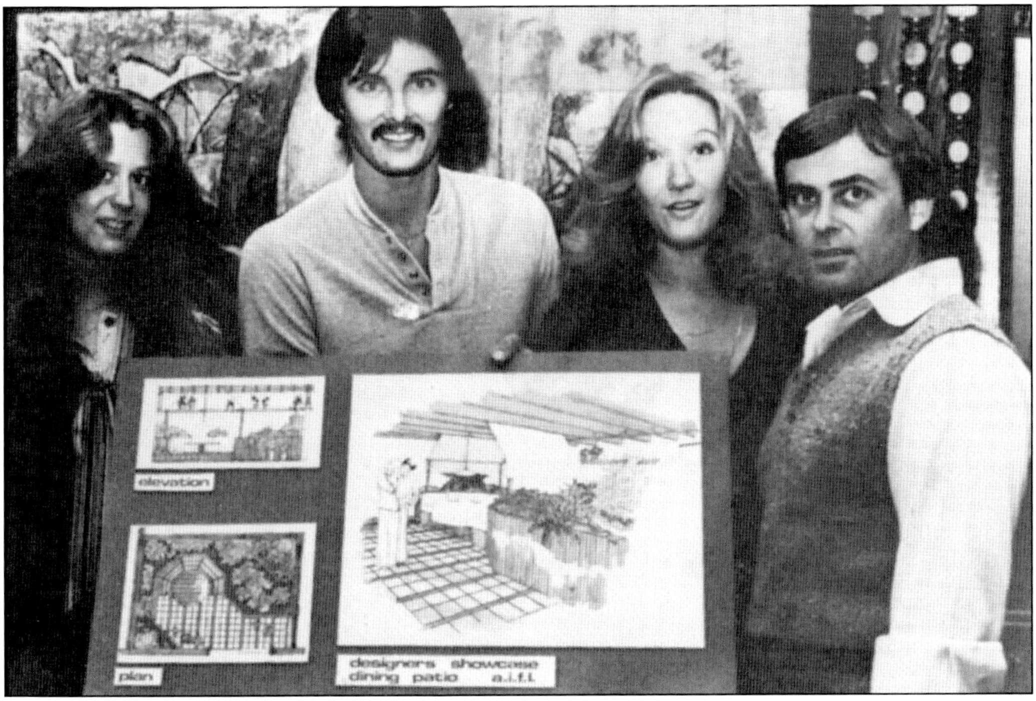

The American Society of Interior Designers' student chapter members are showing off the dining patio they planned for the Designer's Showcase House in July 1980. Interior design department chairman Bill Kobrynich is on the far right.

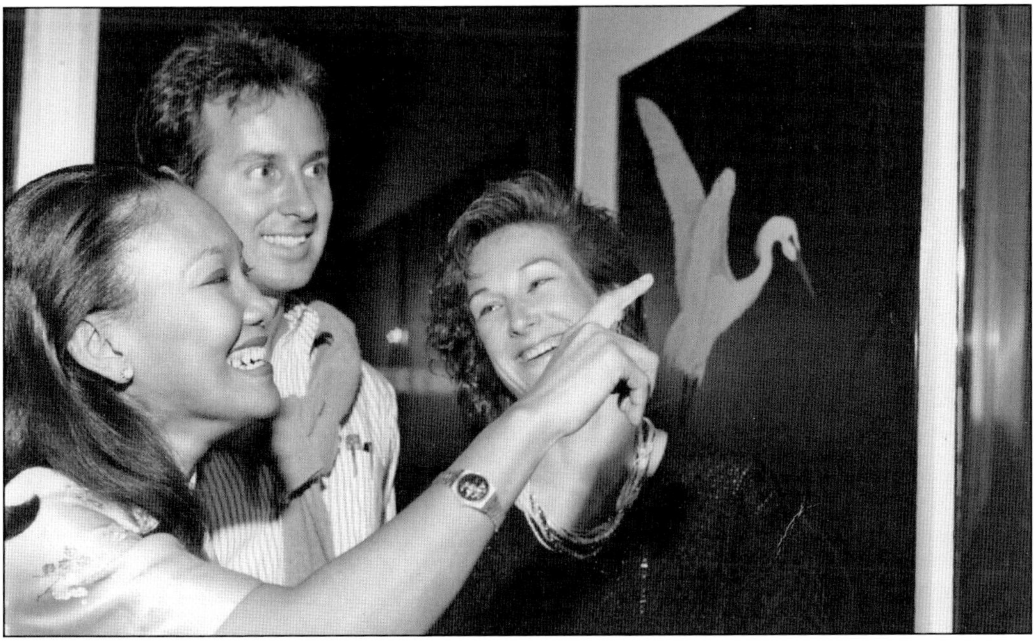

From left to right, Norma Ayee, James "Buck" Miller, and Leslie Stom enjoy a painting of an egret done by Ayee at an exhibition of her paintings and furniture in the school's art gallery. Ayee and Miller started teaching at the school in January 1979, and both were still faculty members in 2008. (Courtesy of Norma Ayee.)

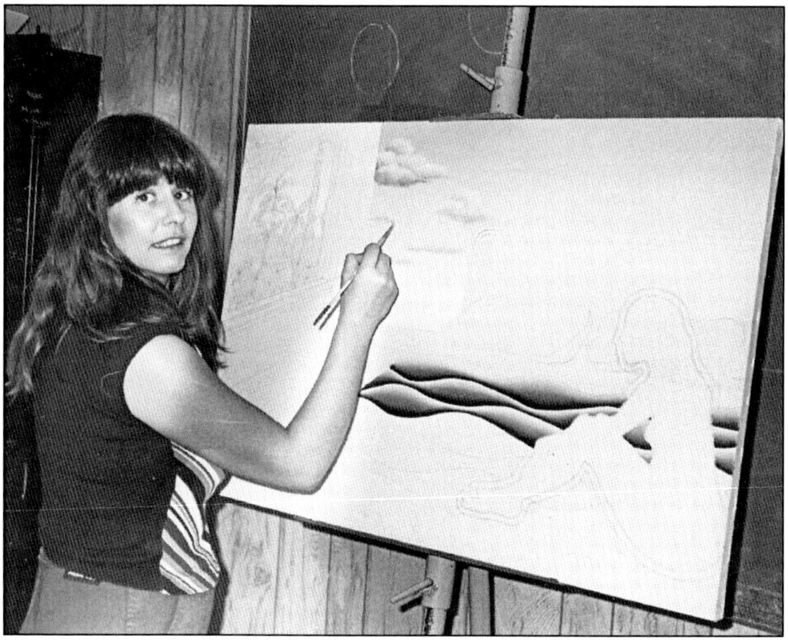

Renowned artist and faculty member Mimi Botscheller is shown working on a painting in 1981. The date July 29, 2008, marks Botscheller's 34th year of teaching at the Art Institute of Fort Lauderdale. No one has been employed at the school longer. (Courtesy of Mimi Botscheller.)

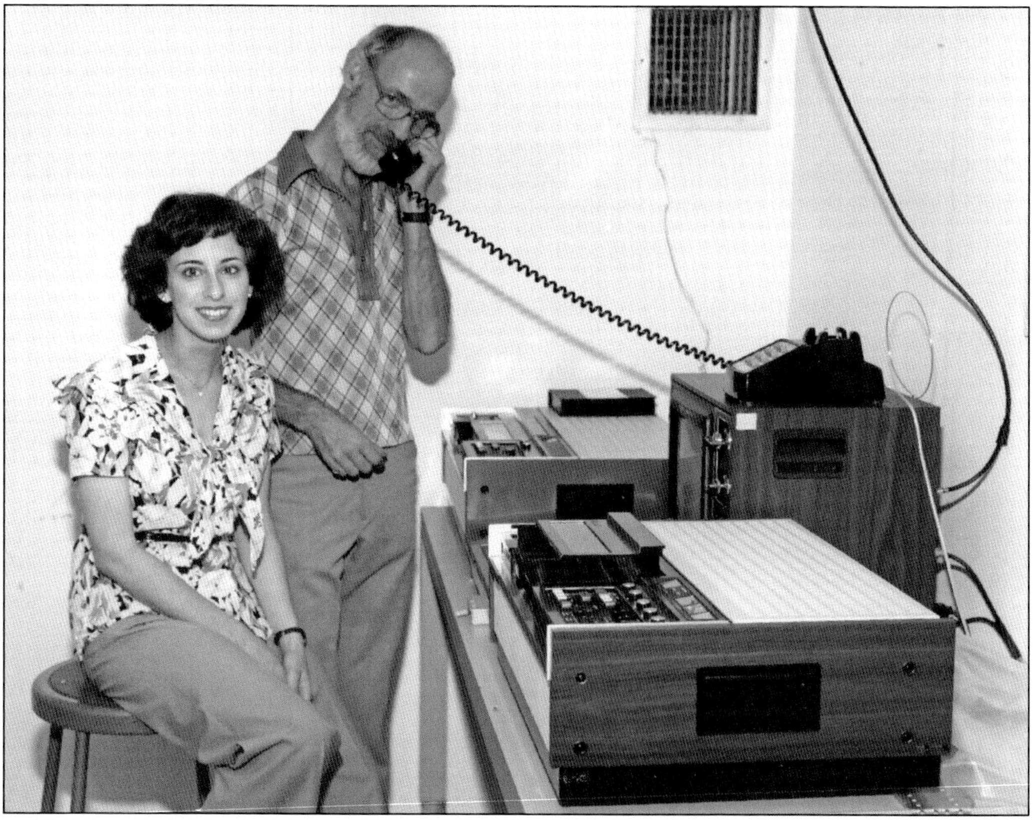

Debbie Rose Myers, a faculty member since September 1979, is shown with Bob Coxen in front of an old-style, three-fourth-inch video-editing setup in 1981. The videocassette station had a small editing machine in the center. (Courtesy of Debbie Rose Myers.)

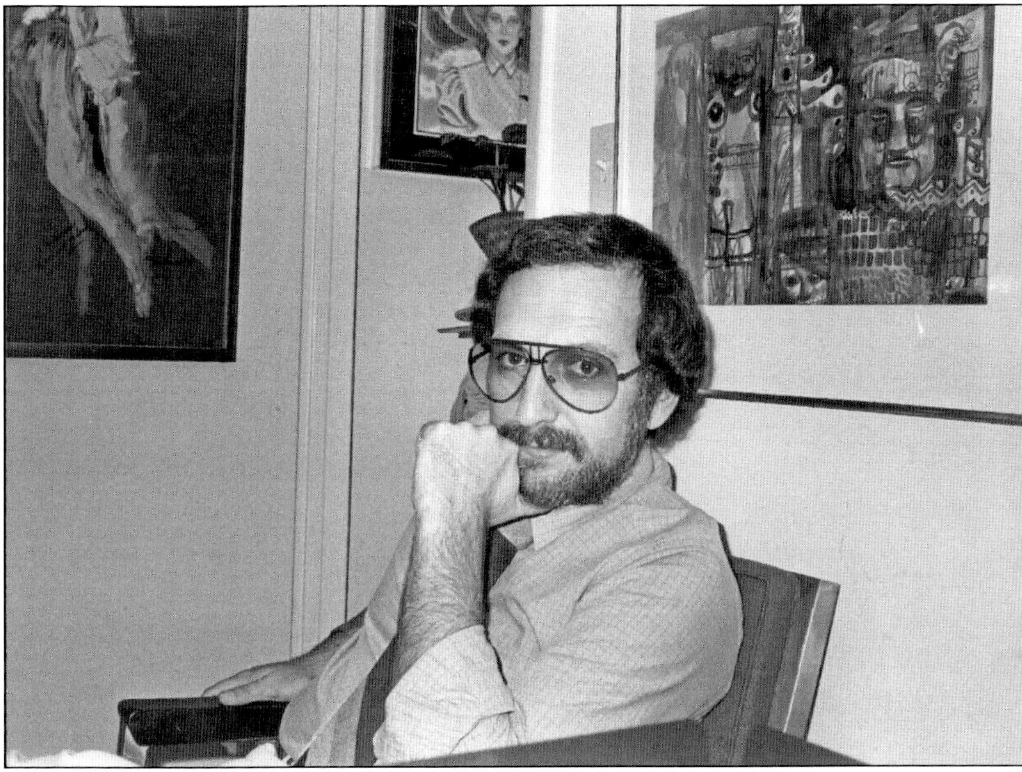

Gary Tepper, the assistant director of advertising design, was hired in January 1980. Tepper was still teaching at the school in 2008.

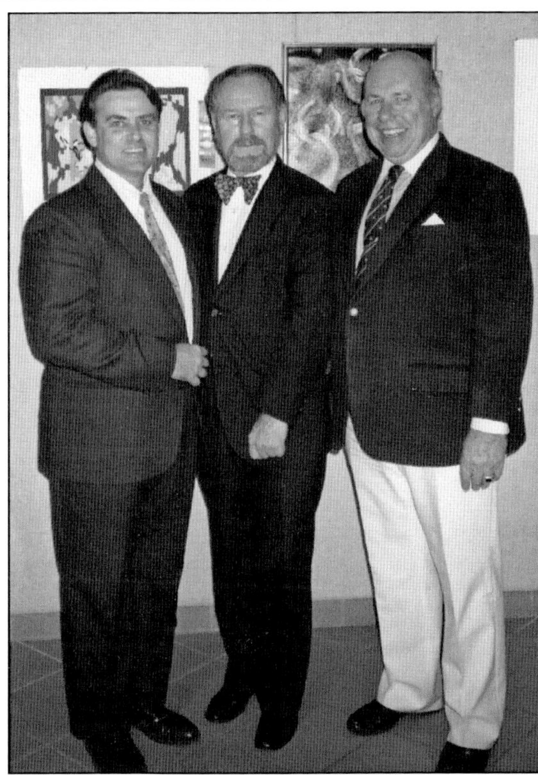

Pictured from left to right are interior design department chair Bill Kobrynich with Wally Jonason, the national president of the American Society of Interior Designers, and interior design instructor John Venters in 1980. Kobrynich joined the school as an instructor in December 1977. Venters started teaching at the school in 1978 and went on to be the first Honored Faculty in the summer of 1991. Both were still with the school in 2008. (Courtesy of Bill Kobrynich.)

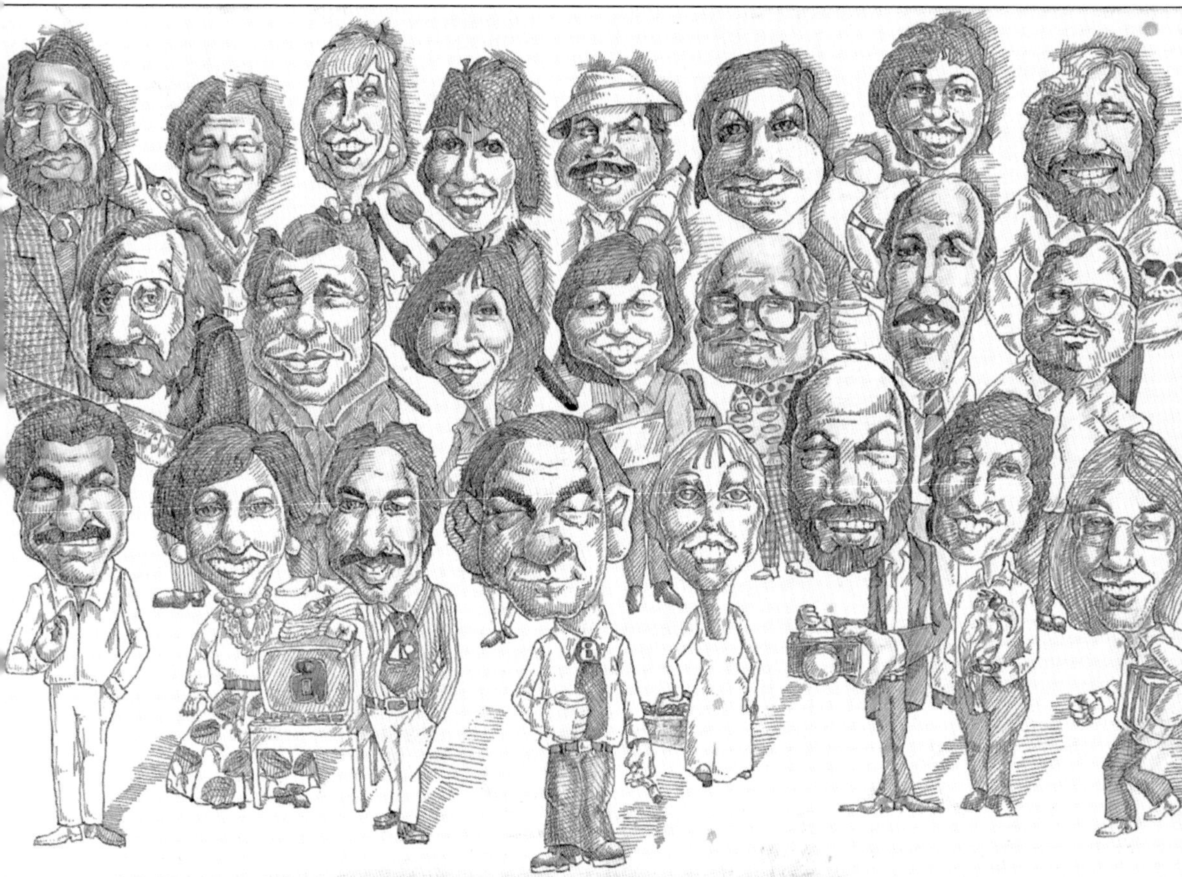

Mike Carnegie, who joined the school in September 1981 and who was still teaching in 2008, sketched a character portrait of the faculty and administrators. Pictured from left to right are (first row) Glenn Toscano, Debbie Rose, Paul Wullschleger, Nevin Meinhardt, Barbara Dix, Howard Sweet, Joy DiLorenzo, and Debbie Weinslinger; (second row) Gary Tepper, Gary Ramey, Linda Vacchiano, Mary Good, Homer Karnes, Ron Kreszswick, and Chuck Schaller; (third row) Frank Raia, Mike Carnegie, Paula Gillam, Mimi Botscheller, Andy Bing, Evelyn Mitchell, Kathy Leisek and Jim Radford.

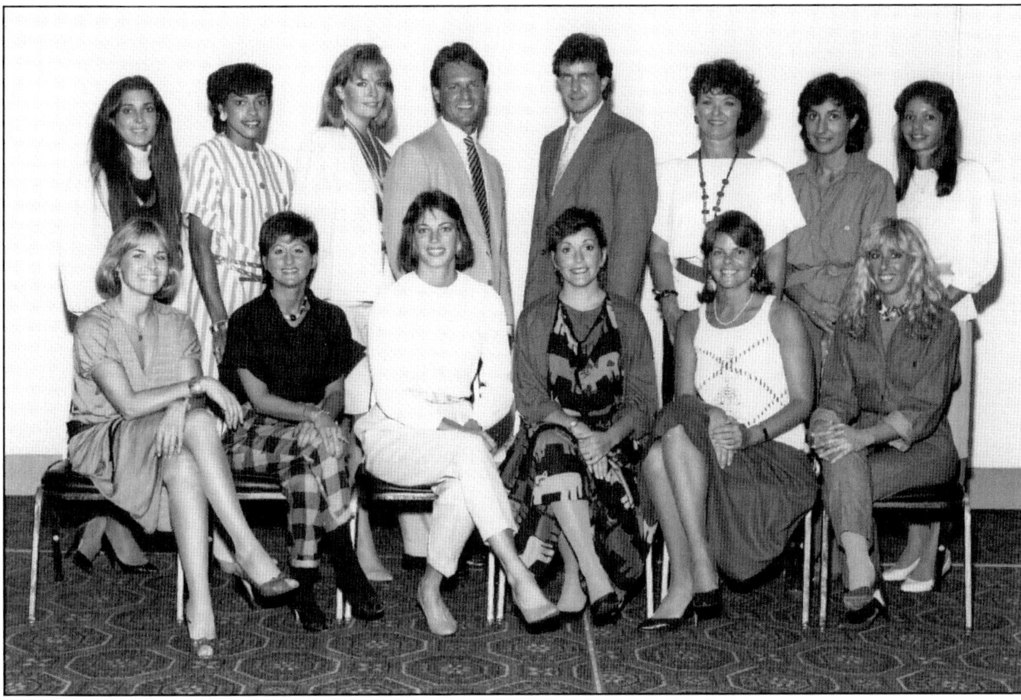

Vice president Robert Peterson (second row, fourth from left) poses with employees from the admissions office in 1981. (Courtesy of Robert Peterson.)

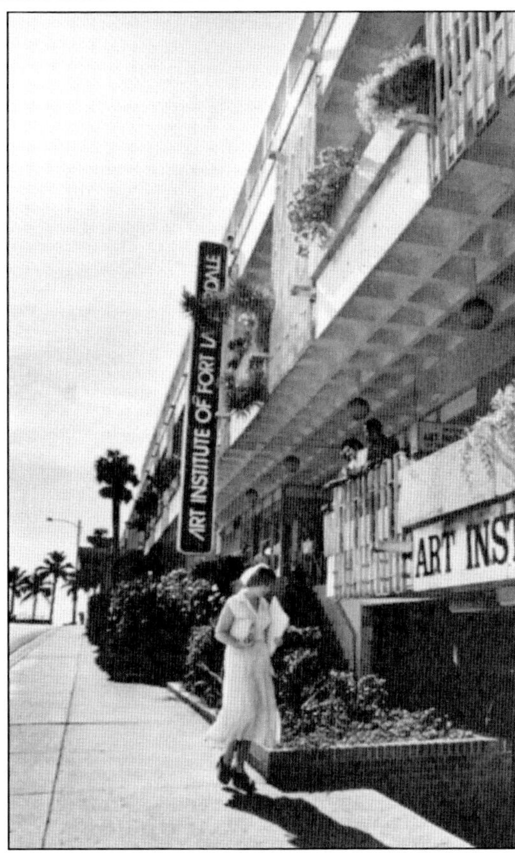

In this *c.* 1981 photograph, the school was advertised as, "merging with palm trees lining the beach."

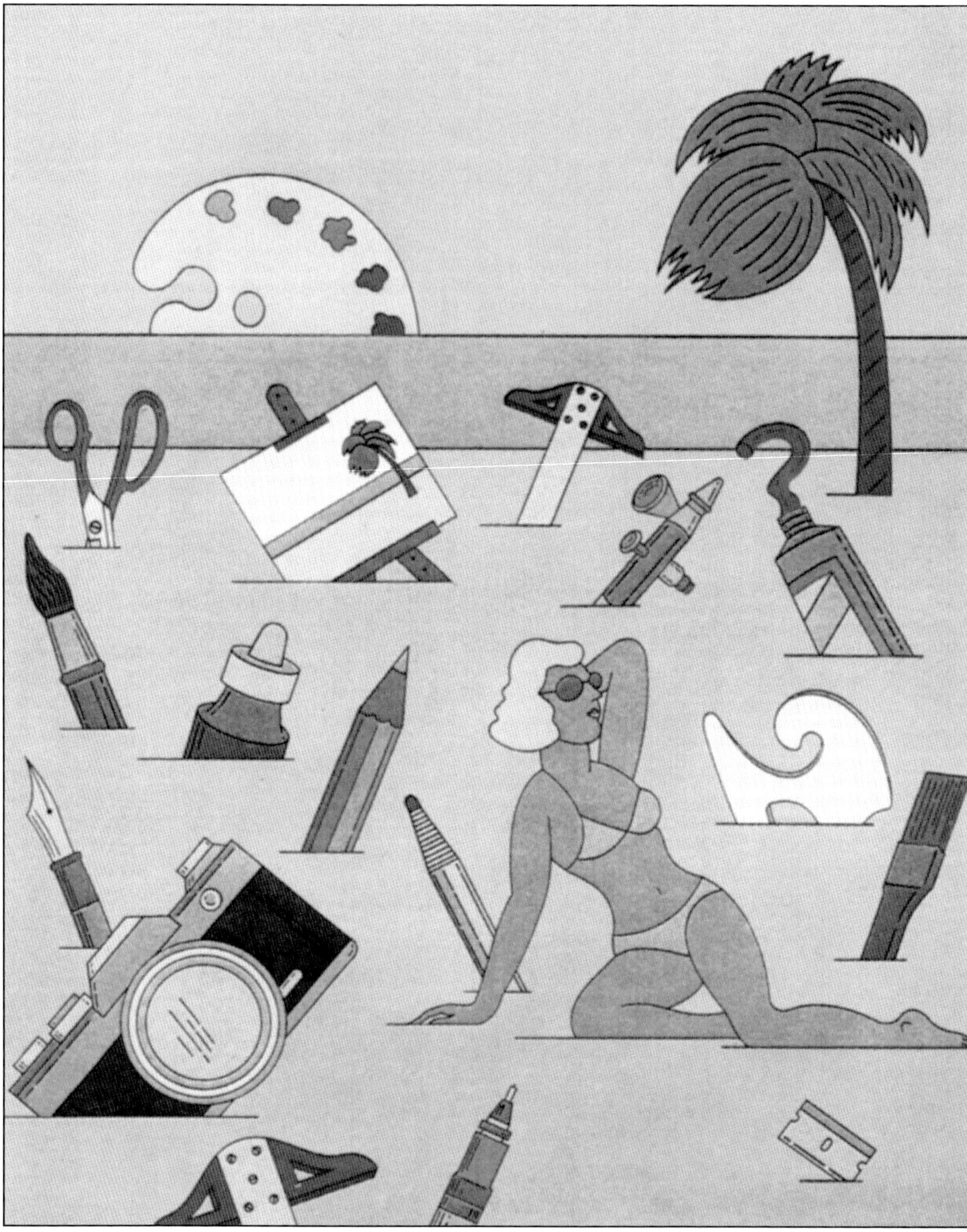

A commercial art and design school set among palm trees, sandy beaches, and bathing beauties graced the cover of the five school catalogs between 1981 and 1988. The cover was created and designed by Seymour Chwast, one of the most renowned and talented artists in the United States at that time. The poster version of the catalog cover was a top prize winner in the 59th-annual competition of the Art Directors' Club of New York, one of only four in its category to receive the distinctive merit award. It was also included in a 1981 exhibition of posters at the Smithsonian Institution's National Museum of Design, the Cooper-Hewitt, in New York City.

This is the September 17, 1982, portfolio, graduation, and awards announcement.

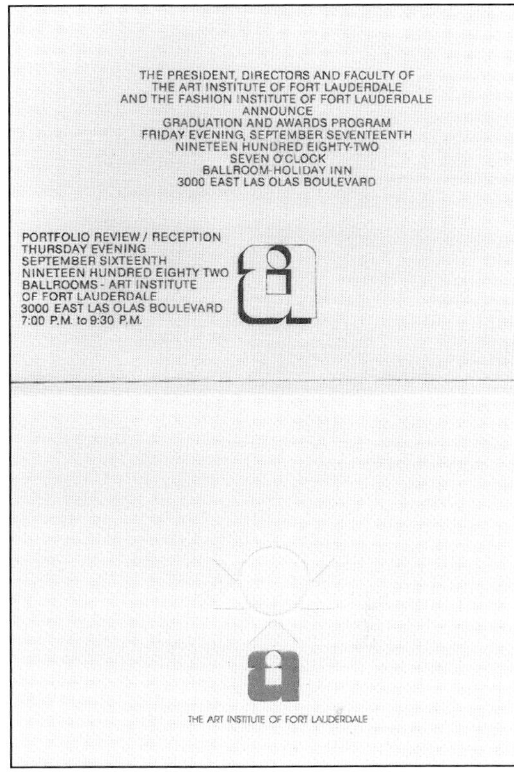

THE PRESIDENT, DIRECTORS AND FACULTY OF
THE ART INSTITUTE OF FORT LAUDERDALE
AND THE FASHION INSTITUTE OF FORT LAUDERDALE
ANNOUNCE
GRADUATION AND AWARDS PROGRAM
FRIDAY EVENING, SEPTEMBER SEVENTEENTH
NINETEEN HUNDRED EIGHTY-TWO
SEVEN O'CLOCK
BALLROOM-HOLIDAY INN
3000 EAST LAS OLAS BOULEVARD

PORTFOLIO REVIEW / RECEPTION
THURSDAY EVENING
SEPTEMBER SIXTEENTH
NINETEEN HUNDRED EIGHTY TWO
BALLROOMS - ART INSTITUTE
OF FORT LAUDERDALE
3000 EAST LAS OLAS BOULEVARD
7:00 P.M. to 9:30 P.M.

THE ART INSTITUTE OF FORT LAUDERDALE

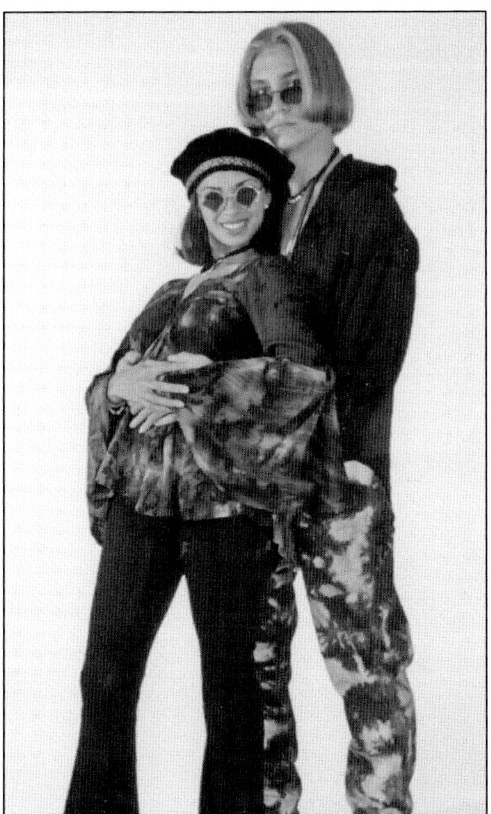

This photograph is from a fashion show in the early 1980s. (Courtesy of Kathy Colussy.)

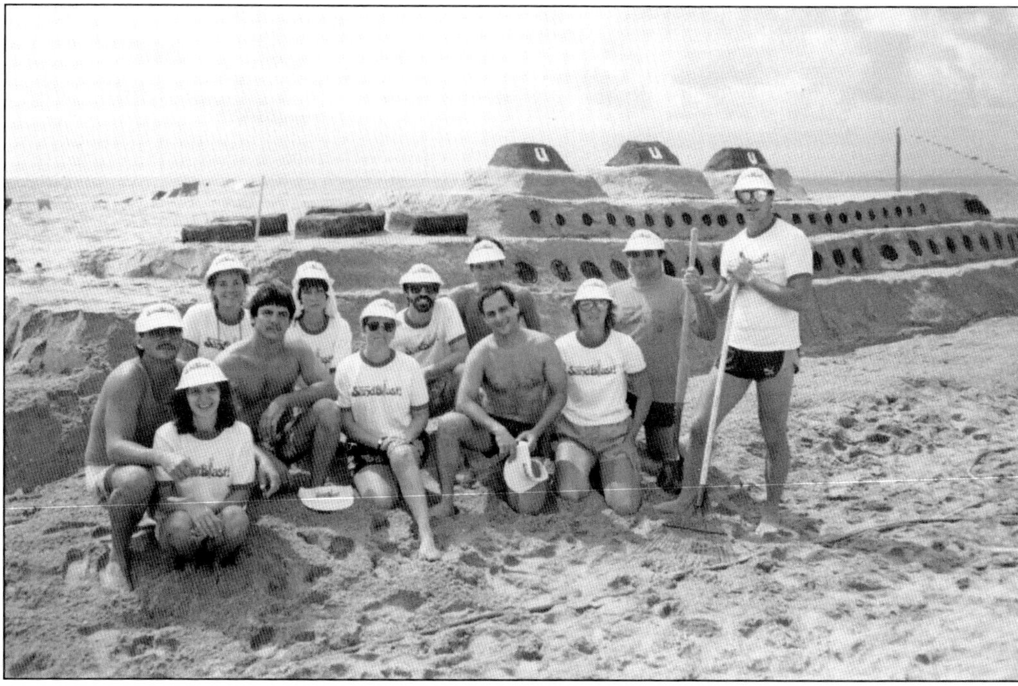

Art and fashion students and staff sculpted the S.S. *Art Institute* cruise ship out of sand at a Fourth of July celebration in the mid-1980s. The sand ship stands 11 feet high and 64 feet long. The three smokestacks were built with the school logo sprayed in red. Dry ice was watered down to make smoke come out of the stacks. The lifeboats were painted in blue.

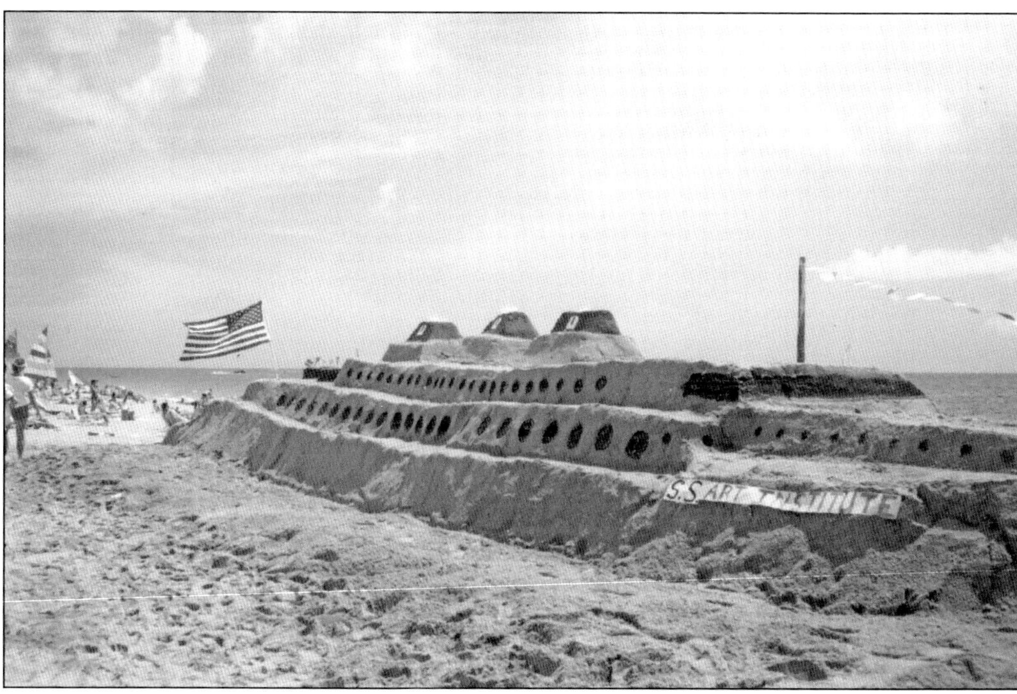

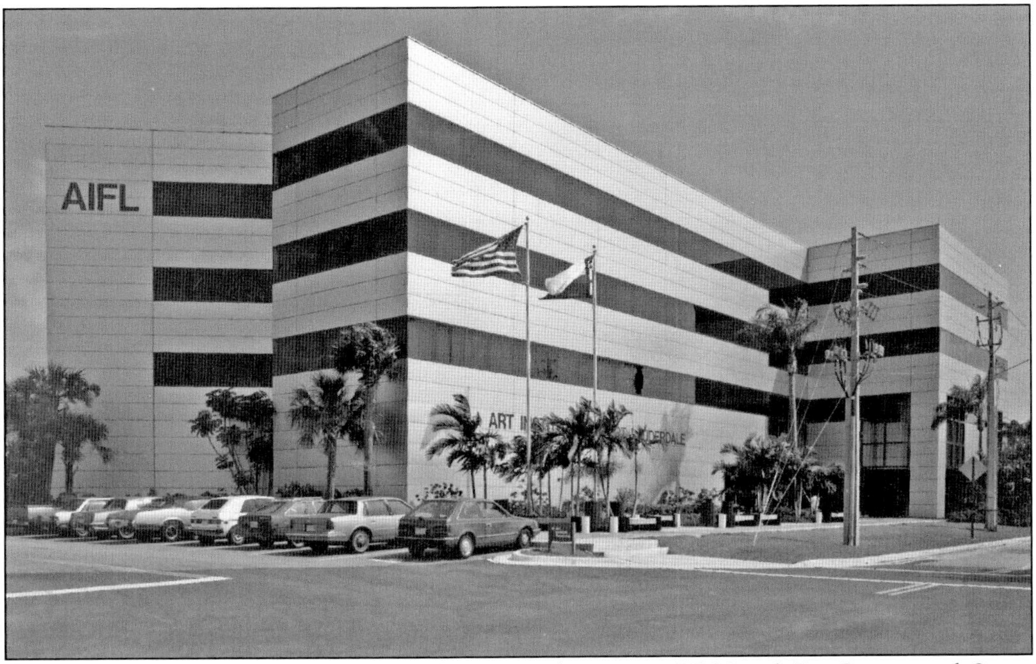

The Art Institute of Fort Lauderdale moved to its new location at 1799 South East Seventeenth Street in 1986. The school's location is one mile from the Atlantic Ocean, just south of the intercoastal waterway and north of Port Everglades.

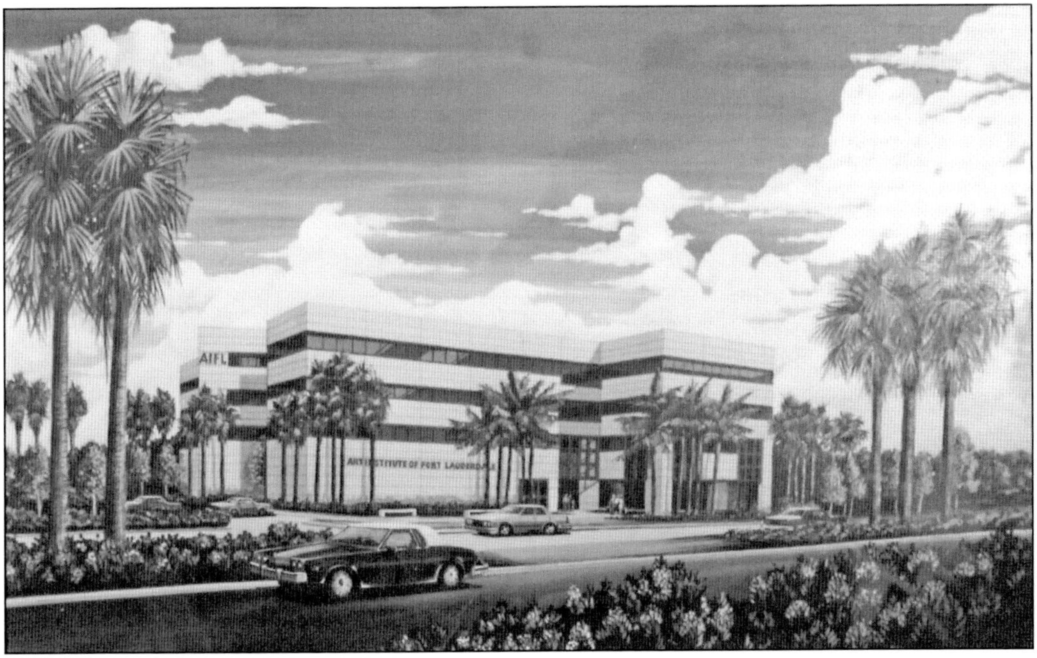

Featured here is Bill Kobrynich's architectural rendering of the new building. The original was sketched on a 3-by-4-foot illustration board.

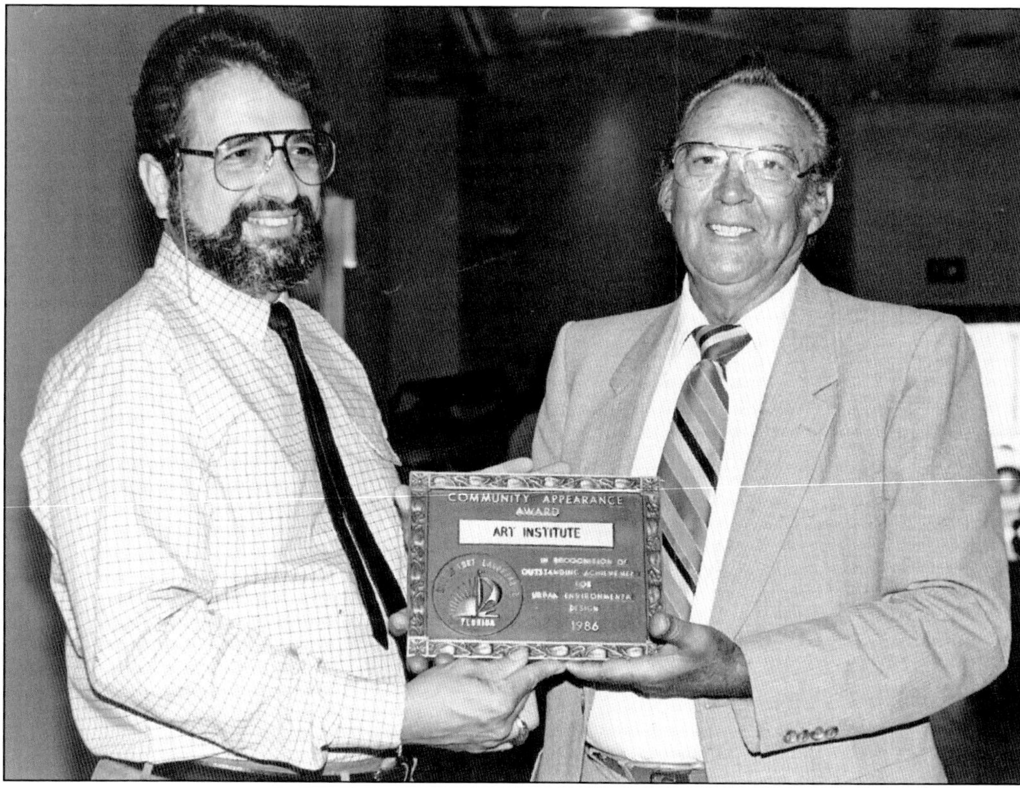

In 1986, school president Mark Wheeler (right) and vice president and director of education Frank Raia show off the Community Appearance Award bestowed upon the new Art Institute of Fort Lauderdale building in recognition of outstanding achievement for urban environmental design.

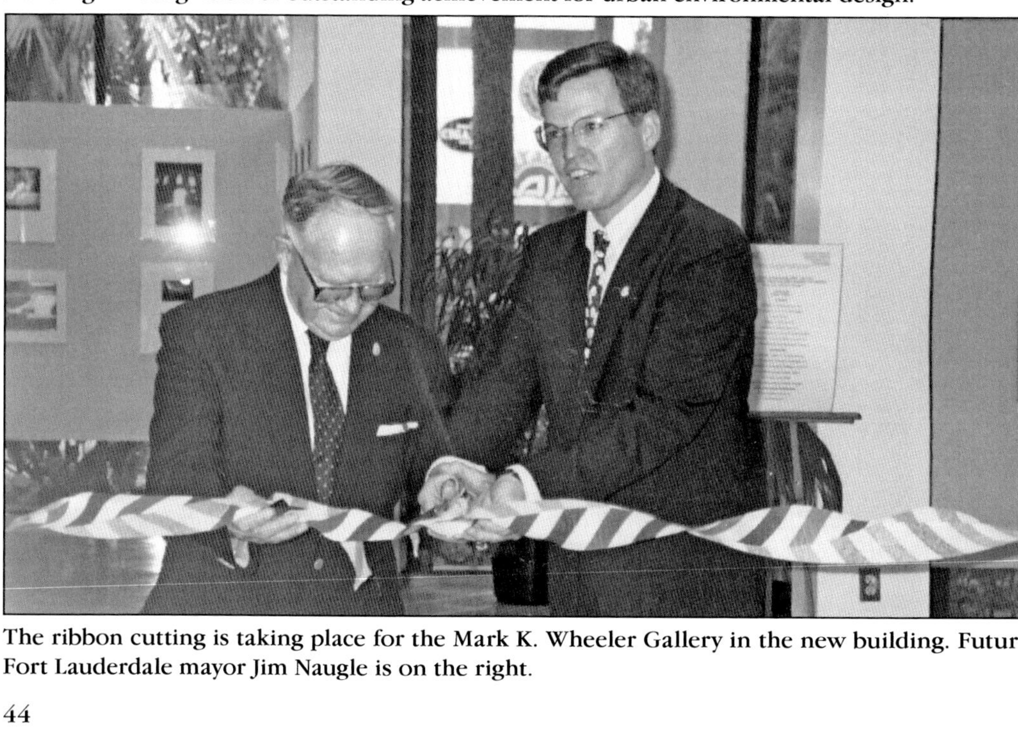

The ribbon cutting is taking place for the Mark K. Wheeler Gallery in the new building. Future Fort Lauderdale mayor Jim Naugle is on the right.

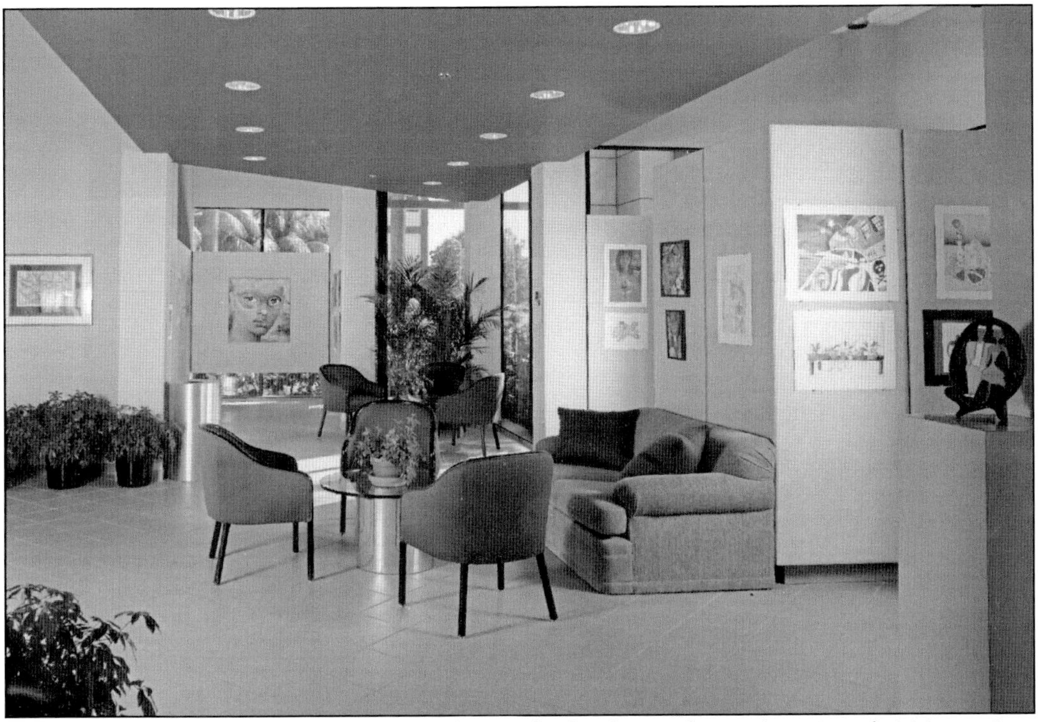

The Mark K. Wheeler Gallery features exhibitions by faculty, students, alumni, and visiting artists. The art gallery has been part of the school since September or October 1978, when it opened in celebration of the school's 10th Anniversary. (Courtesy of Robert Peterson.)

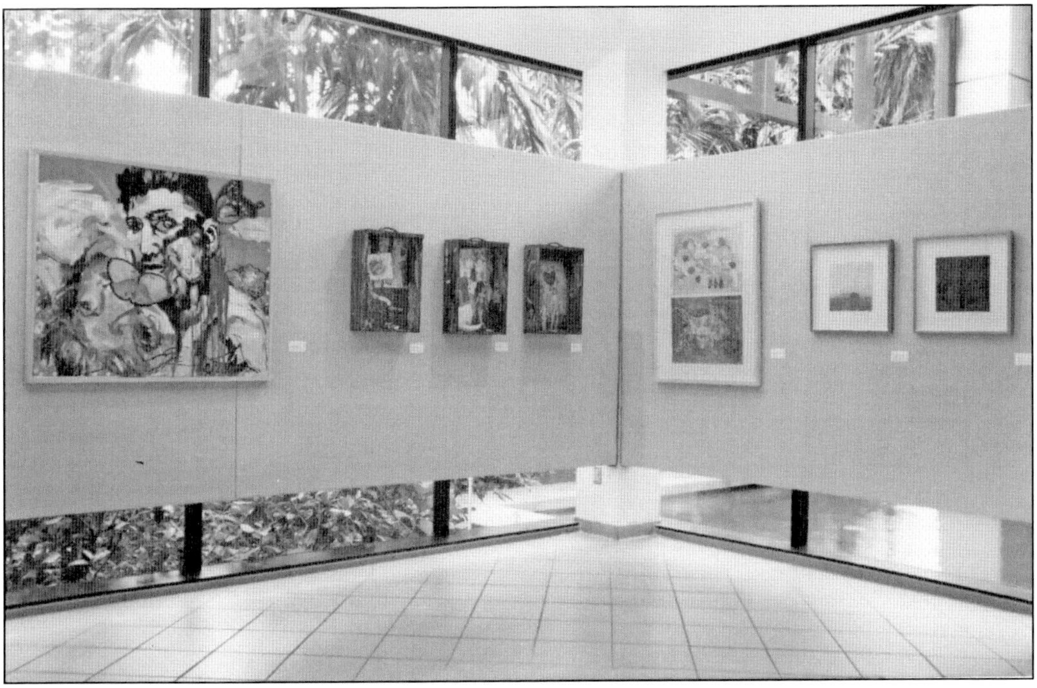

The inside of the Wheeler gallery is a wonderful example of outstanding design, which provides perfect lighting for the art pieces exhibited.

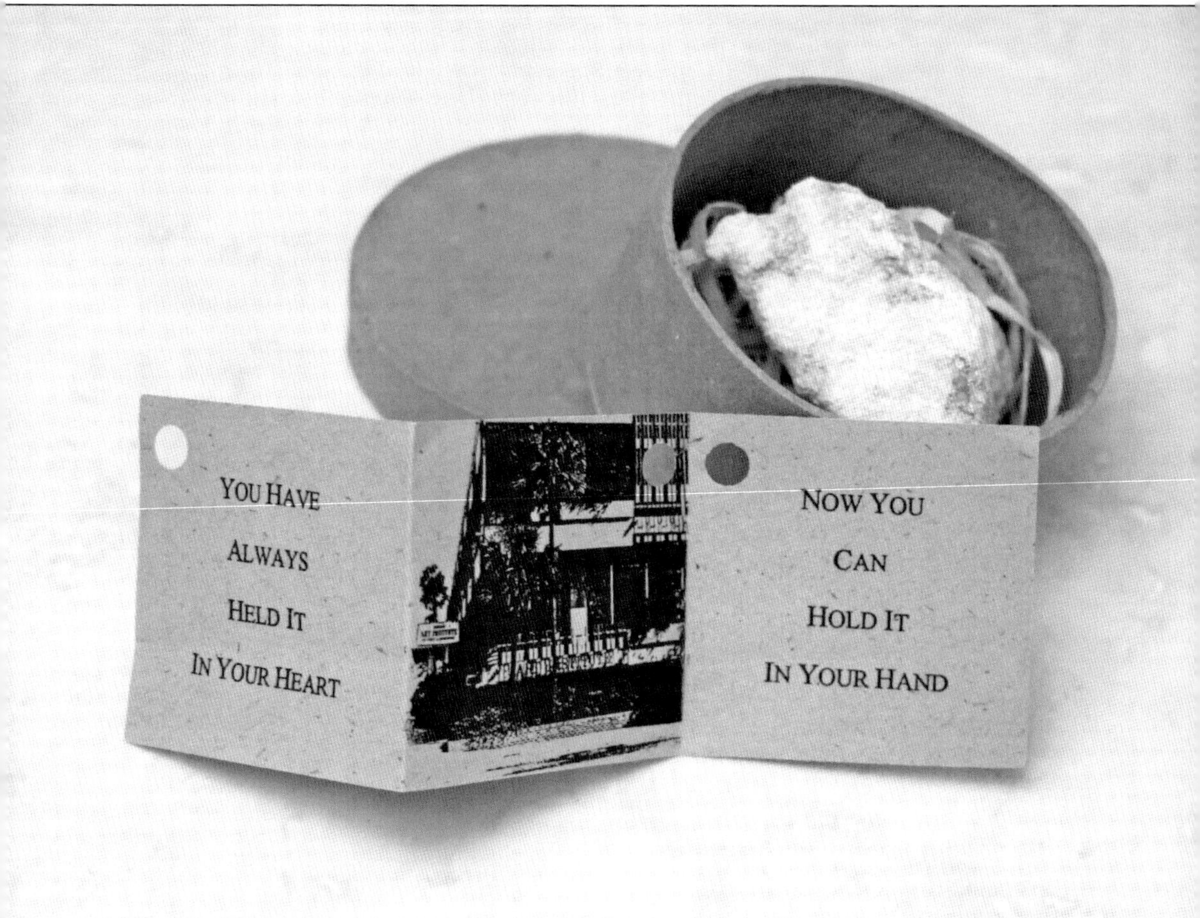

After the school moved, the Oceanside Holiday Inn was torn down. Linda Vacchiano, both an alumna and faculty member, and her husband, Bill Kobrynich, went to the site to collect pieces of concrete, which Vacchiano subsequently turned into gift boxes for her colleagues. (Photograph by Ms. V.)

This is a portrait of Mimi Botscheller taken in 1987.

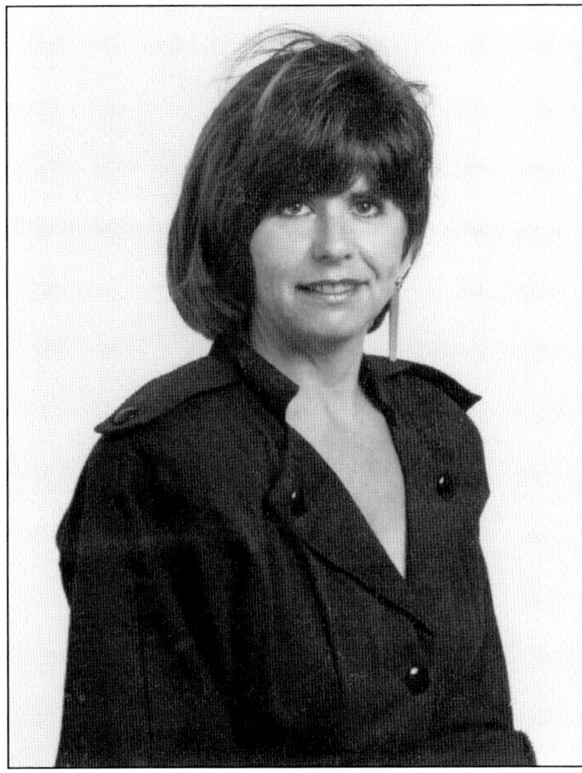

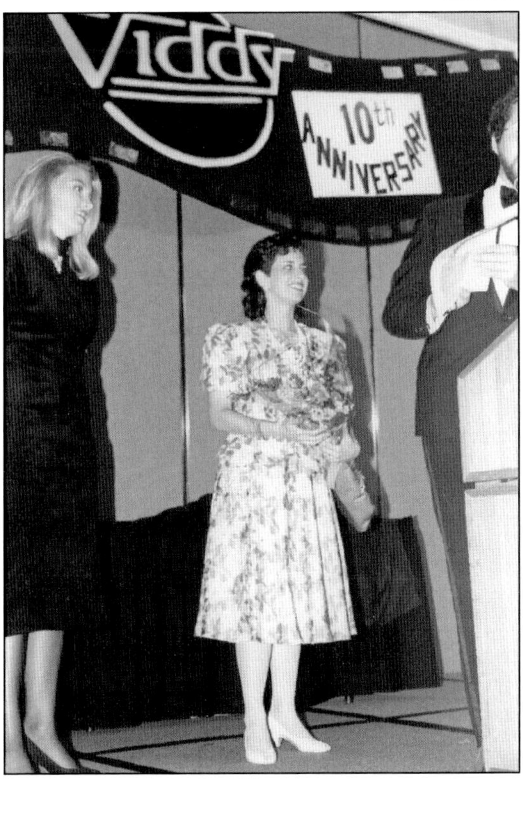

Faculty member Debbie Rose Myers is shown here (center) in 1988 at the 10th-anniversary celebration of the "Viddy" awards, which she started in 1978. "Viddies" were annual video awards given to students for professional excellence in television graphics. The "Viddy" awards contest involved creating different video pieces related to television. It was open to many different departments, with students creating 30- and 60-second commercials, public service announcements, music videos, and animation. Students created storyboards known as "art cards." Industry professionals judged the awards, and a gala event was held once a year at one of the area's hotel ballrooms. (Courtesy of Debbie Rose Myers.)

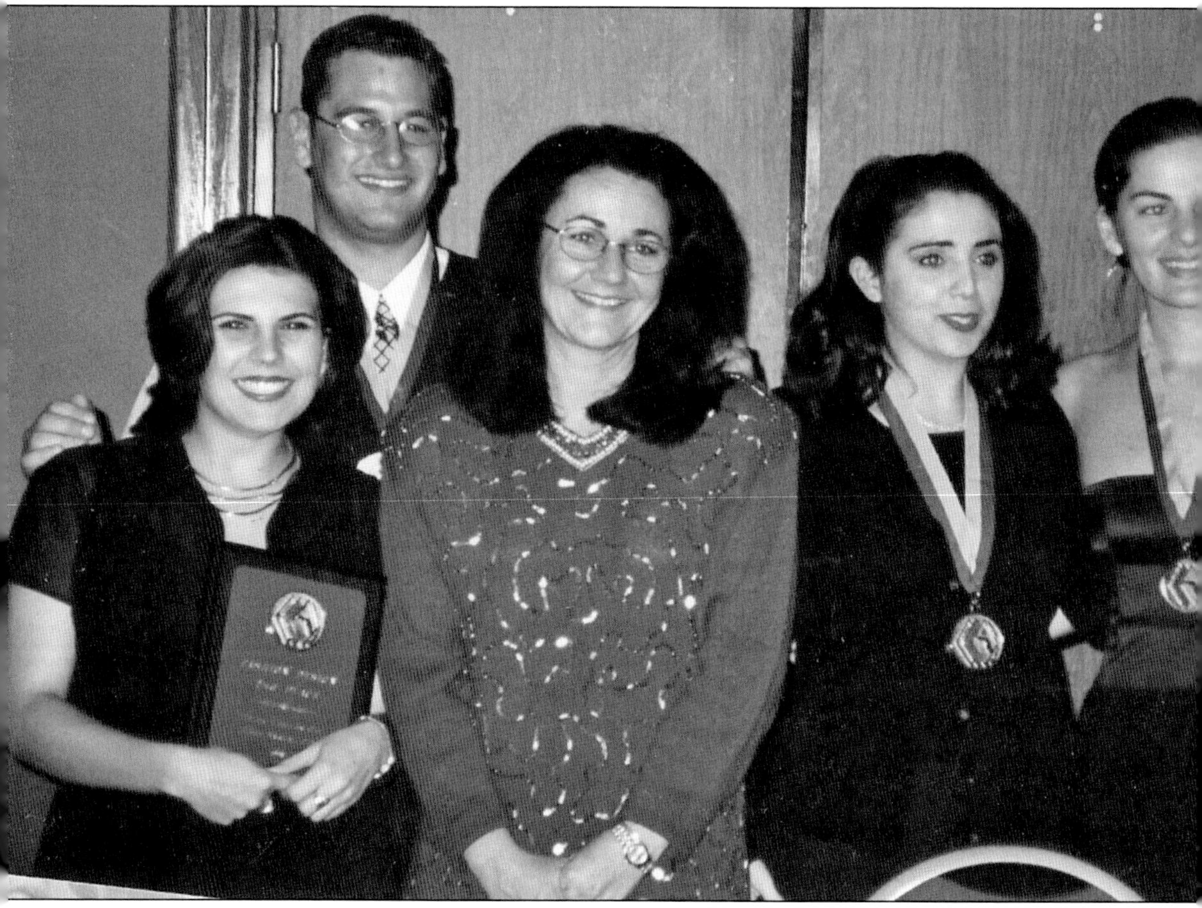

Kathy Colussy (third from left) stands with student members of Delta Epsilon Chi, an international college-level marketing organization. For 20 years, the school was a key player in preparing students for the real world via conferences and competitions held annually. Students conducted research and made presentations in all aspects of apparel, design, and marketing at the state and national levels. Students won at the national level every year the school participated in this organization. (Courtesy of Kathy Colussy.)

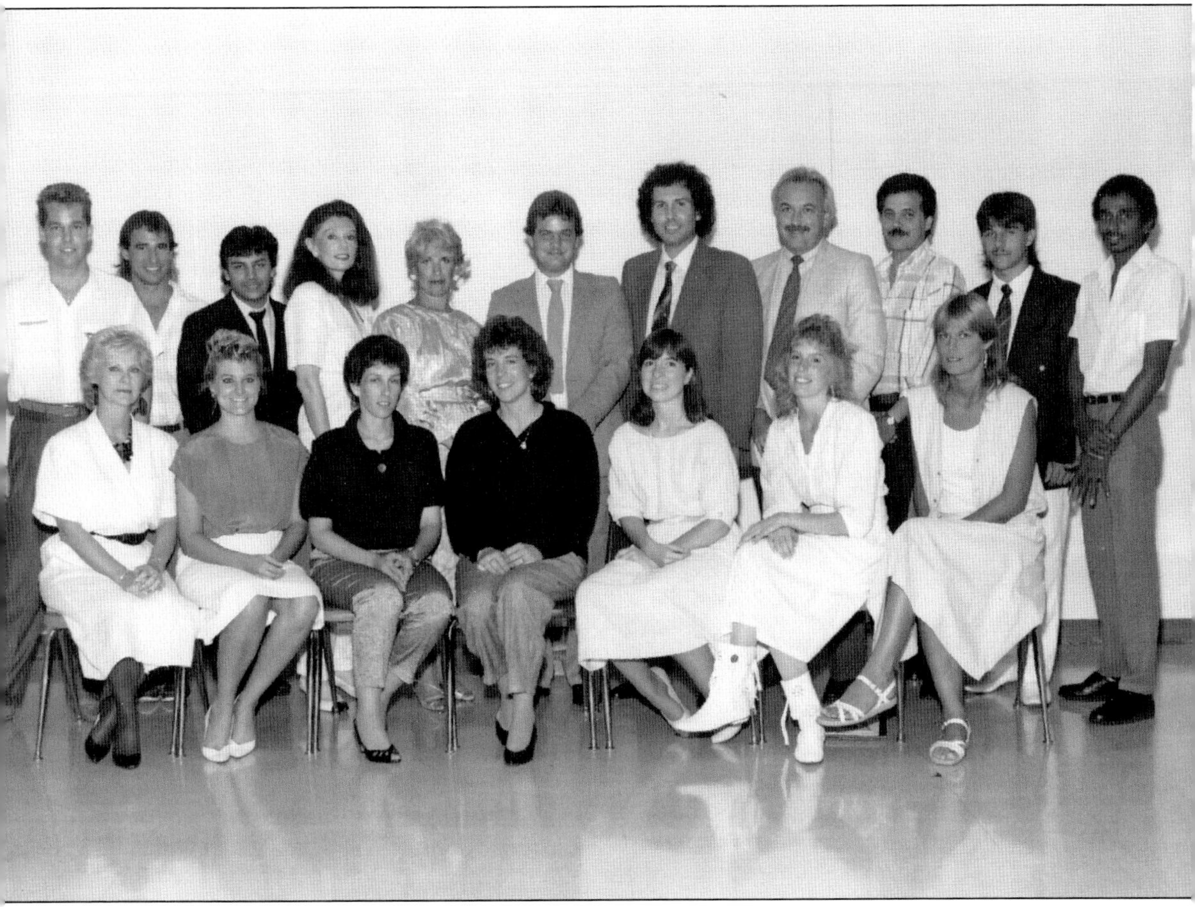

In 1986, the Art Institute of Fort Lauderdale started offering students the opportunity to earn a degree in layout and production art, residential design, and applied photography by going to school exclusively in the evening. This picture shows the first evening division graduate class in 1987. (Courtesy of Robert Peterson.)

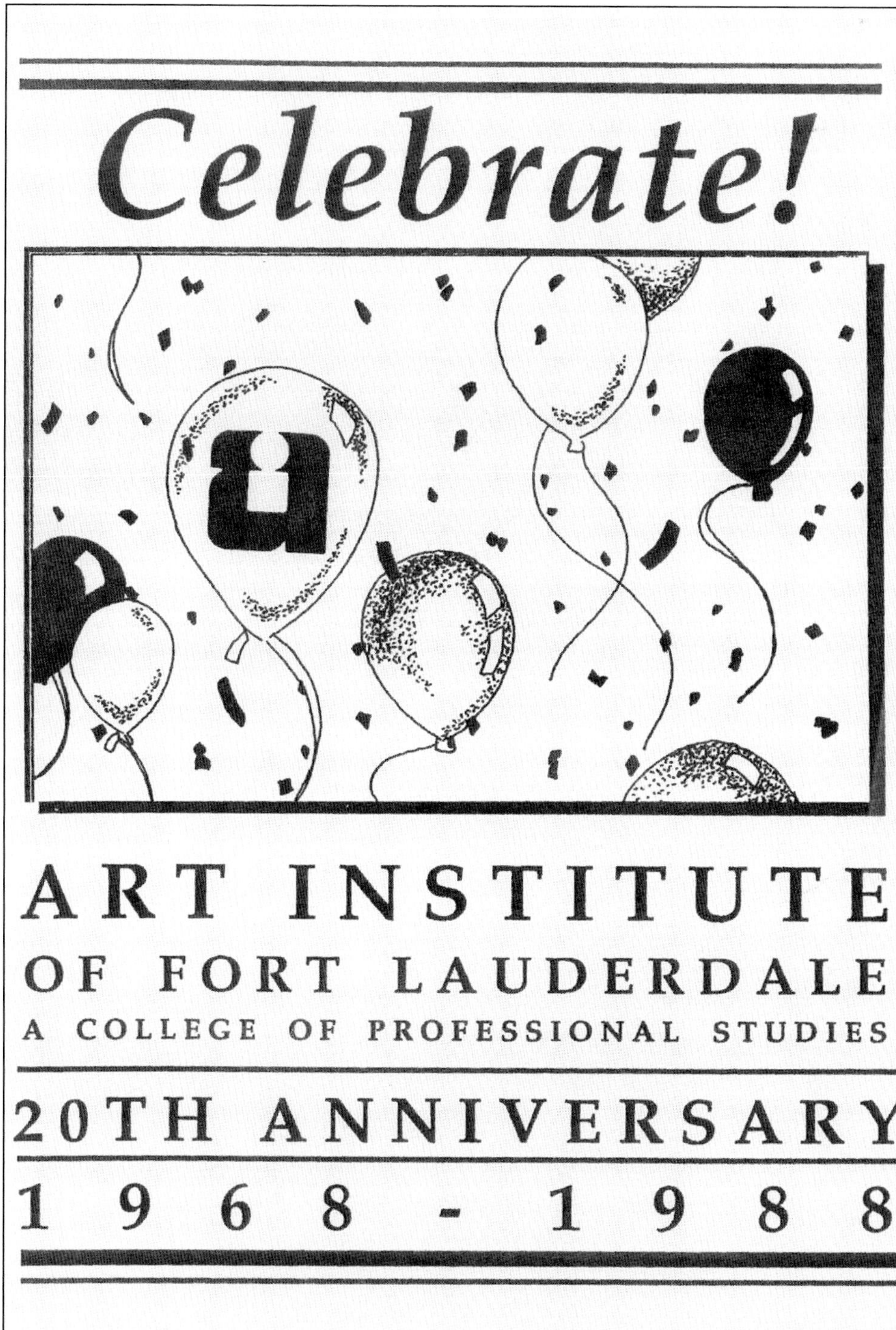

The Art Institute of Fort Lauderdale's 20th-anniversary announcement is shown here. In 1988, the school offered eight associate and two baccalaureate degrees to 1,800 students. At that time, the school was the largest of its type in the southeastern United States. Denise Rodriguez designed the birthday poster pictured here.

Three

GROWTH

The growth of the new associate- and bachelor-level programs that started at the end of the previous decade continued, seemingly exponentially, during the next 10 years. New programs were added, including culinary arts, video production, industrial design, and interactive multimedia programming.

Graduates began to experience unprecedented success in their chosen careers, and many were recognized for their accomplishments by being inducted into the school's "Wall of Fame." Multiple Pulitzer Prize–winning photographer Carol Guzy and renowned artist Jonathan Knight, who would become the school's first graduate to sit on its board of trustees, were among the first inductees. Successful industry professionals continued to join the faculty, and many more visited the school as guest lecturers.

Once again, the Art Institute of Fort Lauderdale found itself facing a familiar dilemma: how to accommodate a growing student body, which had blossomed to 2,000 by 1995. And once again, the school responded by expanding to new facilities—twice. First the Art Institute of Fort Lauderdale moved to a vacant restaurant building adjacent to the main building, and when that proved too small, the school moved again, this time to the Harbor Walk building across the street at 1650 South East Seventeenth Street.

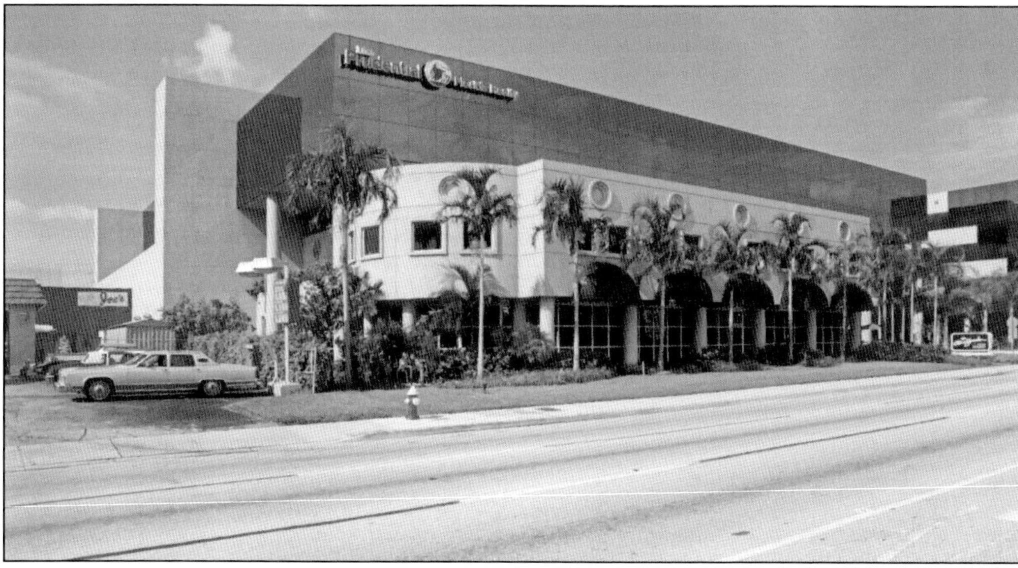

Pictured here is the Harbor Walk building, located at 1650 South East Seventeenth Street. Before the school took over this space, the building housed Prudential Insurance and an Olive Garden restaurant. The price for a gallon of regular unleaded gasoline at that time was $1.059.

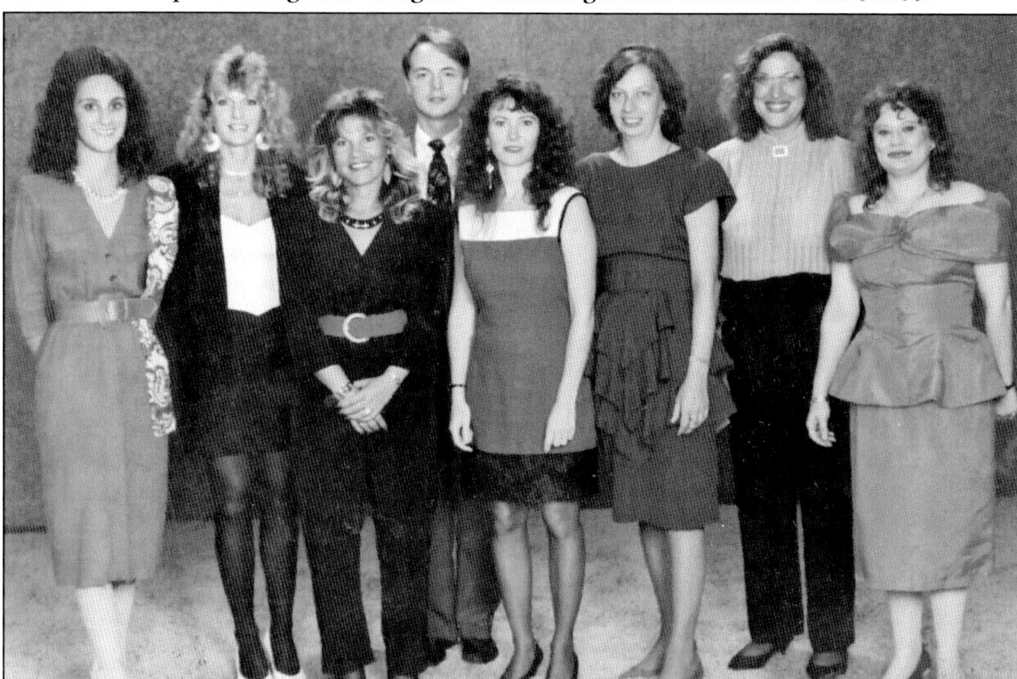

The staff of the career services department included (from left to right) Linda Harrison, Dori Evans, Erika Fleming, Rob Nonweiller, Mary Cober, Vicki Izlar, Susan Pawela, and LuWin Sanchez. Izlar and Sanchez started with the school in 1989 and 1990, respectively, and were still on staff in 2008. Erika Fleming was the president of the Miami International University of Art and Design. Susan Pawela was the long-time chairwoman of the school's general education department. (Courtesy of LuWin Sanchez.)

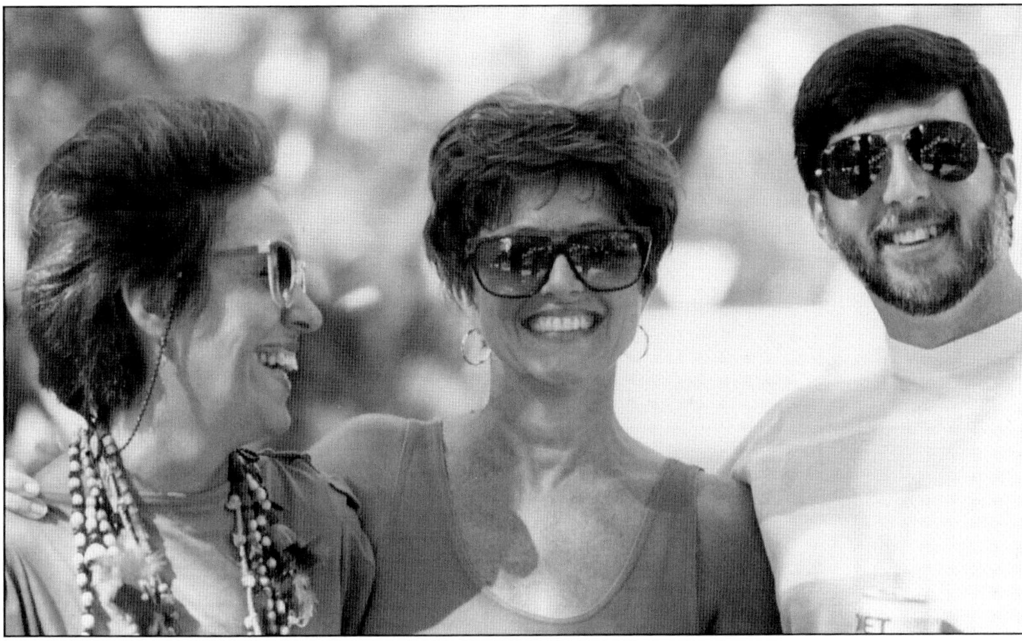

Pictured from left to right are Martha Medina, Connie Yerman, and Ed Galizia at a company picnic in 1989.

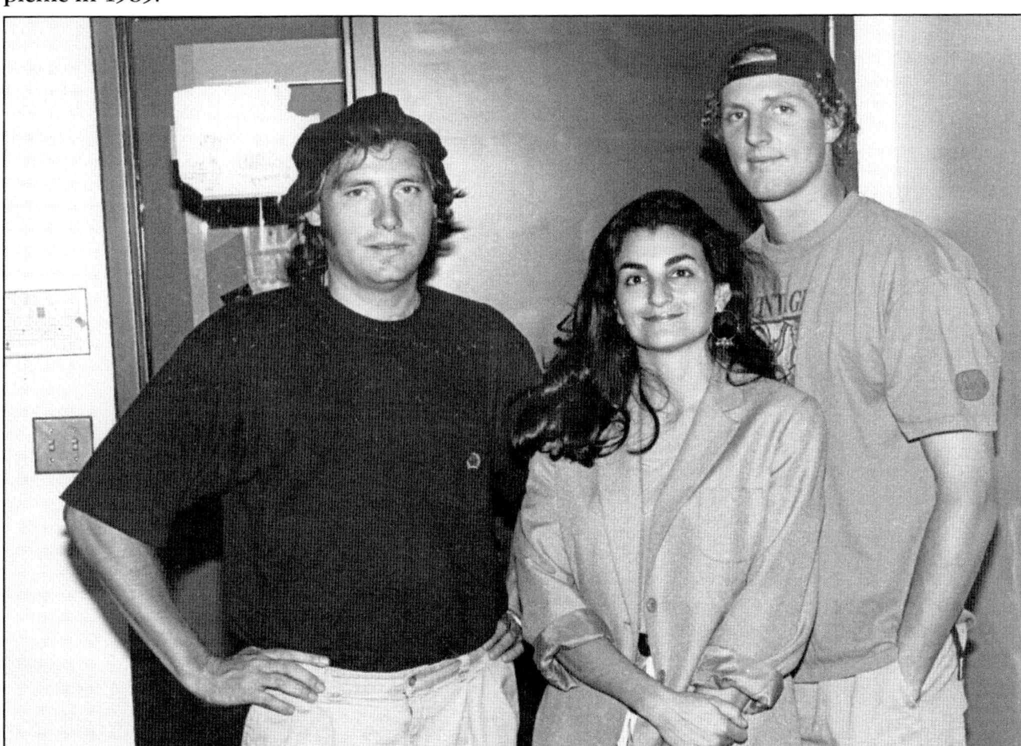

Guest lecturers Dean Felber, bassist (left), and Mark Bryan, guitarist and singer for the music group Hootie and the Blowfish are shown here with music-and-video-business student and promoter Gina Hartley. The group won two Grammy awards for its 1994 debut album *Cracked Rear View.*

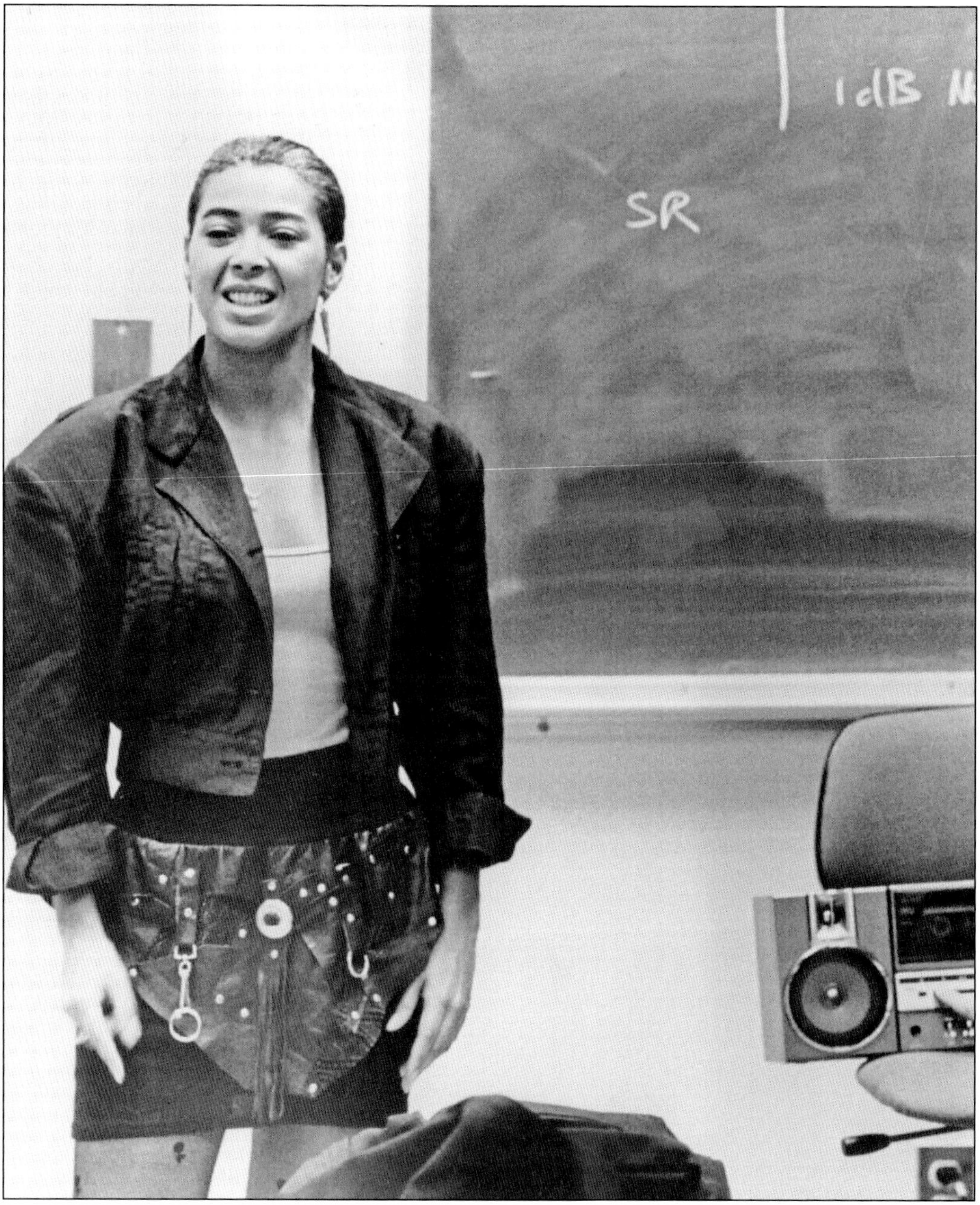

Irene Cara, an actress and singer, teaches students in 1989. Visiting lecturers bring real-world success stories to the classroom. Cara is an Academy Award winner and two-time Grammy award winner for her songs "What a Feeling" (the title song of the movie *Flashdance*) and the title song of the movie *Fame*.

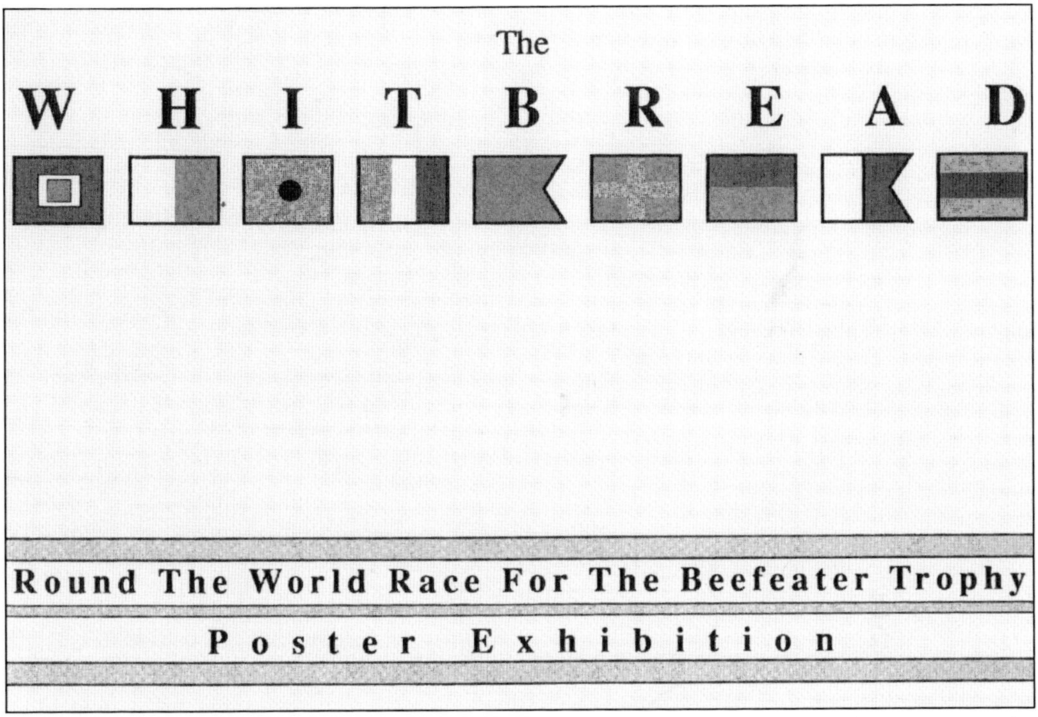

The

WHITBREAD

Round The World Race For The Beefeater Trophy

Poster Exhibition

"You are invited" in December 1989 to the Mark K. Wheeler Gallery to sip champagne at the reception of the poster competition for the 1990 Whitbread Boat Race. This was a round-the-world yacht race for the famous "Beefeater Trophy." The Whitbread race is held every four years and is currently known as the Volvo Ocean Race.

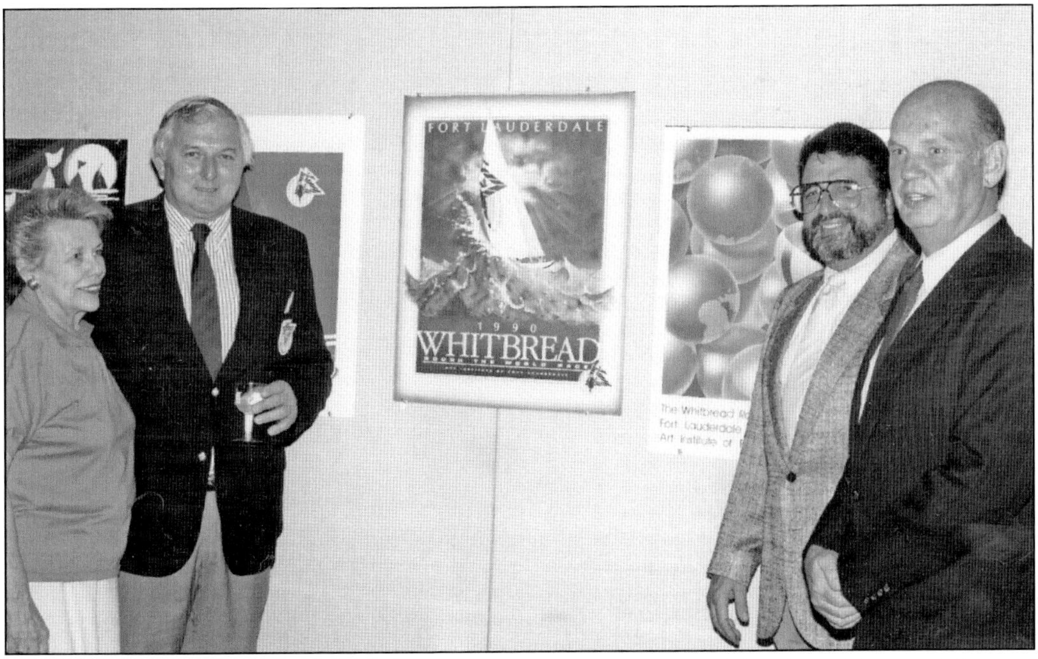

The winning poster, designed by student Bo Huber, is surrounded by (from left to right) Betty Lou Curry, Dick Vander Bosch, Frank Raia, and Hudson Whiting.

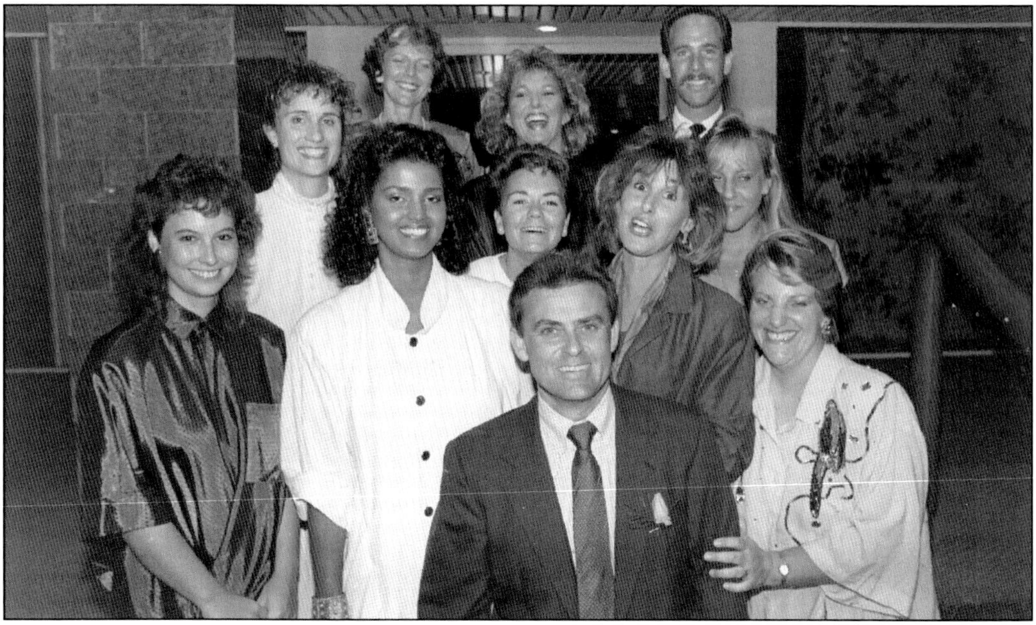

Bill Kobrynich (seated), the chair of the interior design department, poses with students from the American Society of Interior Design (ASID) student chapter at the spring portfolio review held at the Design Center of the Americas (DCOTA). From left to right are (second row) Beth Decker, Miriam DeSilva, Martha Mohr-Franta, Anita Market, and Lisa Grosso; (third row) Patricia Joseph, Gwendolyn Thorton, Terri Gagnon, unidentified, Julie Harris. (Courtesy of Bill Kobrynich.)

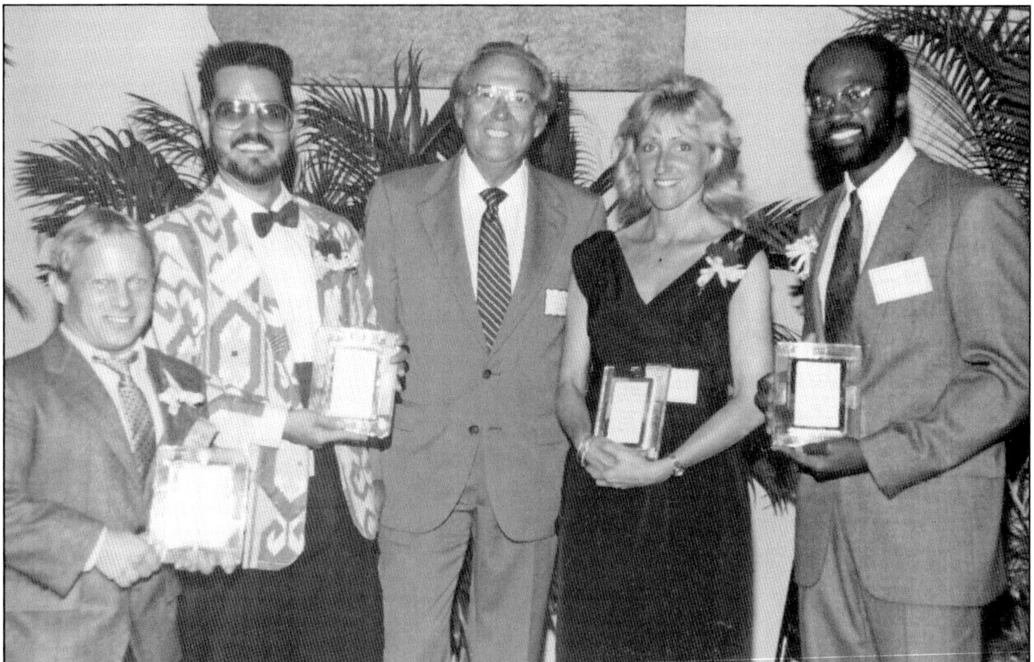

School president Mark K. Wheeler is shown in 1989 with the first inductees to the "Wall of Fame." Pictured from left to right are Alan Keifer, Mark Wygonik, Wheeler, Carol Guzy, and Jonathan Knight.

This announcement invites the public and possible employers to attend the portfolio review for the first bachelor's degree graduating class in fashion design, on March 20, 1990.

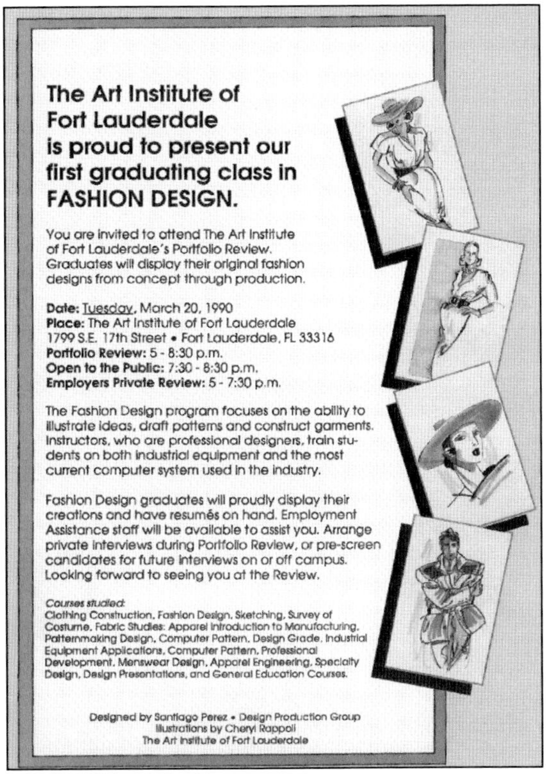

The Art Institute of Fort Lauderdale is proud to present our first graduating class in FASHION DESIGN.

You are invited to attend The Art Institute of Fort Lauderdale's Portfolio Review. Graduates will display their original fashion designs from concept through production.

Date: Tuesday, March 20, 1990
Place: The Art Institute of Fort Lauderdale
1799 S.E. 17th Street • Fort Lauderdale, FL 33316
Portfolio Review: 5 - 8:30 p.m.
Open to the Public: 7:30 - 8:30 p.m.
Employers Private Review: 5 - 7:30 p.m.

The Fashion Design program focuses on the ability to illustrate ideas, draft patterns and construct garments. Instructors, who are professional designers, train students on both industrial equipment and the most current computer system used in the industry.

Fashion Design graduates will proudly display their creations and have resumés on hand. Employment Assistance staff will be available to assist you. Arrange private interviews during Portfolio Review, or pre-screen candidates for future interviews on or off campus. Looking forward to seeing you at the Review.

Courses studied:
Clothing Construction, Fashion Design, Sketching, Survey of Costume, Fabric Studies: Apparel Introduction to Manufacturing, Patternmaking Design, Computer Pattern, Design Grade, Industrial Equipment Applications, Computer Pattern, Professional Development, Menswear Design, Apparel Engineering, Specialty Design, Design Presentations, and General Education Courses.

Designed by Santiago Perez • Design Production Group
Illustrations by Cheryl Rappoli
The Art Institute of Fort Lauderdale

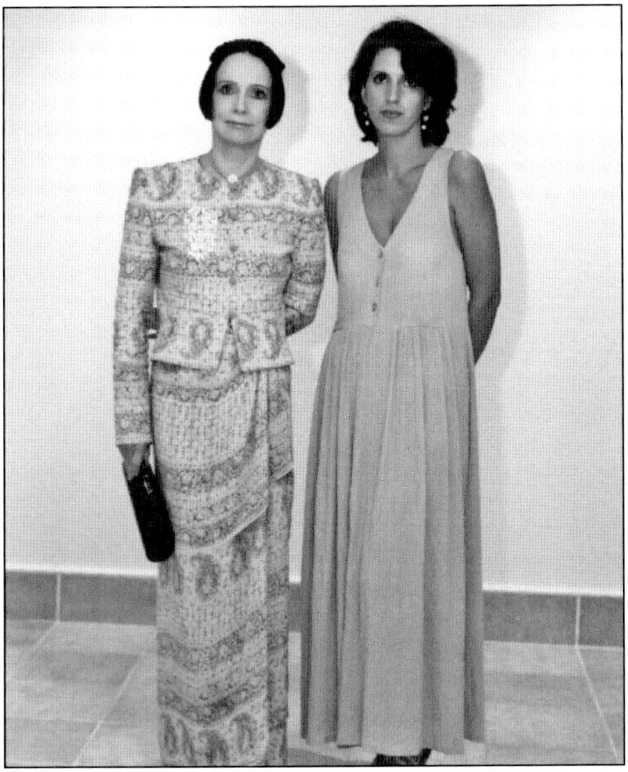

Haute-couture designer Mary McFadden (left) is pictured here with fashion instructor Chrisa Tatakis. The University of Pennsylvania Museum called McFadden the "high priestess of high fashion." (Courtesy of Kathy Colussy.)

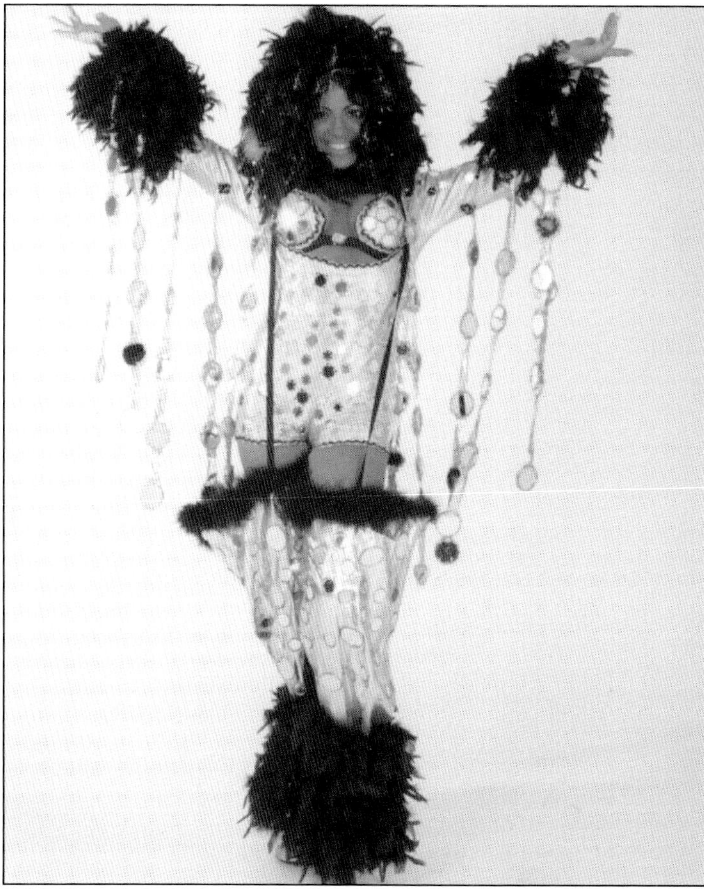

An outfit from a fashion show in the early 1990s is pictured here. (Courtesy of Kathy Colussy.)

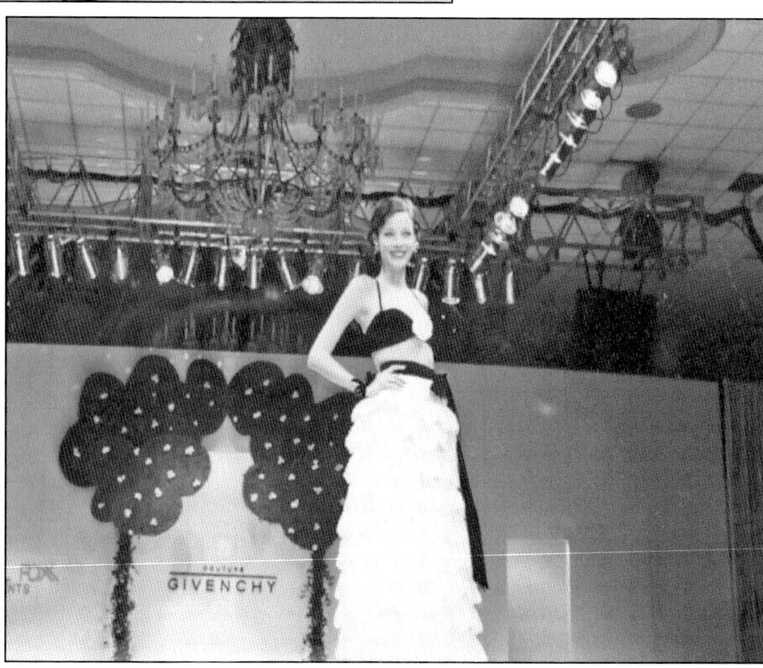

Count Hubert James Marcel Taffin de Givenchy opened his own fashion design house in Paris in 1952. He was Audrey Hepburn's favorite designer and became the first high-fashion designer to produce ready-to-wear clothing in 1956. This photograph shows an outfit from the fashion design department's celebration of his work. (Courtesy of Kahty Colussy.)

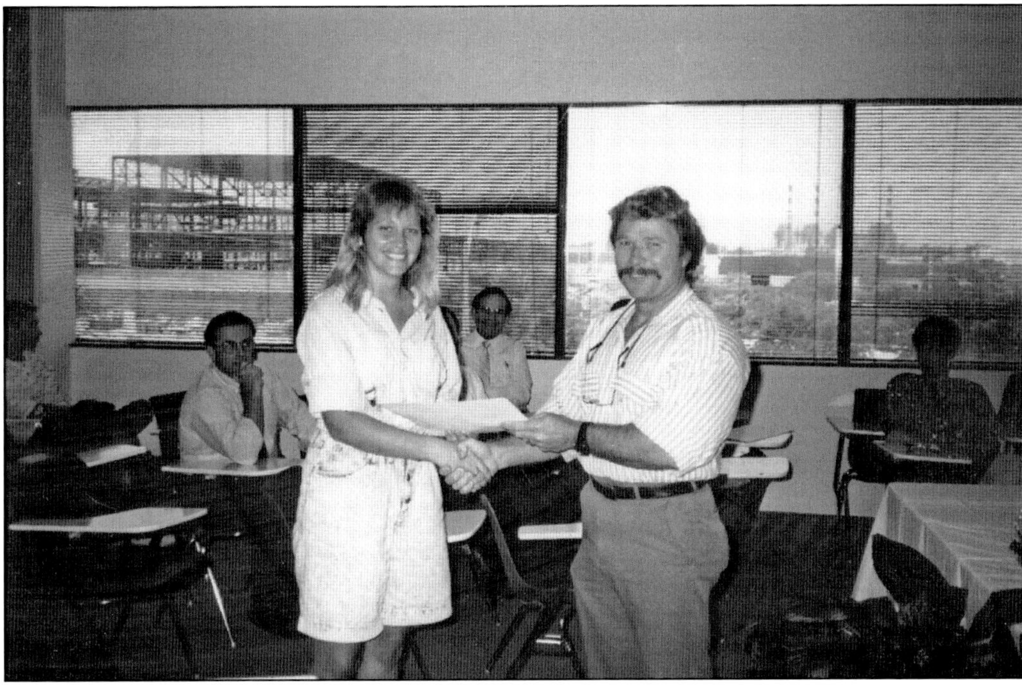

Faculty member Jim Radford presents a scholarship to an unidentified student. The construction of the Broward County Convention Center can be seen in the background.

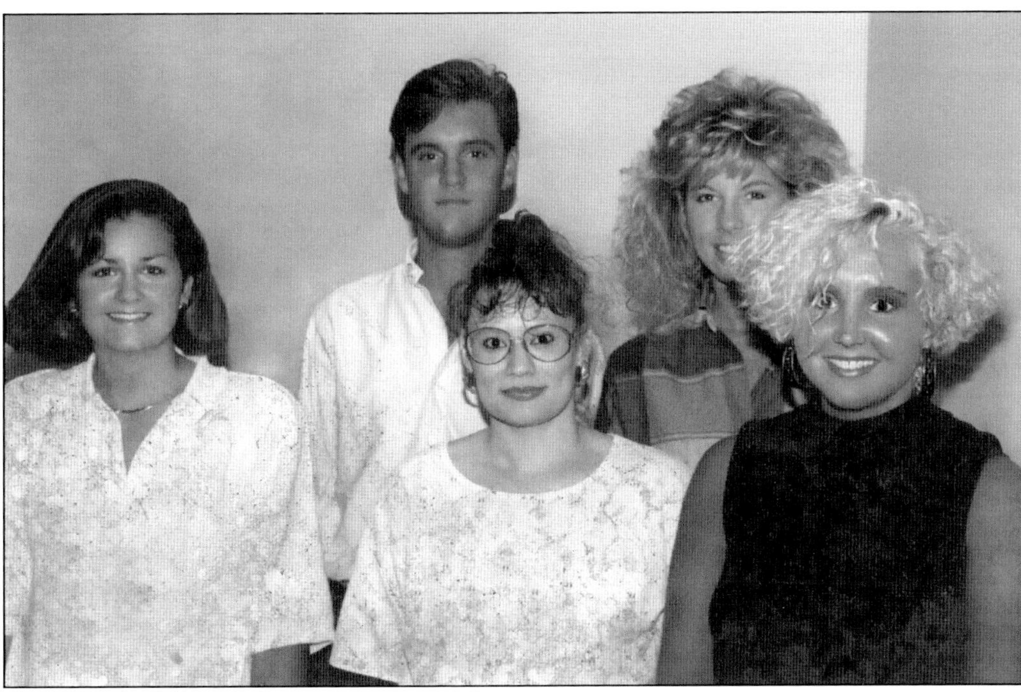

Pictured here, in March 1990, are career services staff members who were also Honor Roll students. From left to right are Christina Churchill, Kevin Staffens, LuWin Sanchez, Lorraine Coles Wood, and Nancy Lavin. (Courtesy of LuWin Sanchez.)

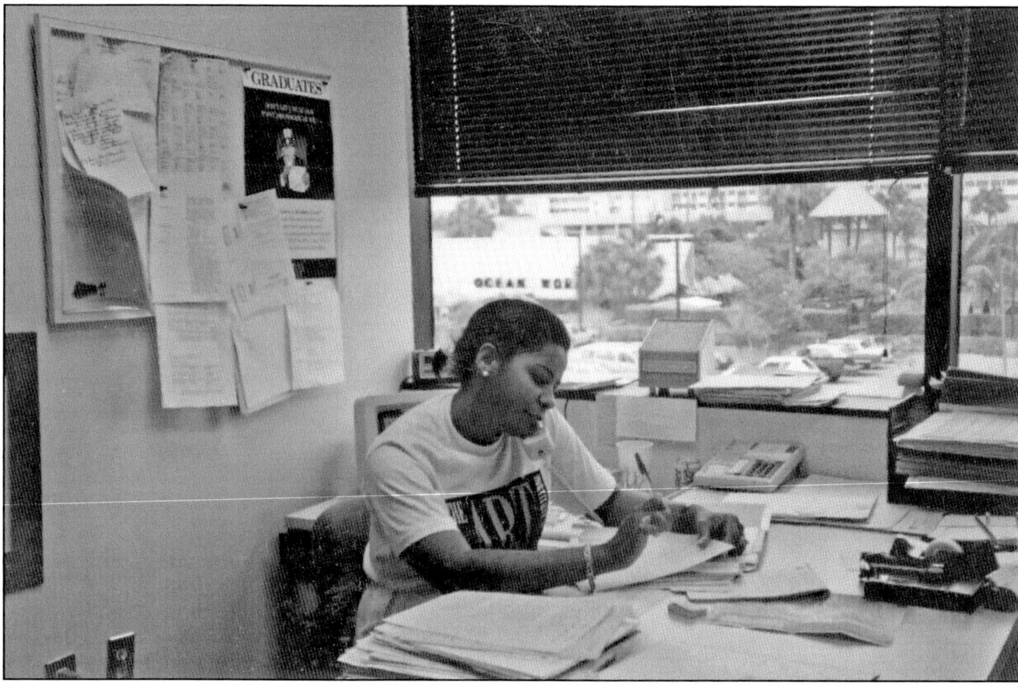

A Ms. Carol from financial services is working, and the sign for Ocean World is visible in the background of this June 20, 1990, photograph. (Courtesy of Laura Waterman.)

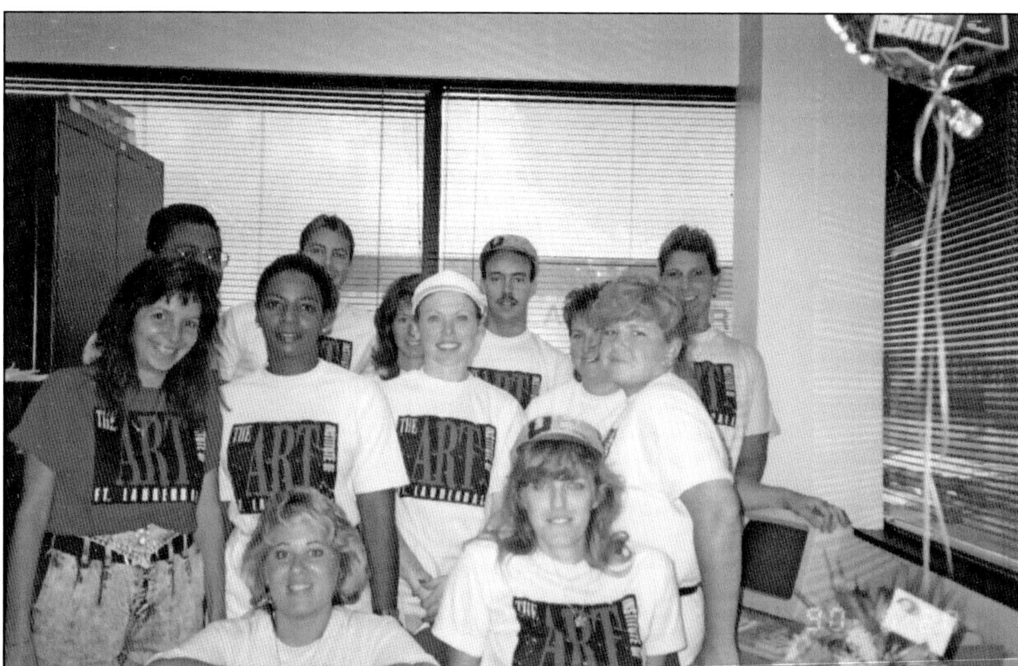

Members of the student financial services office are shown during a team work-a-thon, held to help move new students through the financial aid process in the summer of 1990. (Courtesy of Laura Waterman.)

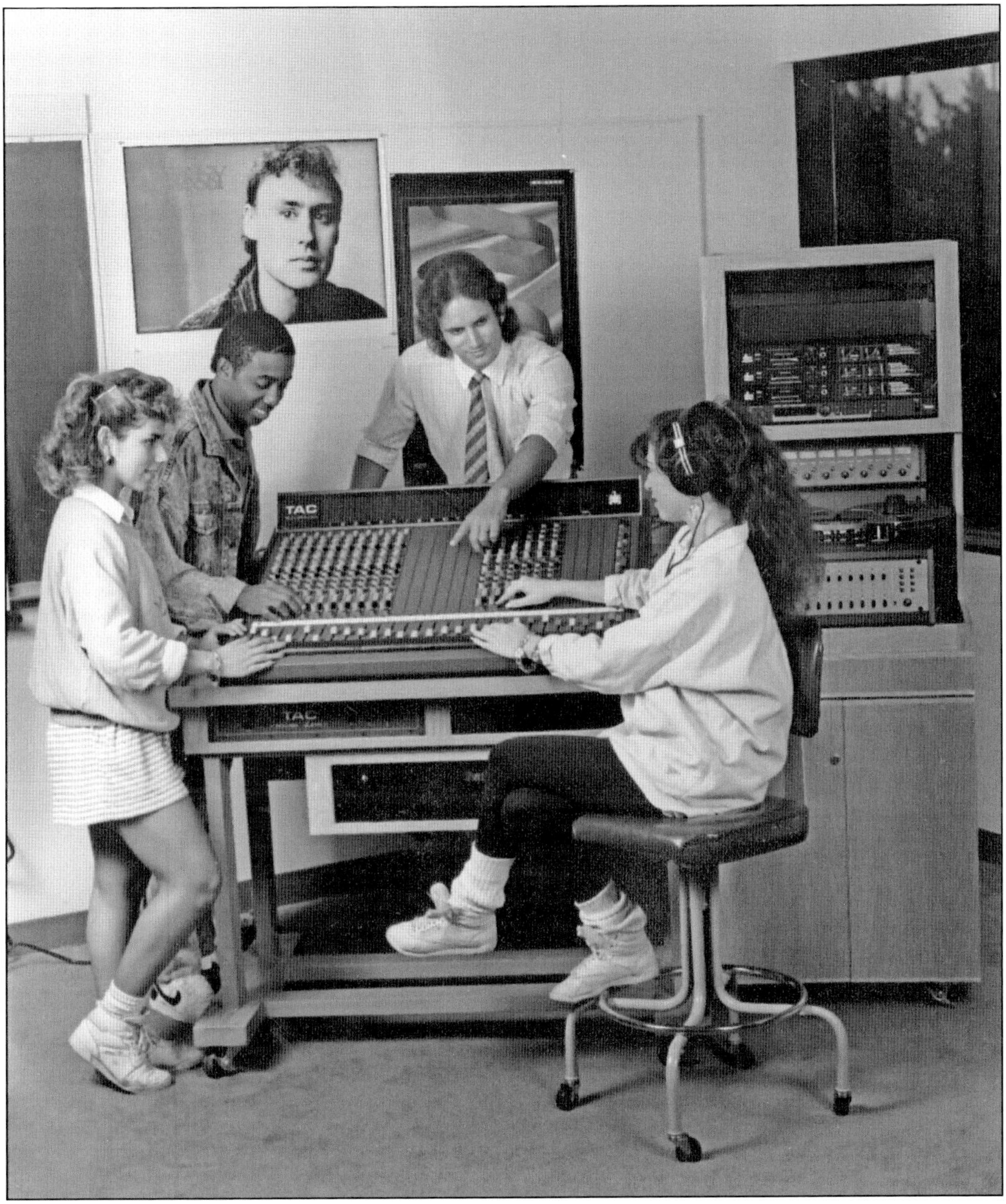

Music-and-video business instructor George Papabeis teaches students how to operate a TAC audio console in the fall of 1990.

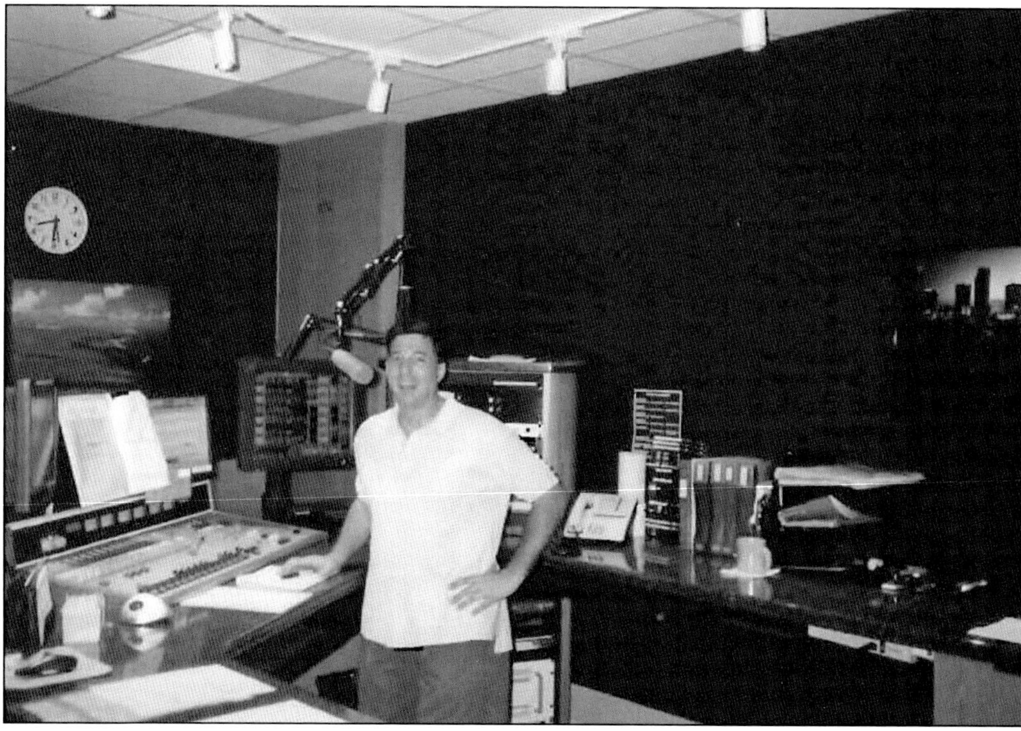

Ed Galizia is pictured in the 101.5 Lite FM music radio station studio. Galizia was the long-time chairman of the broadcasting department before he served as the dean of education from 2005 to 2007. (Courtesy of Ed Galizia.)

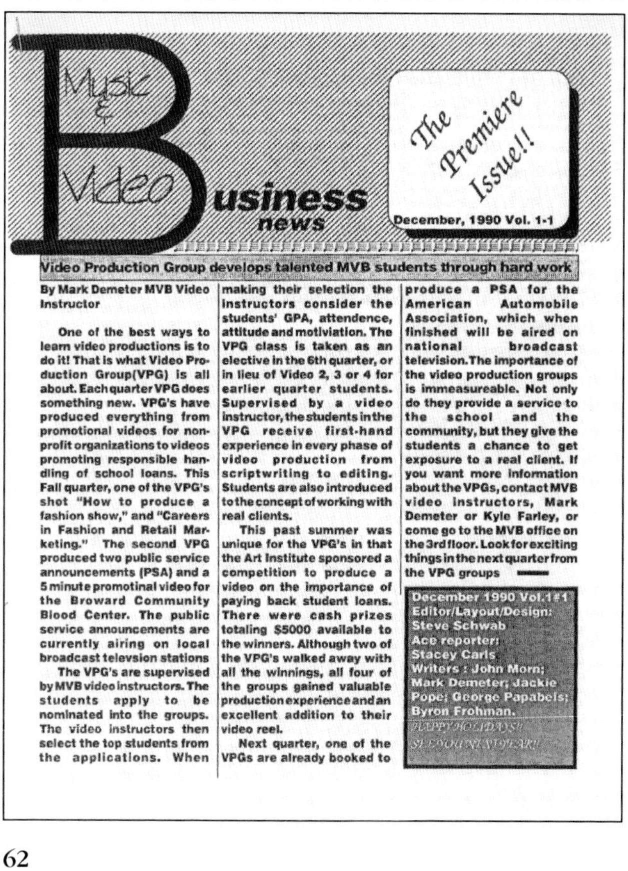

Music & Video Business news

The Premiere Issue!!

December, 1990 Vol. 1-1

Video Production Group develops talented MVB students through hard work

By Mark Demeter MVB Video Instructor

One of the best ways to learn video productions is to do it! That is what Video Production Group(VPG) is all about. Each quarter VPG does something new. VPG's have produced everything from promotional videos for non-profit organizations to videos promoting responsible handling of school loans. This Fall quarter, one of the VPG's shot "How to produce a fashion show," and "Careers in Fashion and Retail Marketing." The second VPG produced two public service announcements (PSA) and a 5 minute promotinal video for the Broward Community Blood Center. The public service announcements are currently airing on local broadcast televsion stations

The VPG's are supervised by MVB video instructors. The students apply to be nominated into the groups. The video instructors then select the top students from the applications. When making their selection the instructors consider the students' GPA, attendence, attitude and motiviation. The VPG class is taken as an elective in the 6th quarter, or in lieu of Video 2, 3 or 4 for earlier quarter students. Supervised by a video instructor, the students in the VPG receive first-hand experience in every phase of video production from scriptwriting to editing. Students are also introduced to the concept of working with real clients.

This past summer was unique for the VPG's in that the Art Institute sponsored a competition to produce a video on the importance of paying back student loans. There were cash prizes totaling $5000 available to the winners. Although two of the VPG's walked away with all the winnings, all four of the groups gained valuable production experience and an excellent addition to their video reel.

Next quarter, one of the VPGs are already booked to produce a PSA for the American Automobile Association, which when finished will be aired on national broadcast television. The importance of the video production groups is immeasureable. Not only do they provide a service to the school and the community, but they give the students a chance to get exposure to a real client. If you want more information about the VPGs, contact MVB video instructors, Mark Demeter or Kyle Farley, or come go to the MVB office on the 3rd floor. Look for exciting things in the next quarter from the VPG groups

December 1990 Vol.1#1
Editor/Layout/Design: Steve Schwab
Ace reporter: Stacey Carls
Writers : John Morn; Mark Demeter; Jackie Pope; George Papabeis; Byron Frohman.

December 1990 saw the premier issue of the *Music and Video Business News*.

Bonnie Lallky Seibert, a local artist, went on to work for a Fort Lauderdale newspaper, the *Sun Sentinel*, for many years. She is shown here with her Judges Recognition Award for alumni in 1991.

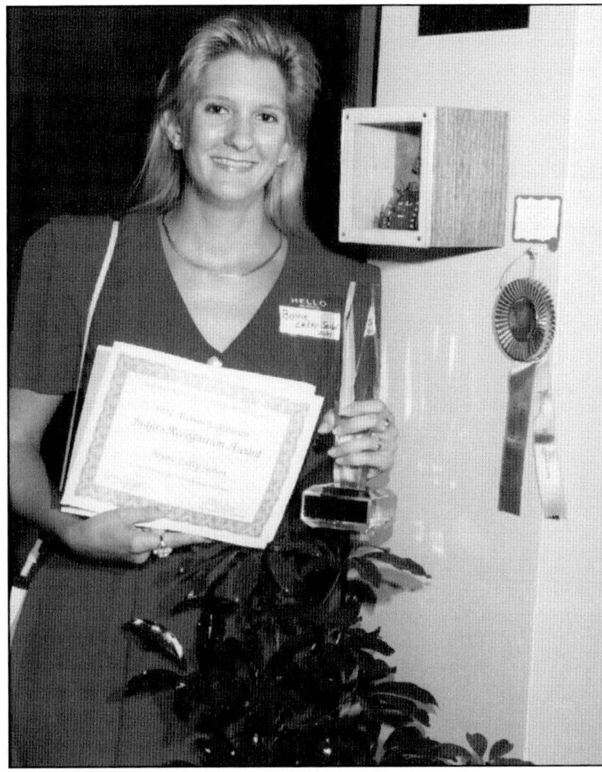

Mark Wheeler, outgoing president (left), and Skip Higley, incoming president (right) are shown with Joan Roy in 1991. Roy, a graduate from the interior design program, holds the Distinguished Alumni award she received.

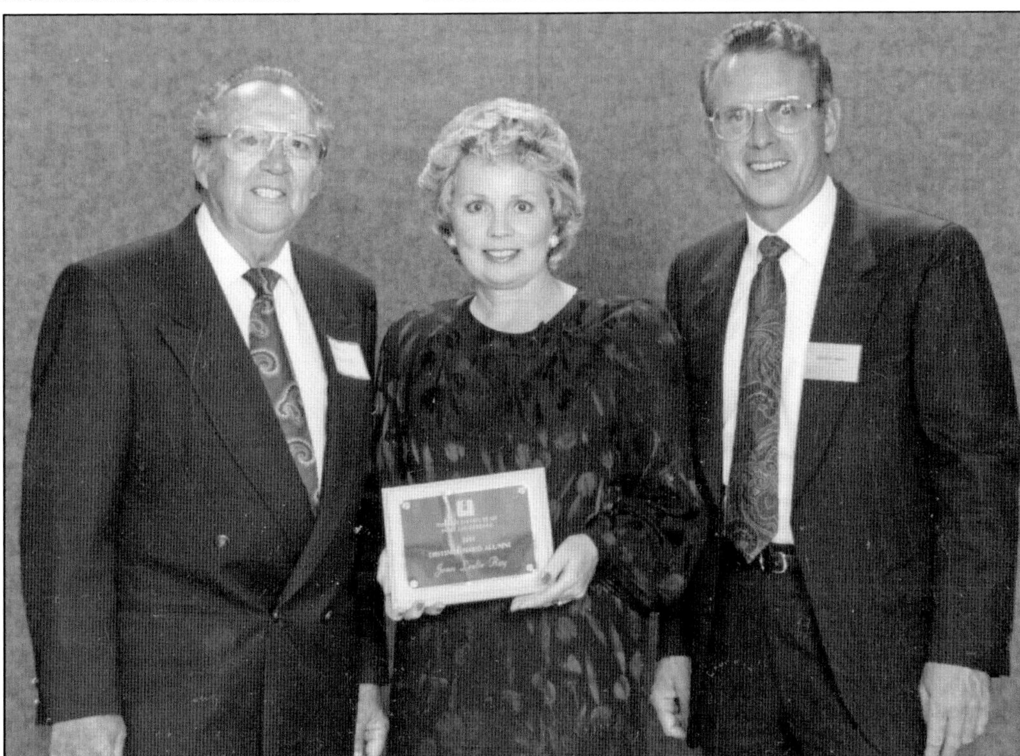

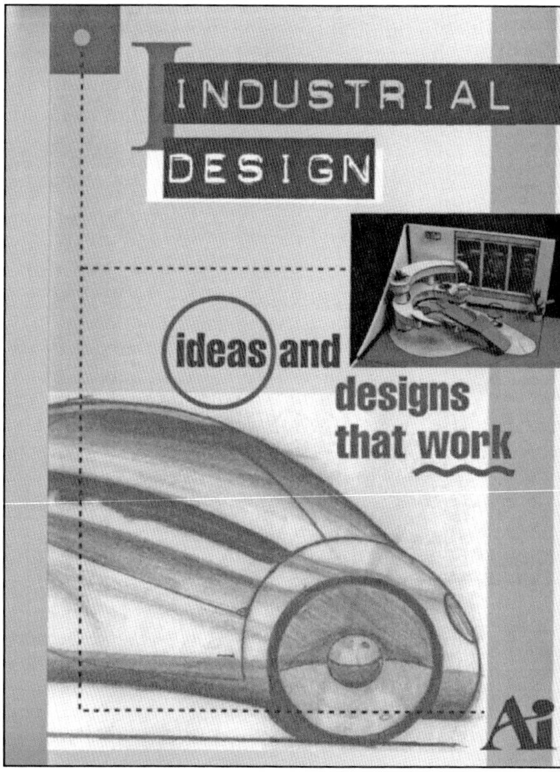

The industrial design department began operations in the fall of 1991. This is the first advertisement announcing the new department. Faculty member Andy Bing designed the front cover. (Courtesy of Brian Wood.)

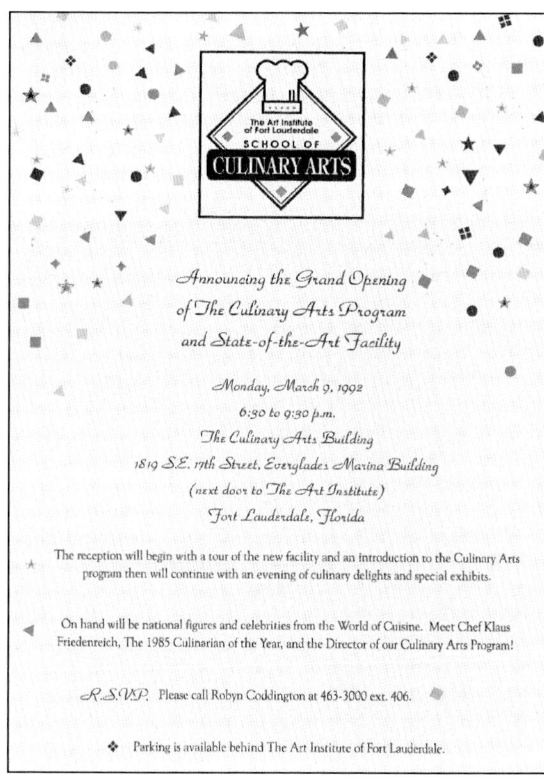
The Art Institute of Fort Lauderdale
SCHOOL OF
CULINARY ARTS

Announcing the Grand Opening
of The Culinary Arts Program
and State-of-the-Art Facility

Monday, March 9, 1992
6:30 to 9:30 p.m.
The Culinary Arts Building
1819 S.E. 17th Street, Everglades Marina Building
(next door to The Art Institute)
Fort Lauderdale, Florida

The reception will begin with a tour of the new facility and an introduction to the Culinary Arts program then will continue with an evening of culinary delights and special exhibits.

On hand will be national figures and celebrities from the World of Cuisine. Meet Chef Klaus Friedenreich, The 1985 Culinarian of the Year, and the Director of our Culinary Arts Program!

R.S.V.P. Please call Robyn Coddington at 463-3000 ext. 406.

❖ Parking is available behind The Art Institute of Fort Lauderdale.

On March 9, 1992, an invitation announced the grand opening of the new state-of-the-art culinary facilities.

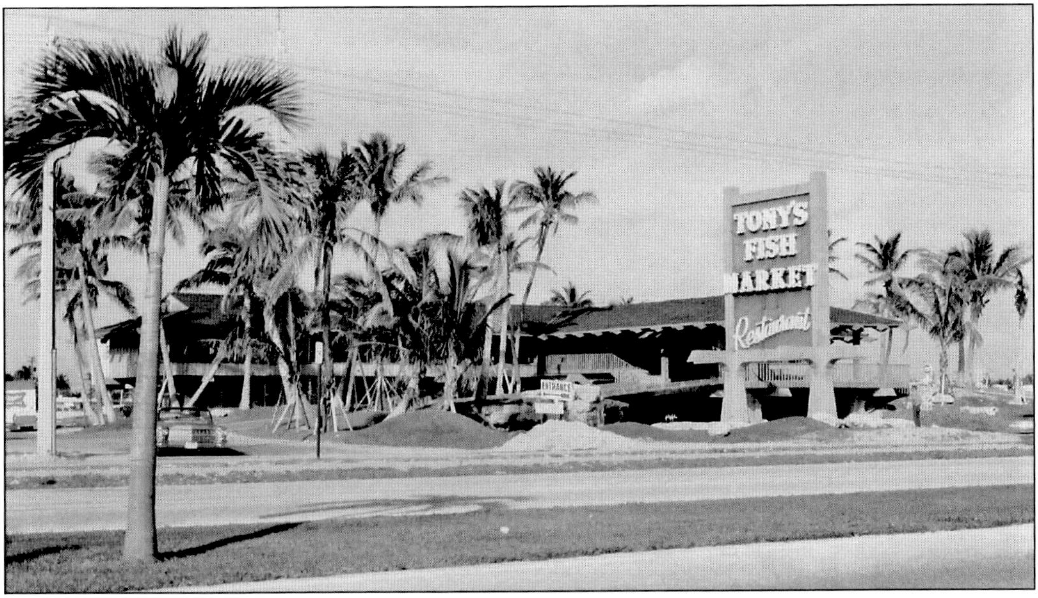

This is a 1964 photograph of Tony's Fish Market on Seventeenth Street. In 1992, the abandoned building, located directly east of the school's main building, became home to the industrial design and culinary arts departments. The building was designed by architect George L. Bennett of Fort Lauderdale and featured a second floor that gave the illusion of hanging over the waterfront and a newly created lagoon. The building was cantilevered from unusual, cross-shaped, concrete piers resembling petals. The dining area consisted of heavy wood timbers reminiscent of early building and ship construction techniques. Oregonian, rough-sawn fir timbers were used for columns, beams, and the exposed trussed ceiling. On top was a roof made of hand-split cedar shingles. Most unusual was the entrance drive, which crossed the lagoon by means of a heavy timber bridge. (Photograph by Floyd Pyles; courtesy of the Broward County Historical Commission.)

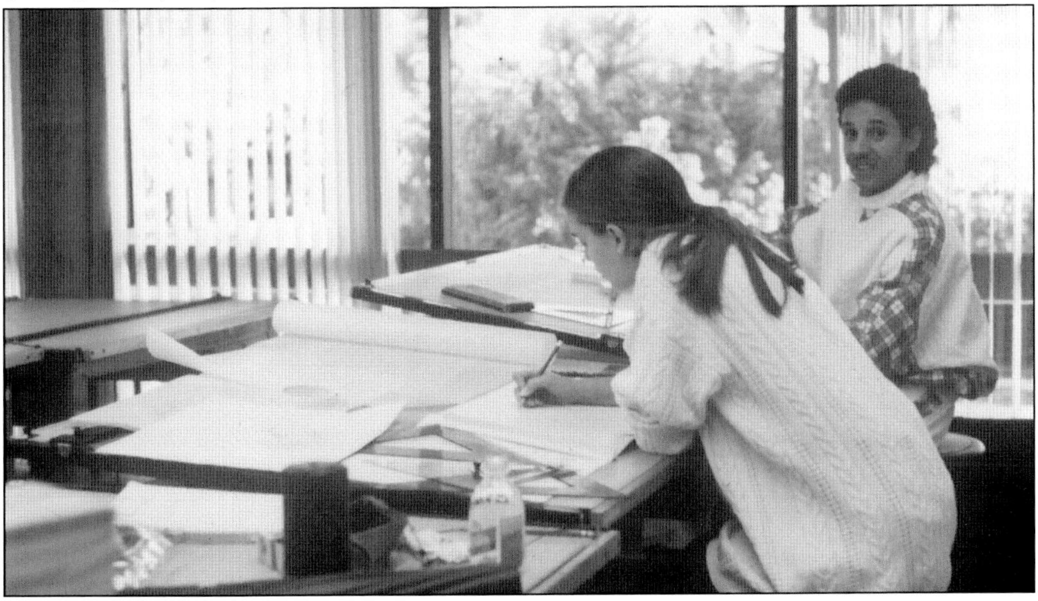

Two students are seen at work in the industrial design department's new home. (Courtesy of Brian Wood.)

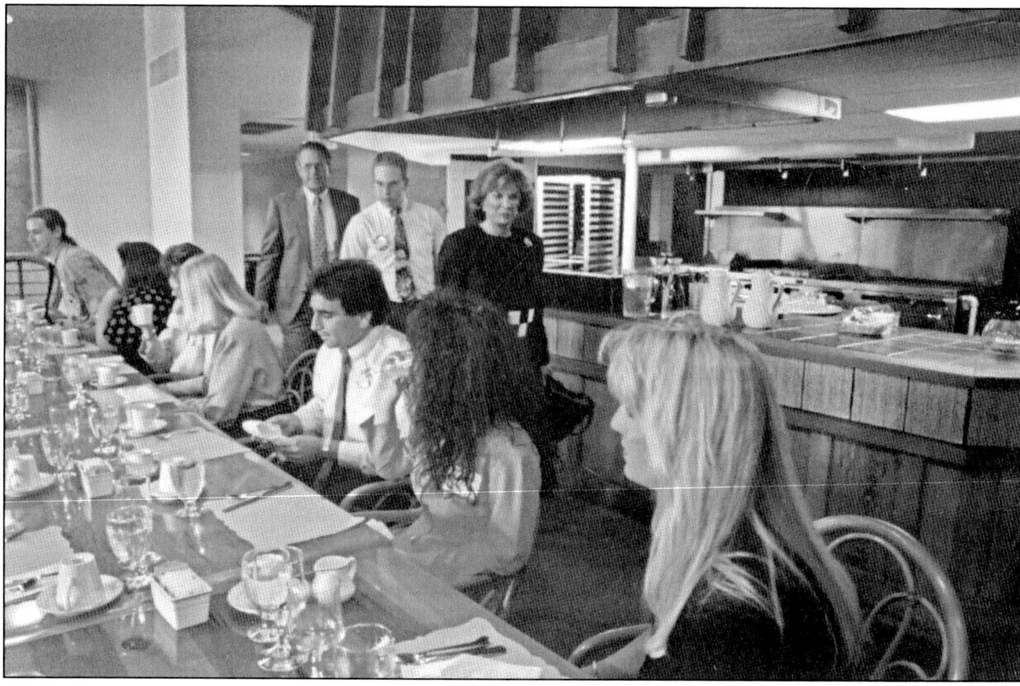

Gwen Margolis, a Florida state senator (standing), was a guest at the grand opening of the culinary arts program. Senator Margolis was elected to the Florida Senate in 1980 and served as its first female president from 1990 to 1992. From this picture, it is easy to get a glimpse of the wood timbers that were characteristic of the building.

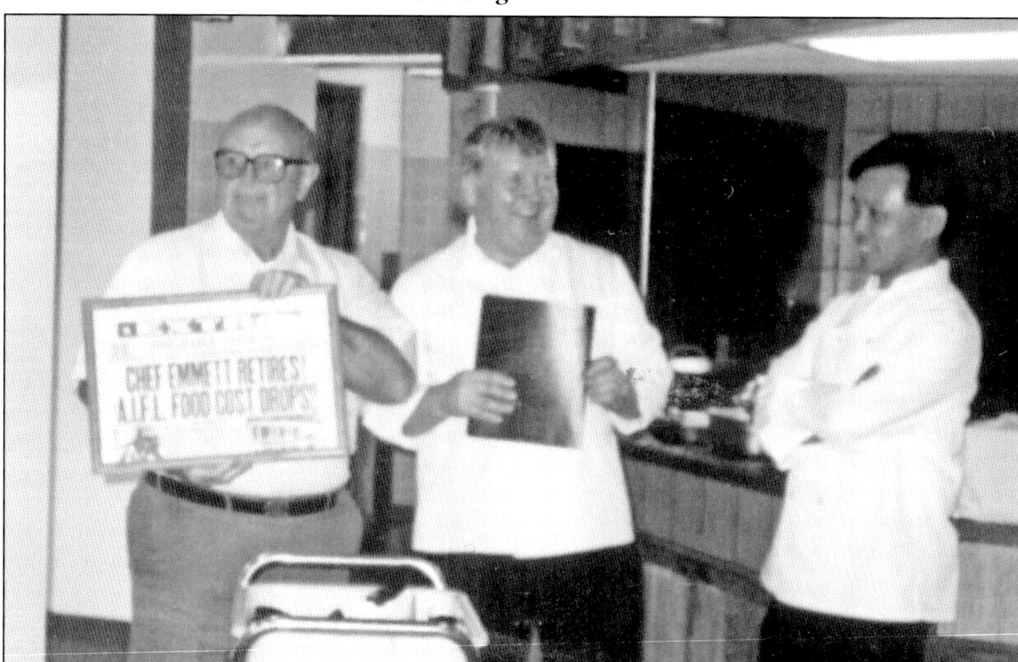

Chef Emmet Hodgkins (left), who started the culinary arts program, retired on June 4, 1992, and handed over the leadership of the program to master chef Klaus Friedenreich (center).

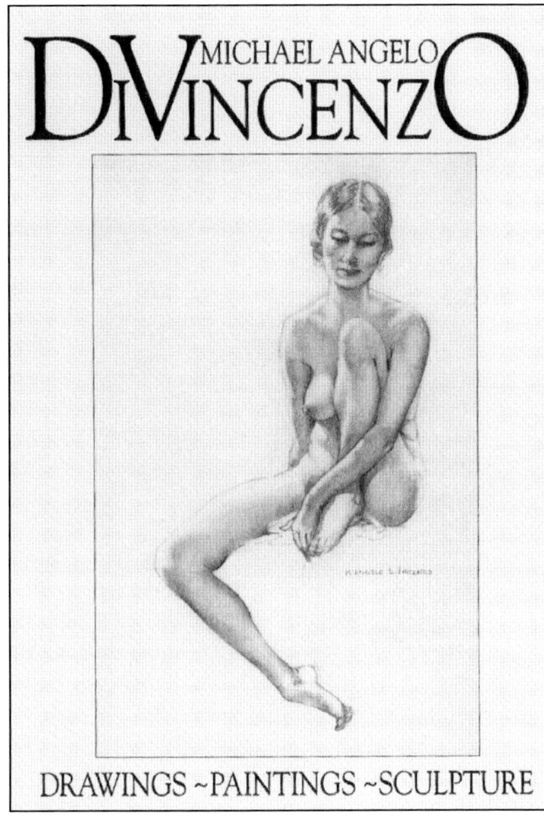

On November 13, 1991, a reception was held in honor of faculty member Michael Angelo DiVincenzo's work.

THE ART INSTITUTE
OF FORT LAUDERDALE
proudly hosts the works
of
Michael Angelo DiVincenzo

in the

Mark K. Wheeler Gallery
1799 S.E. 17th Street
Fort Lauderdale, Florida 33316
November 1 - 30th, 1991

Reception will be held
November 13th, 1991
5:30 - 8:30 p.m.
The artist will be present.

Free Admission
Open to the public

Gallery Hours
Mon ~ Thurs 8 a.m. - 8 p.m.
Fri 8 a.m. - 5 p.m.
Sat 8 a.m. - Noon

As this logo retires...

On January 25, 1993, on the occasion of the school's 25th anniversary, the school's logo was retired.

Ai

The Art Institute
of Fort Lauderdale®

Ai The Art Institute
of Fort Lauderdale®

Ai The Art Institute of Fort Lauderdale®

This was the new school logo, including three ways to depict the school's name.

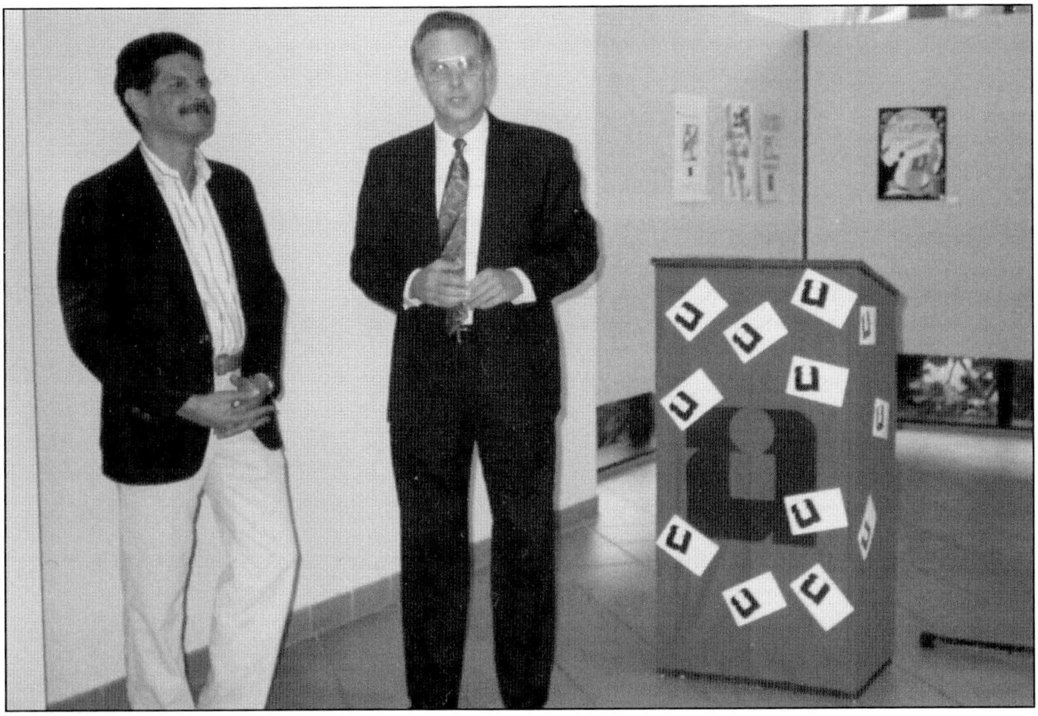

School president Skip Higley (right) gets ready to unveil the school's 25th-anniversary logo, created by instructor Andy Bing (left).

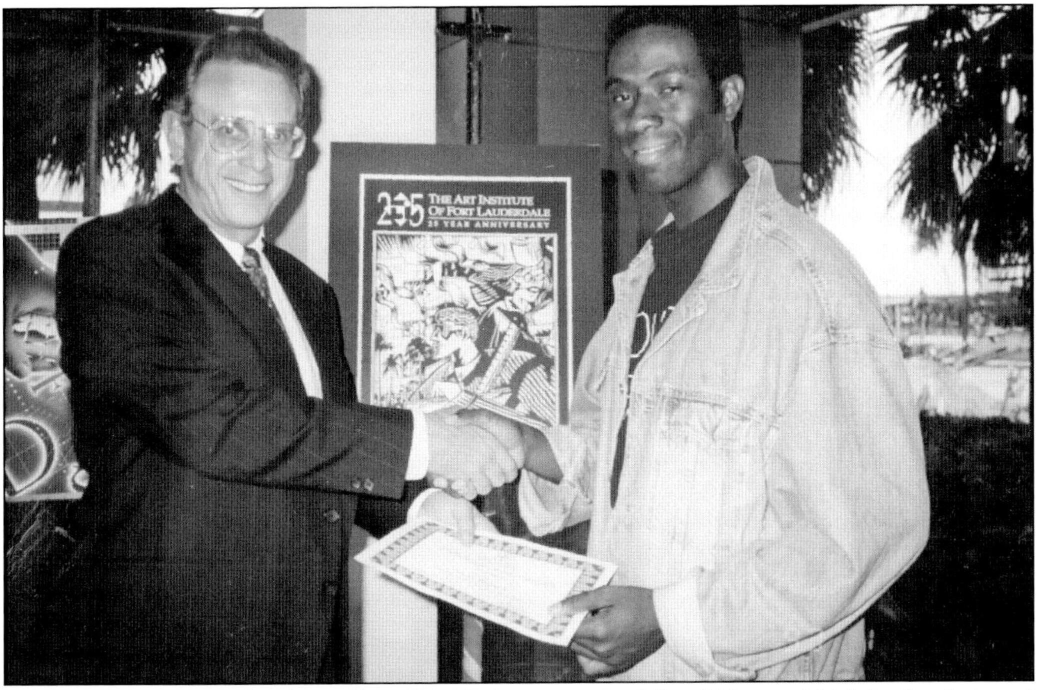

On January 25, 1993, school president Skip Higley recognized Geoff Maynard (right), who designed the winning poster for the school's 25th anniversary. Instructor Andy Bing's logo can be seen on the upper left side of the poster.

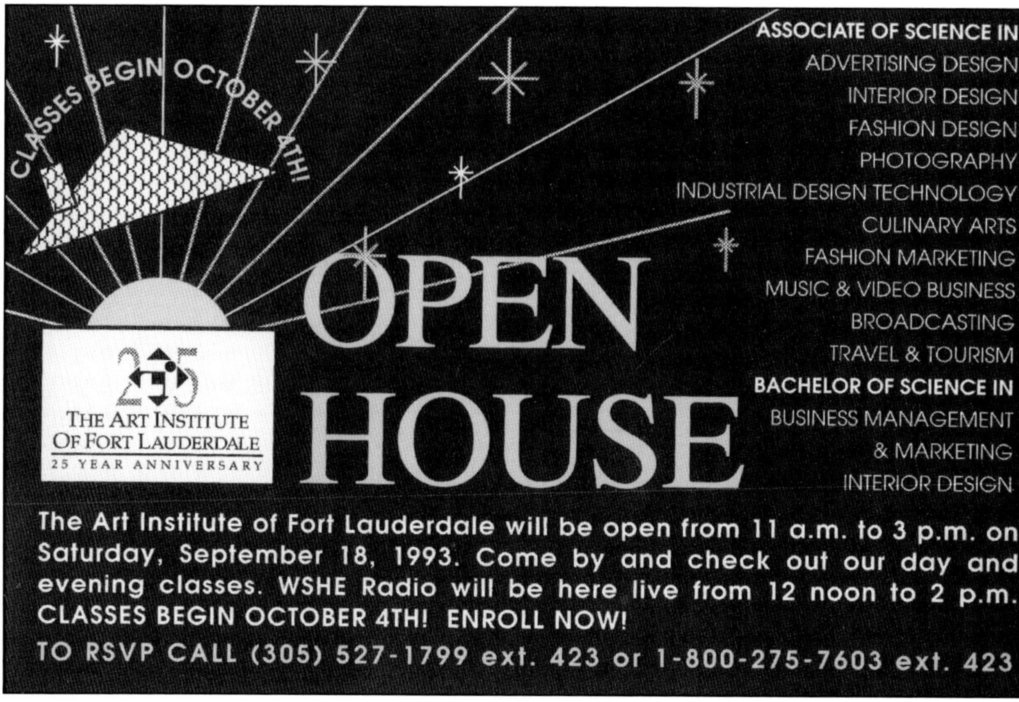

An Open House invitation, on September 18, 1993, lists the growing fields of study and degree programs. The invitation also includes the 25th-anniversary logo.

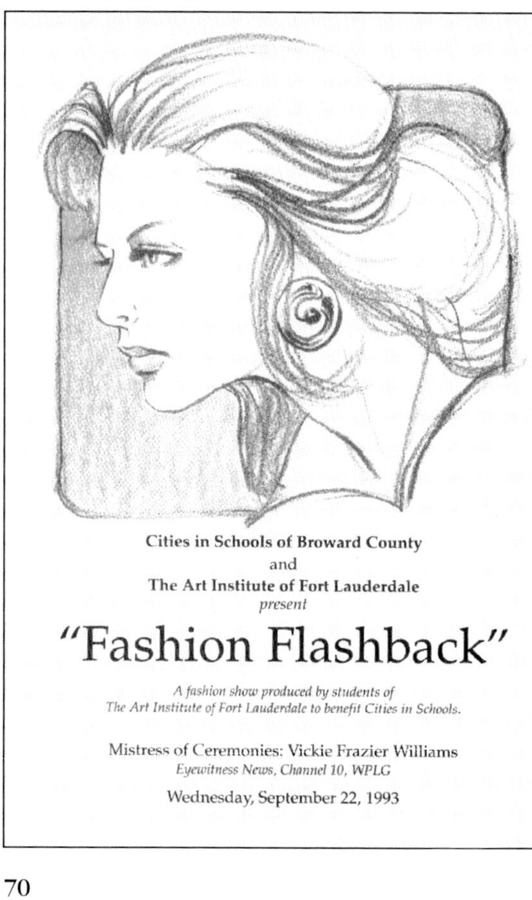

To benefit the "Cities in Schools" program of Broward County, students of the fashion department presented "Fashion Flashback," a show celebrating 25 years of fashion.

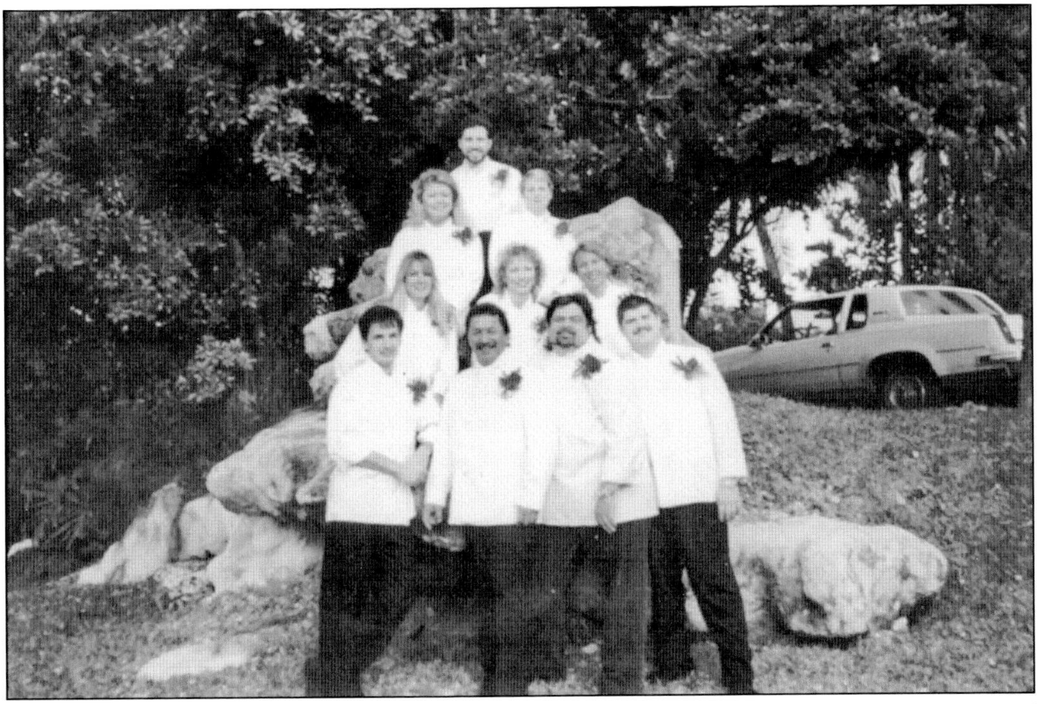

The year 1993 saw the first graduating class from the culinary arts department. (Courtesy of Sheila Getman.)

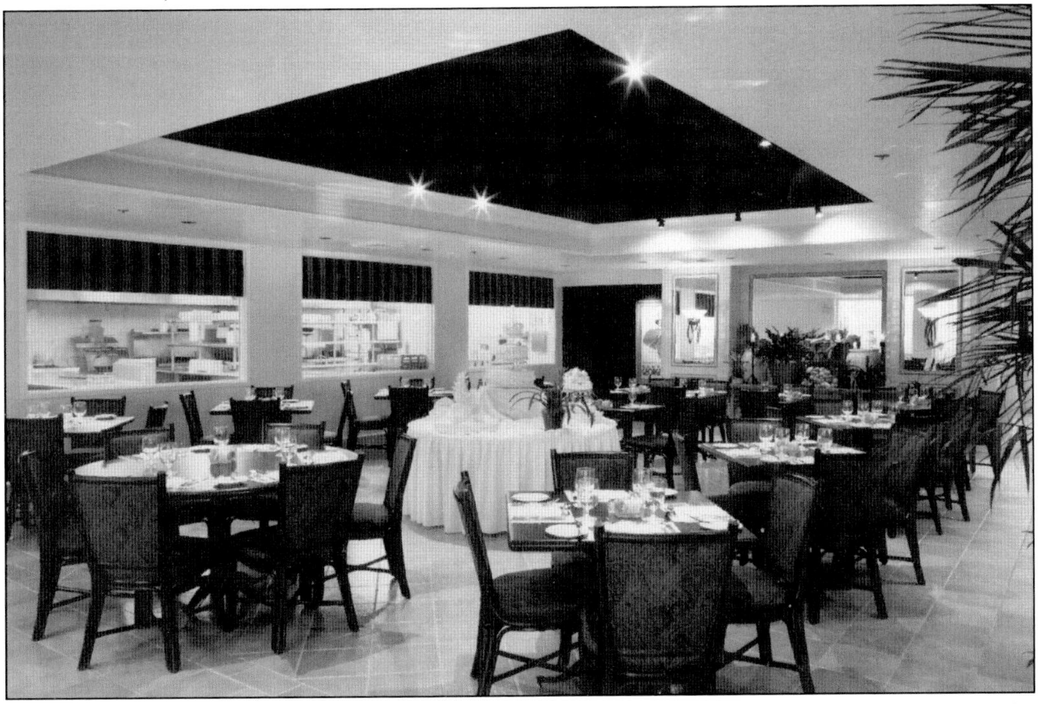

On April 17, 1995, culinary arts classes were relocated to the Harbor Walk building. This is the dining room of the new Chef's Palette restaurant, with the main kitchen in the background. (Courtesy of Jack Kane.)

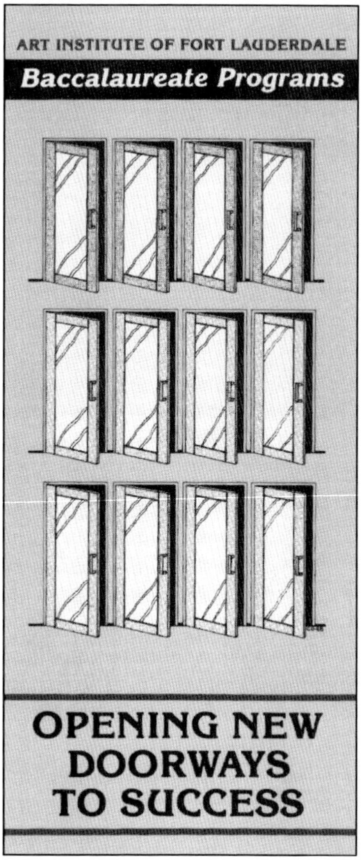

This brochure, designed by instructor Andy Bing, announces the new baccalaureate programs in computer animation, graphic design, industrial design, and interior design. (Courtesy of Andy Bing.)

Below, a computer animation student in a two-dimensional, traditional, hand-drawing class uses a character board while working on a light table.

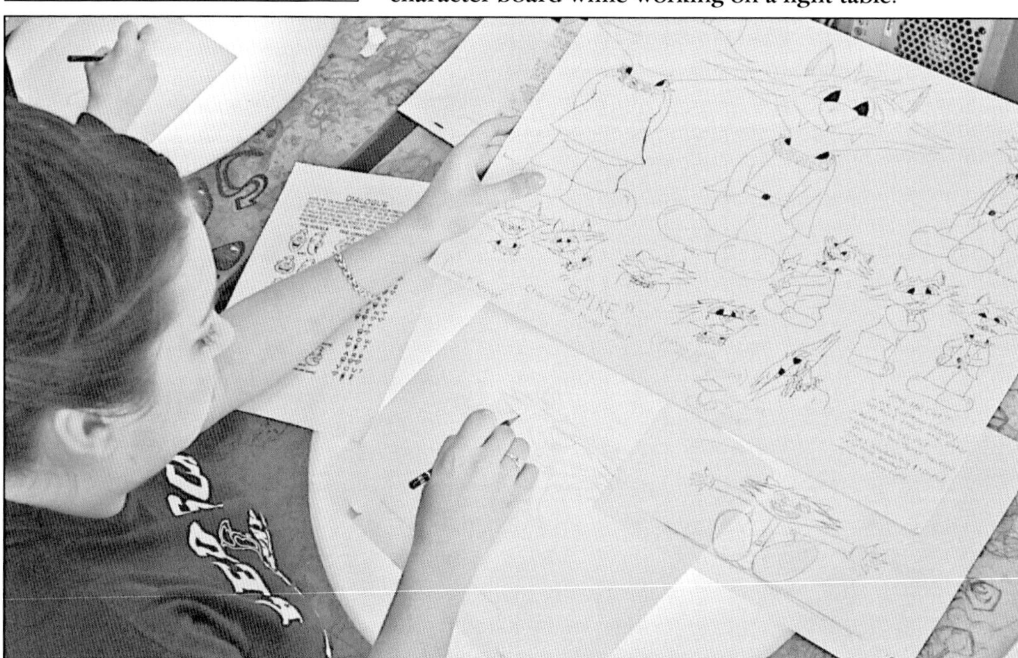

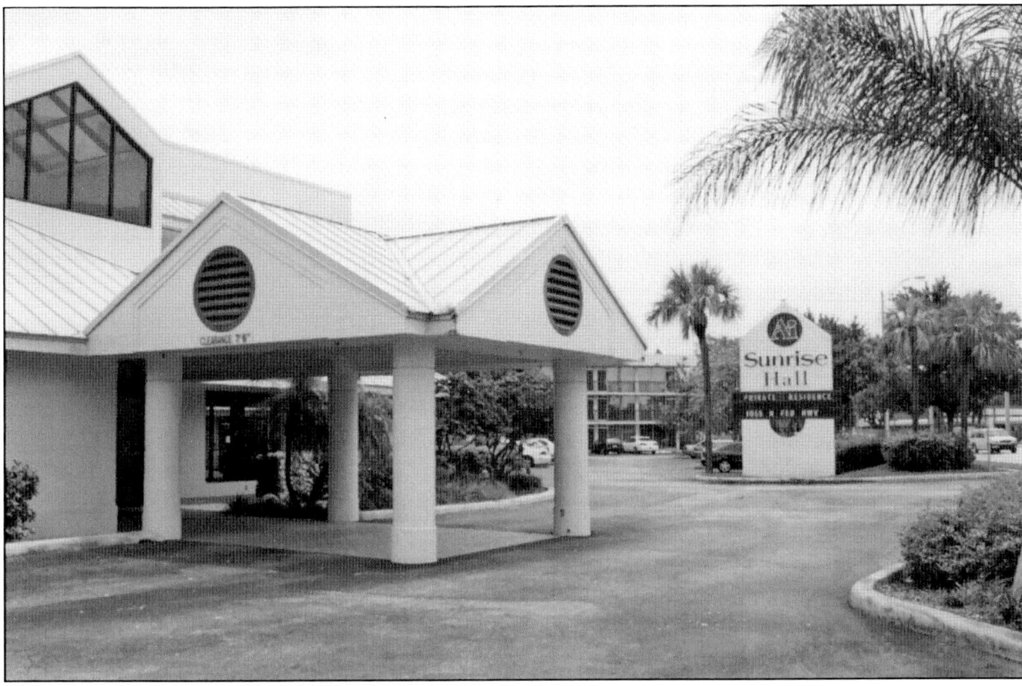

Above, the entrance to the Sunrise Hall student dormitory is pictured. Shown below is the dormitory's pool area.

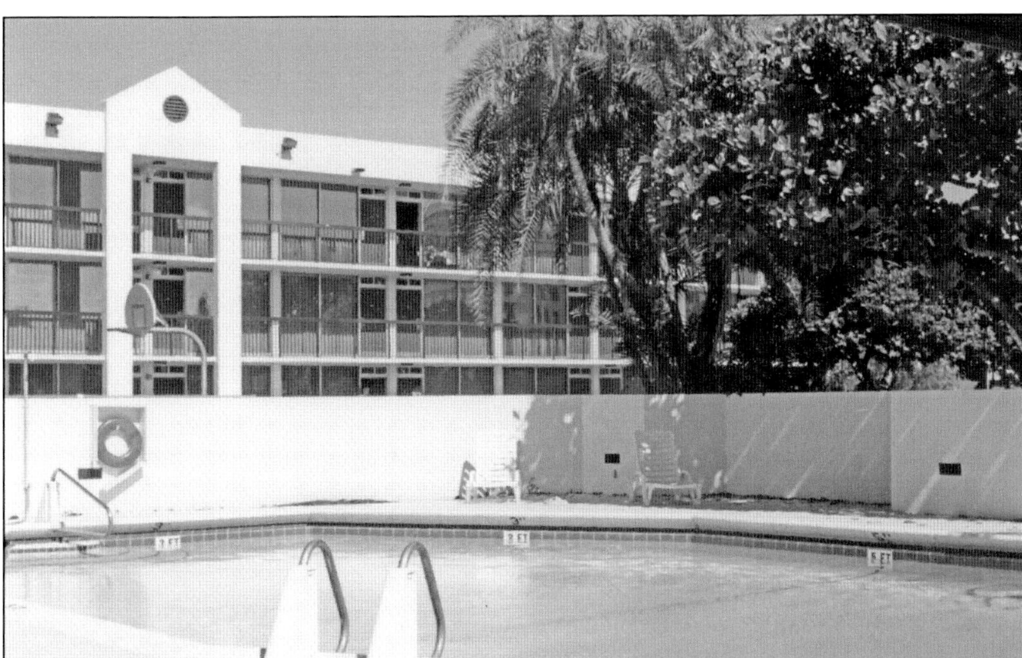

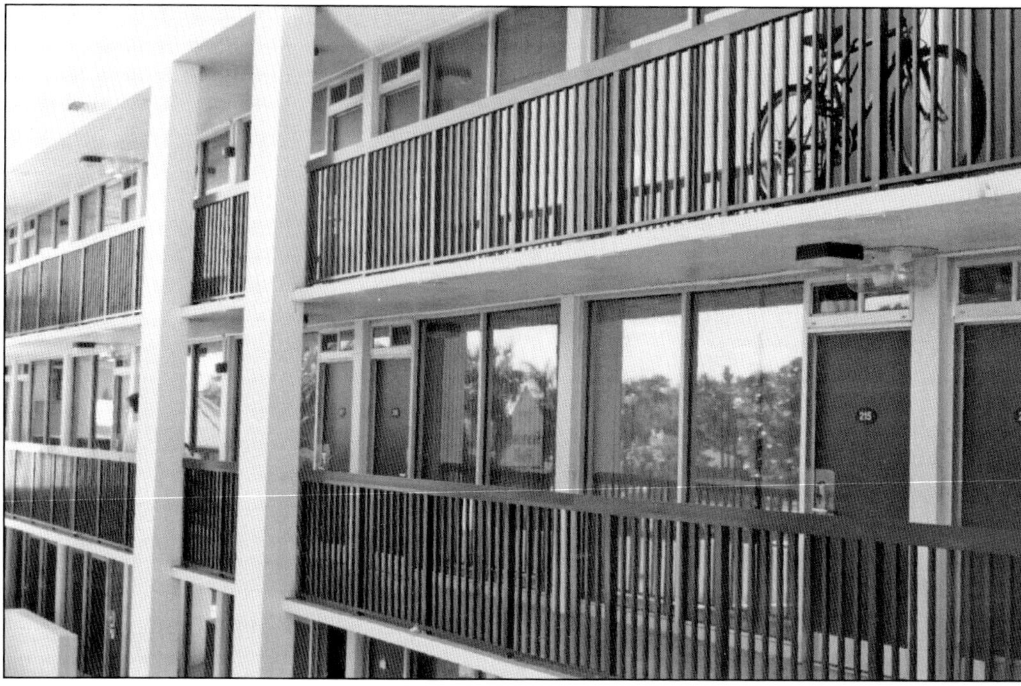

Sunrise Hall was purchased in 1998 and was still providing housing for students in 2008.

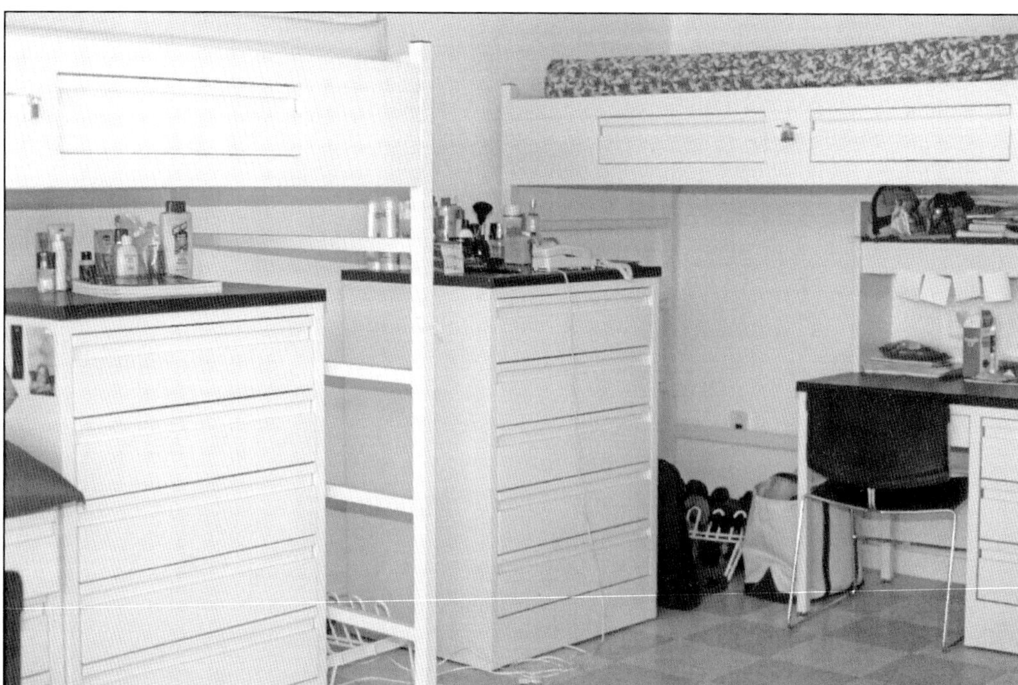

Four

MATURITY

In 2000, the school's enrollment reached 3,000. International students from 58 countries equaled 15 percent of the school's total enrollment. This was the same year that the school was accredited by the Accrediting Council for Independent Colleges and Schools. The Art Institute of Fort Lauderdale was also named the "Career College of the Year" in 2001.

As the school matured, more faculty members became celebrated artists and authors, and received statewide recognition as teachers of the year. A world-renowned yacht designer helped to establish a new program, and the school's first major motion picture, *Gringo Wedding*, was released. The school's work with local community groups garnered still more prestigious awards. Culinary students cooked for a president, and graduation placement rates reached 93 percent.

On September 16, 2008, the school celebrated its 40th anniversary.

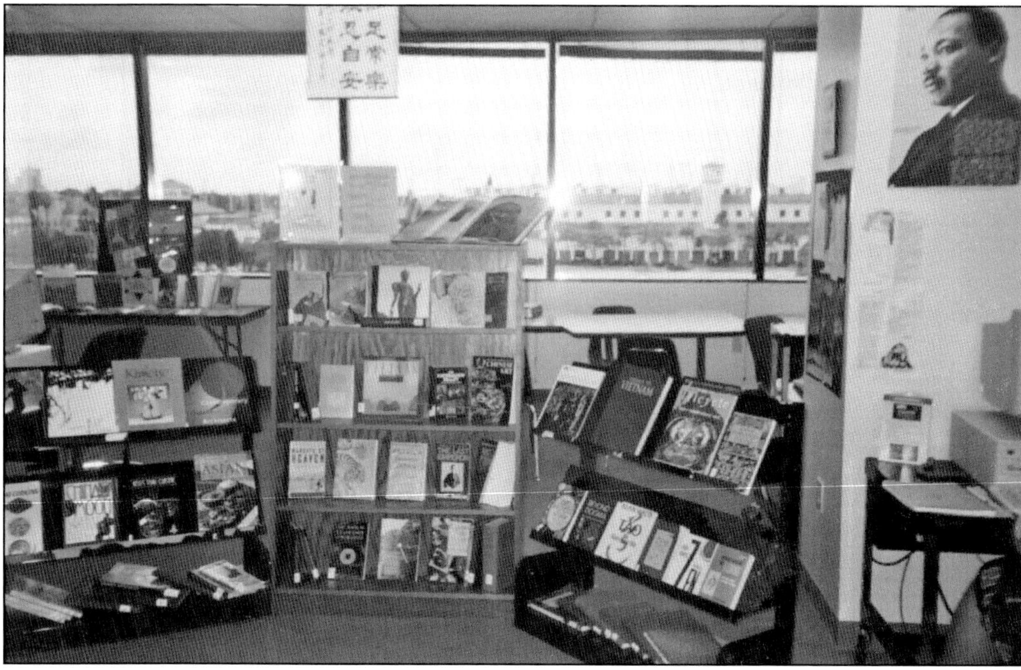

This is the Meinhardt Memorial Library in 1999, when it was located on the fourth floor of the Harbor Walk building.

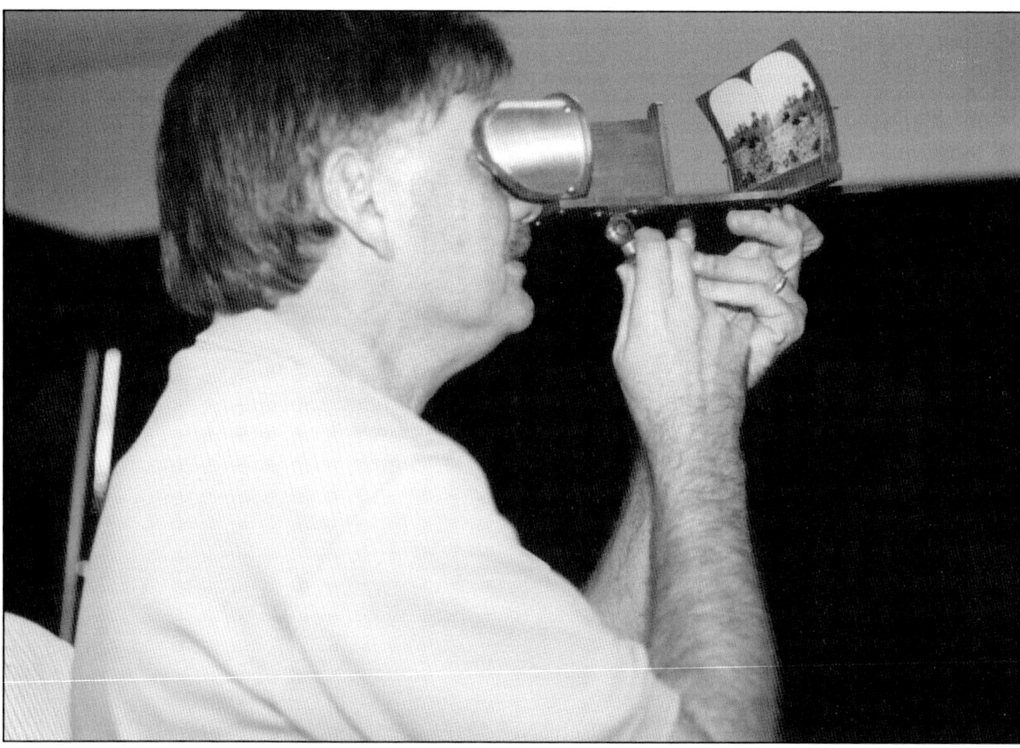

Instructor Don Sheffield looks through a stereoscope in 1999.

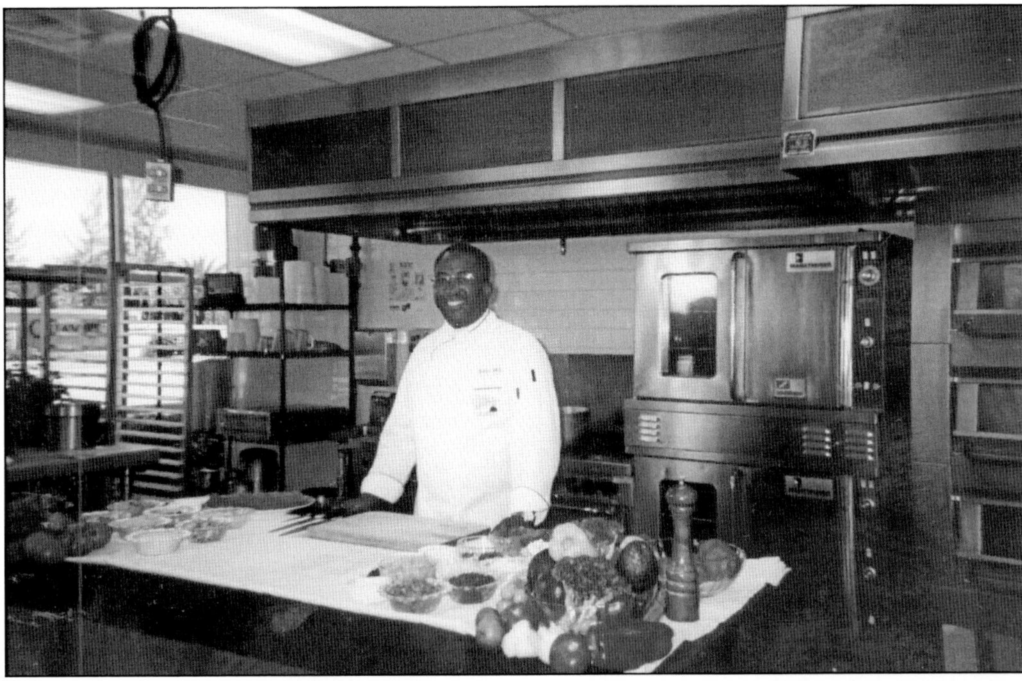

Richard Willis (above) served as the chair of the culinary arts department in 1998–1999.

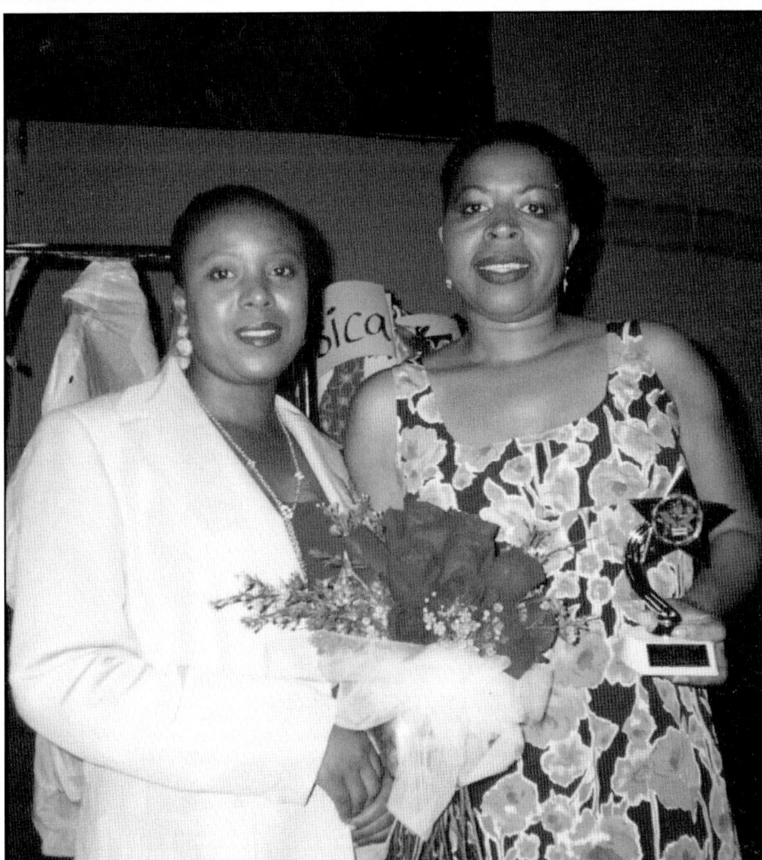

Sandra Robinson (right) received the "Exceptional Student Design" award during the July 1999 "Fashion Fusion" fashion show. Robinson graduated several months later, when she also won for best portfolio and highest achievement. Today she owns her own business, Saje Robinson Collection. (Courtesy of Sandra Robinson.)

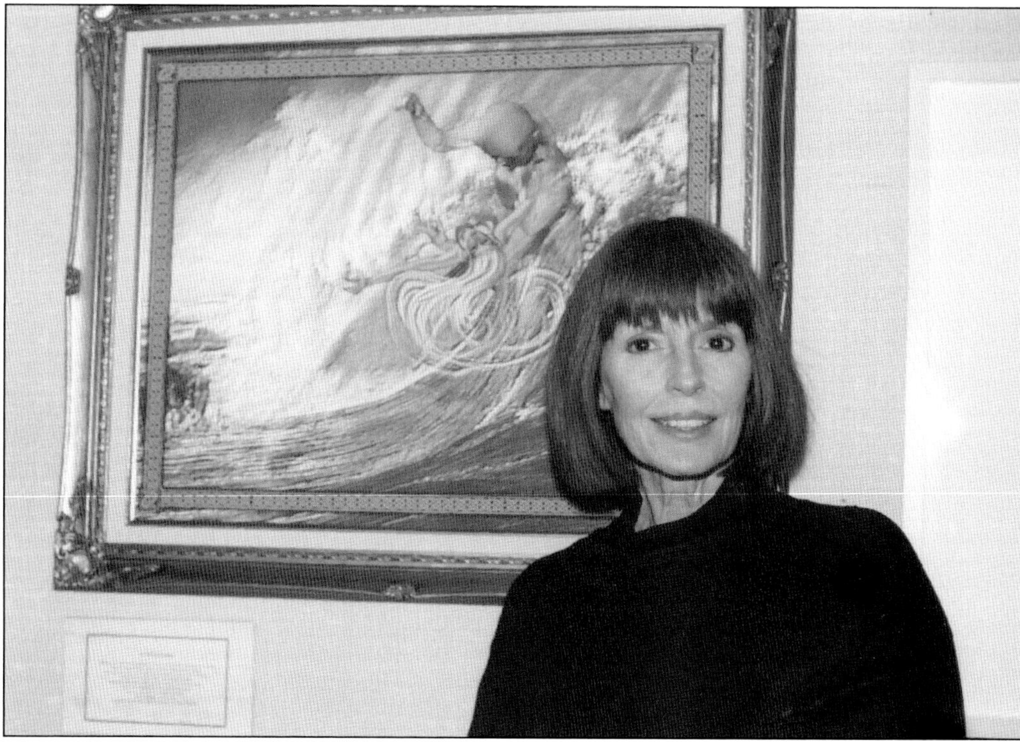

Valan Evers, known as "Ms. V." around campus, stands in front of her painting, entitled *The Wave of Cliodhna*. Ms. V was a student in the photography department in the 1970s before joining the faculty. After working in Italy, Evers returned to full-time teaching at her alma mater in 1987.

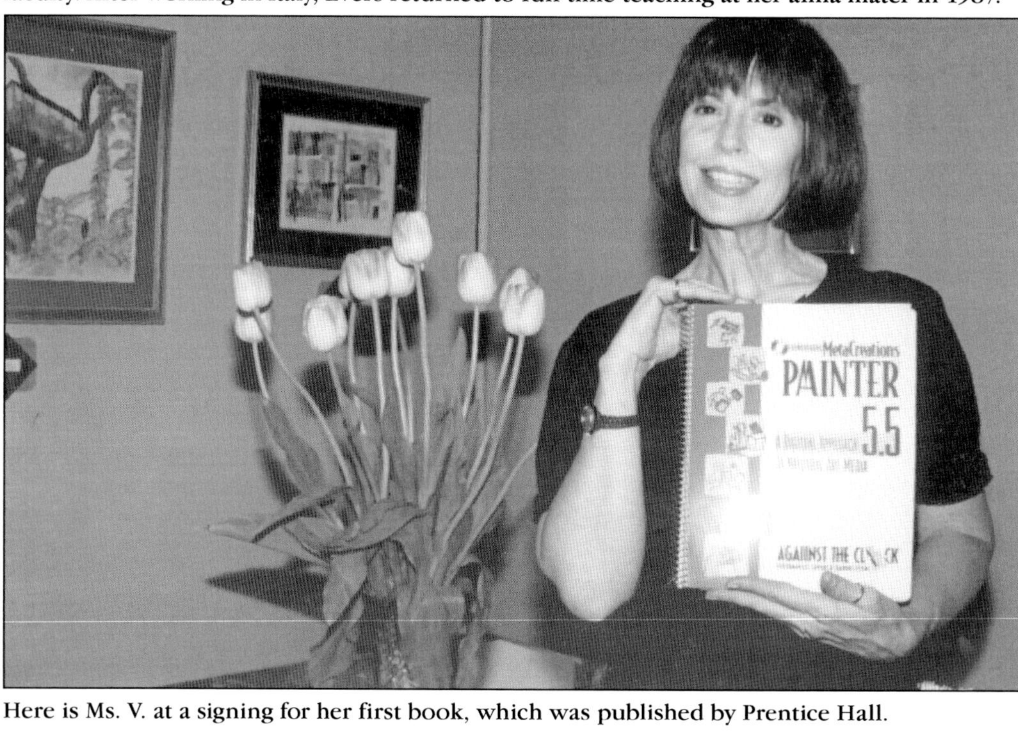

Here is Ms. V. at a signing for her first book, which was published by Prentice Hall.

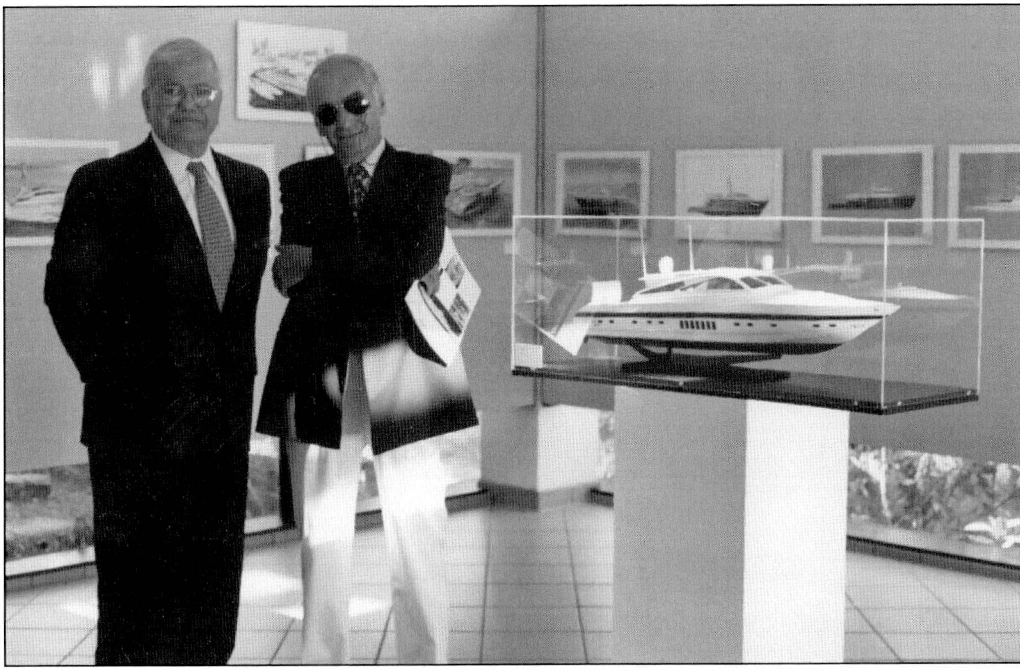

World-renowned yacht designer Paolo Caliari (right) is pictured here in April 1999 with school president Bill Kalaboke. He became the mentor of five yacht-and-marine-design students.

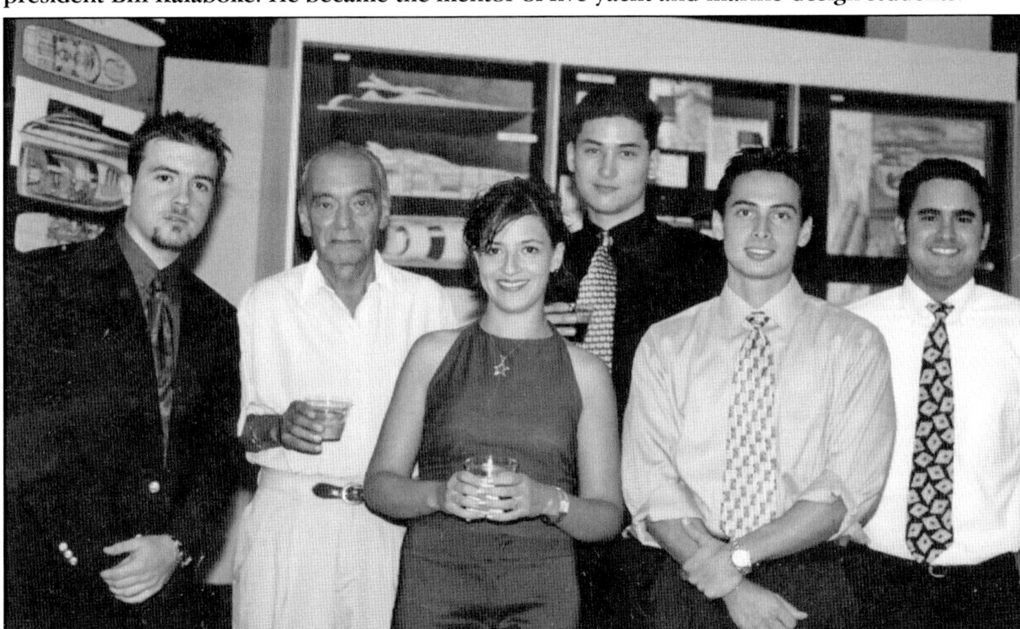

This February 2000 Marriott Yacht Design exhibit features (from left to right): John Hodgson, mentor Paolo Caliari, Andrea Fazzolari, Renato Daina, Mark Ello, and Juan Tome. The exhibit focused on the comprehensive stages of marine design. Caliari, born in Genoa, Italy, graduated from Italy's famous Politecnico Institute in Turin, Italy, with degrees in architecture and engineering. Caliari is a direct descendent of the famous muralist known as "Veronese," whose work is still visible in many cathedrals and castles in Italy.

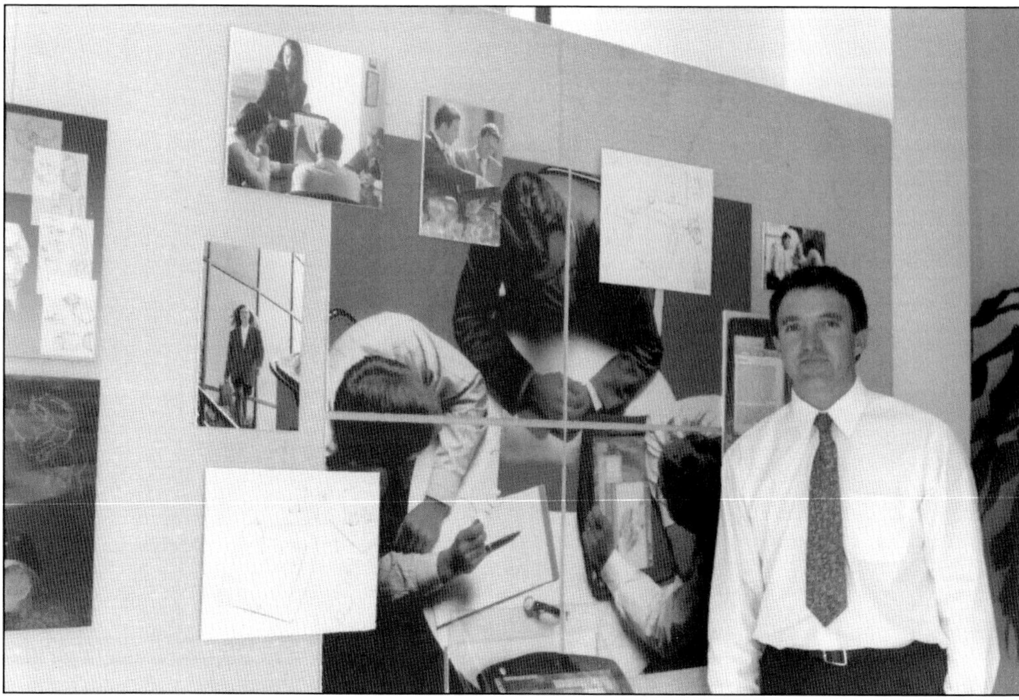

This is part of Brian Wood's visual presentation of his master's thesis, entitled *Paper or Plastic: A Transition to Digital Media in the Design Professions*, shown in the Wheeler gallery. Wood is the chair of the industrial design department.

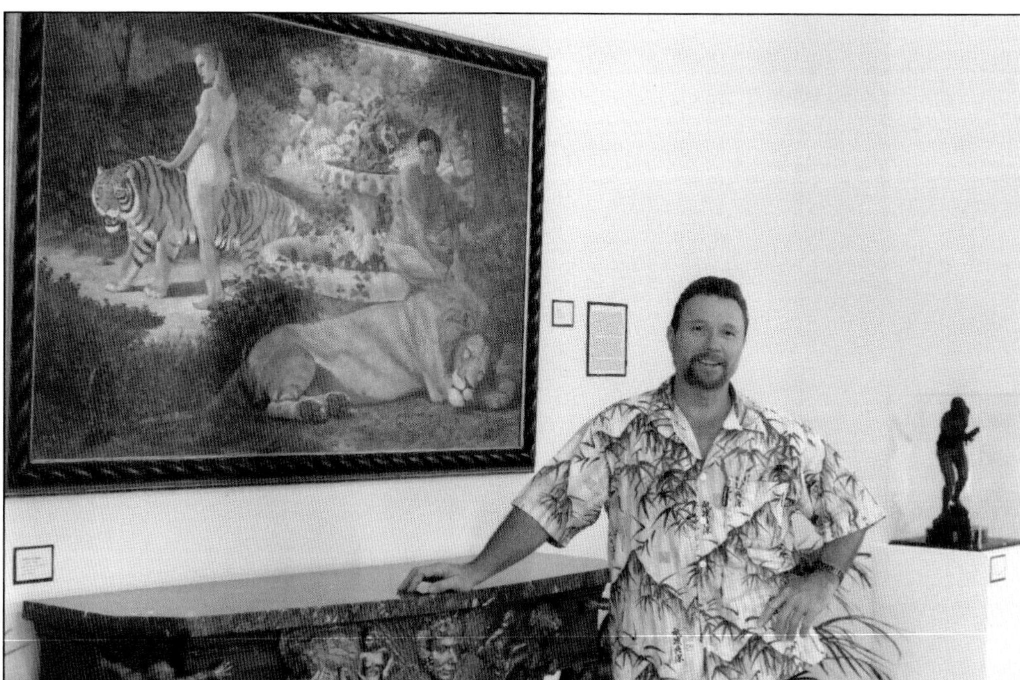

Jim Radford's MFA thesis was a combination of painting and sculpture.

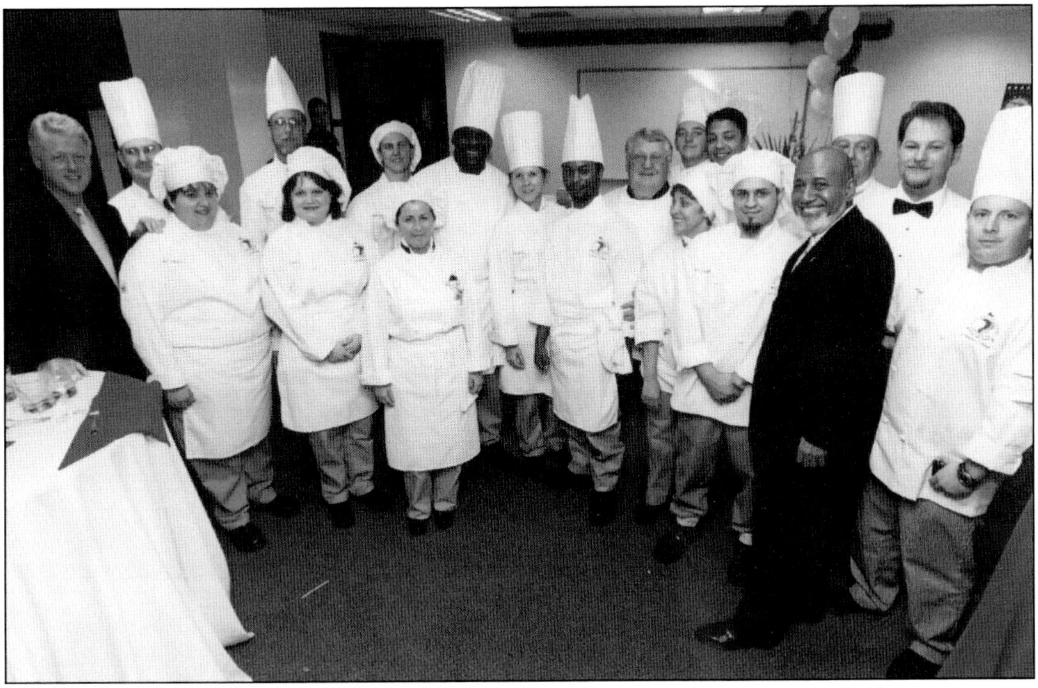

Former U.S. president Bill Clinton (left) poses with culinary arts students and Congressman Alcee Hastings (third from right) in December 1999. President Clinton helped to raise funds for Congressman Hastings at an event where the students prepared a reception for more than 700 guests.

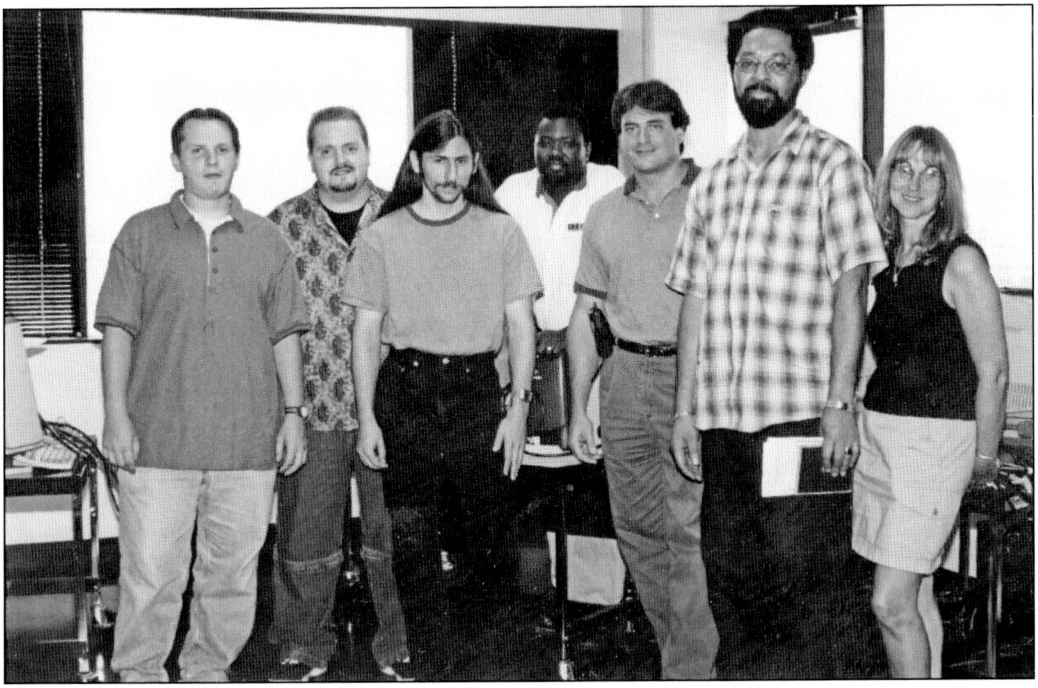

Here are the members of the technology department in 1999. From left to right are Bob David, Chris Zaharek, Brian Aranoff, Rob Diggs, Jon Sloan, Orville Thompson, and Jane Vigna.

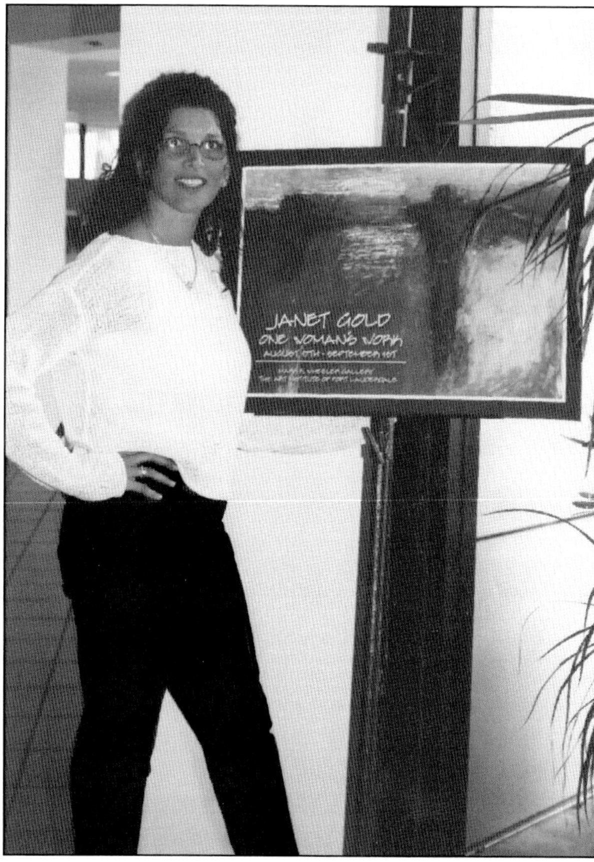

This is Janet Gold at the opening of her show, entitled One Woman's Work . . . What I do when I am not Teaching, in the Mark K. Wheeler Gallery. The show ran in 2000 from August through September.

Mimi Botscheller demonstrates a painting technique to a student in 2000.

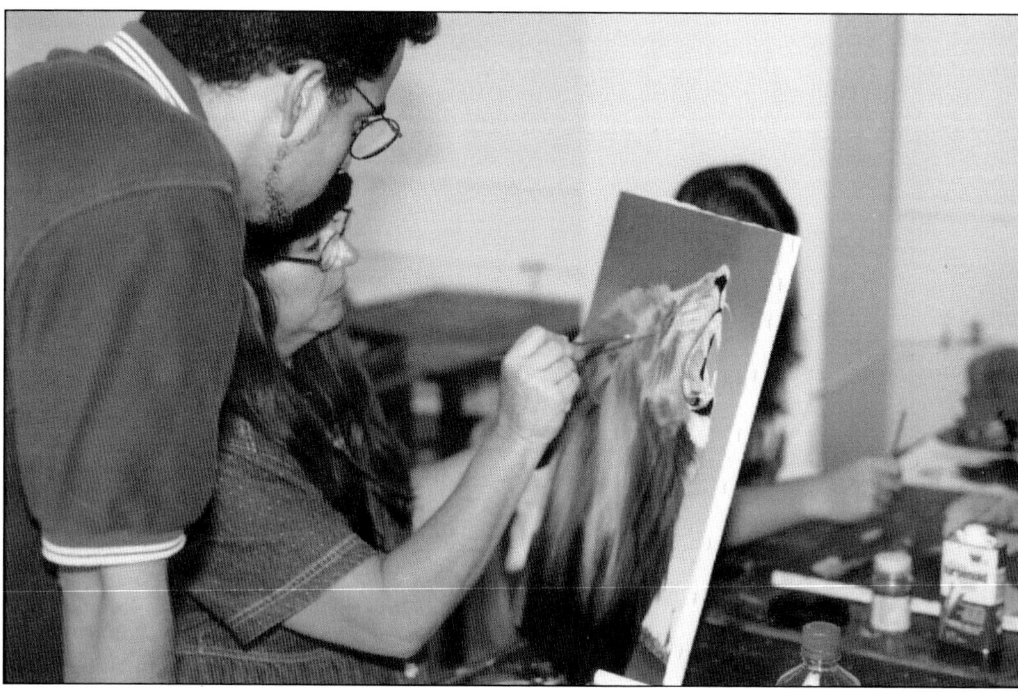

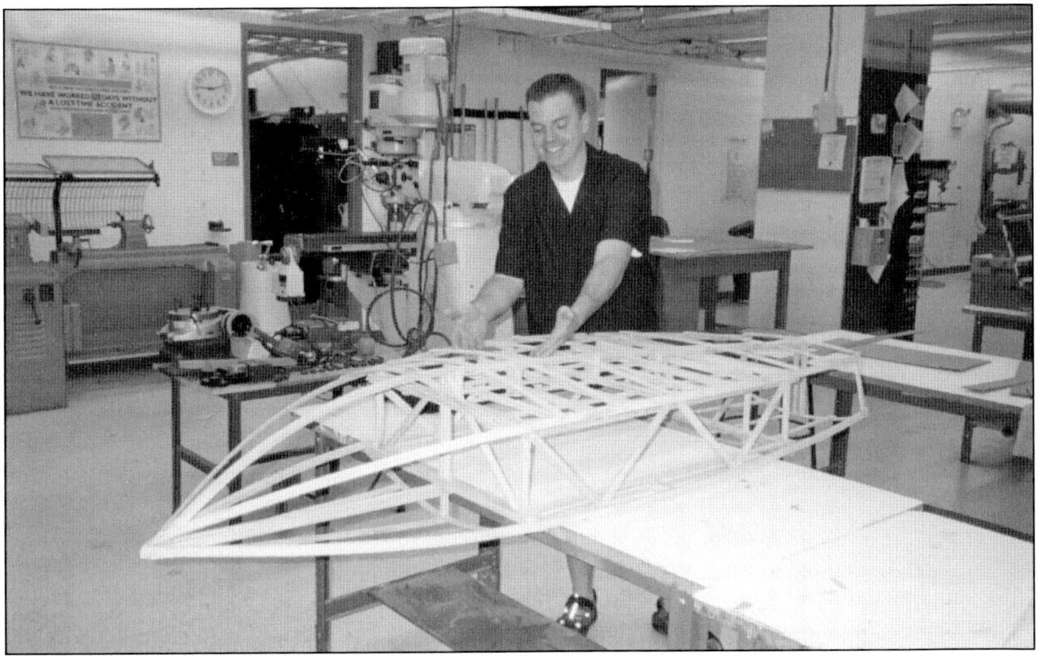

February 2000 saw the first "Float in the Moat" competition. For this event, students were required to build a boat that could hold their weight. The boats are made entirely from one-fourth-inch-by-three-fourths-inch wood sticks covered with one layer of brown paper and one coat of waterproof varnish. The boats cannot exceed 12 inches in depth and must have a "V" shaped bottom in order to be able to float in the school's 16-inch-deep reflecting pool. The event is now called the "Annual Love Boat Regatta" and takes place around Valentine's Day each year. (Courtesy of Winston Menish.)

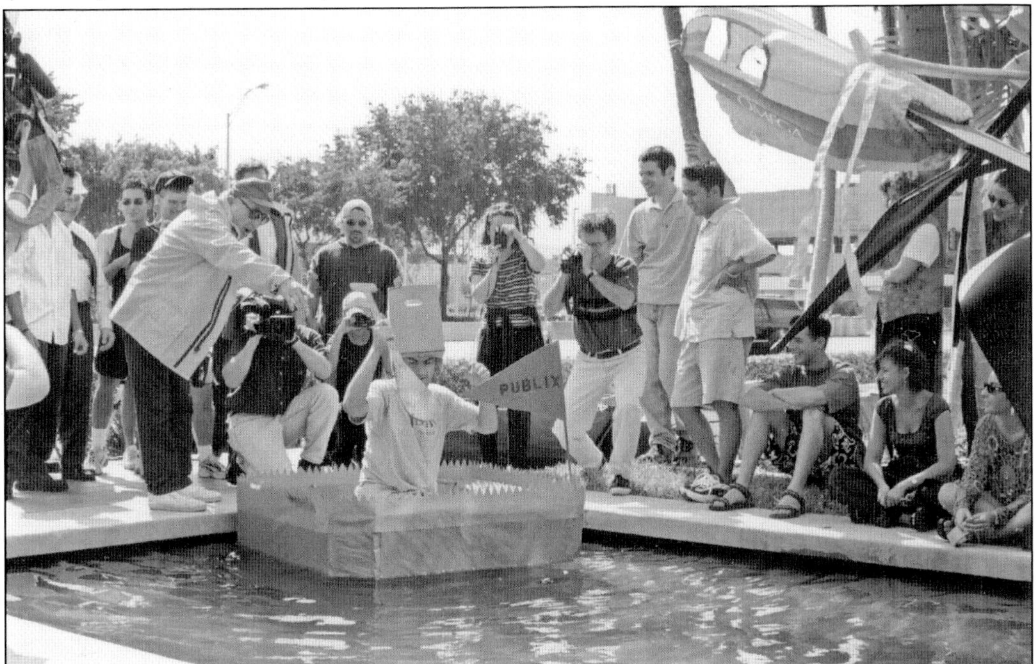

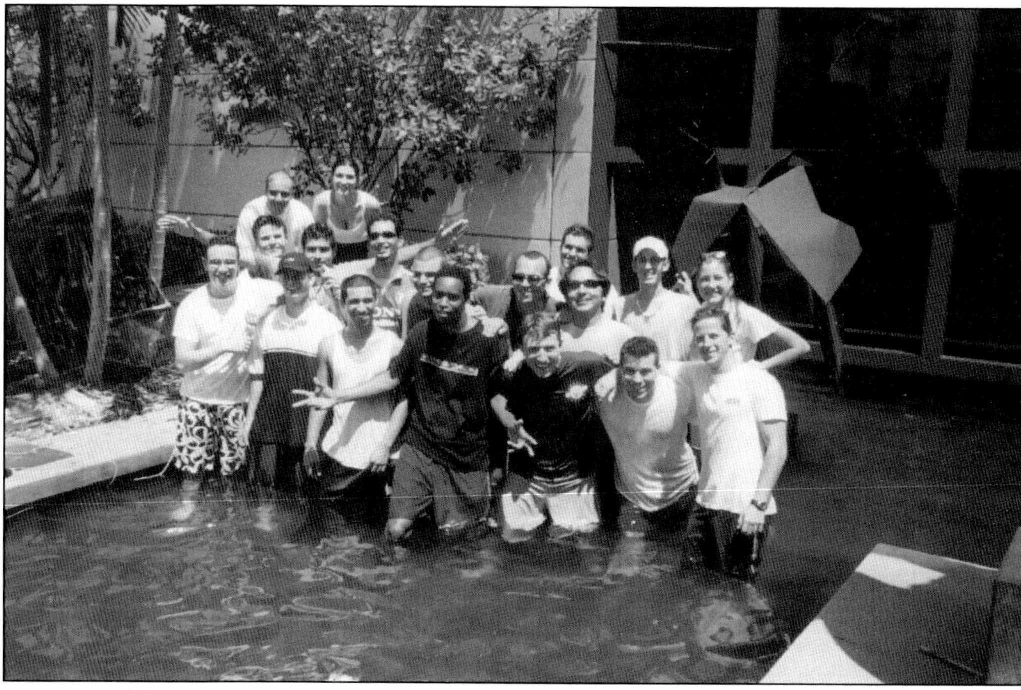

Students celebrate in the moat after the float. (Courtesy of Winston Menish.)

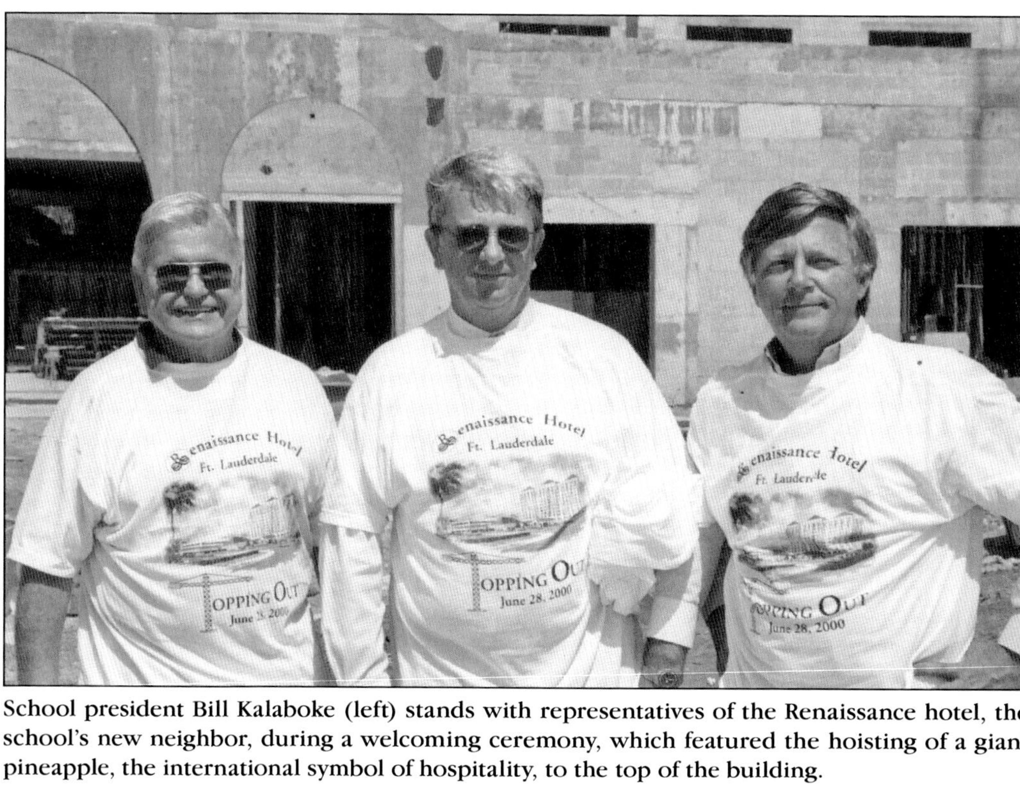

School president Bill Kalaboke (left) stands with representatives of the Renaissance hotel, the school's new neighbor, during a welcoming ceremony, which featured the hoisting of a giant pineapple, the international symbol of hospitality, to the top of the building.

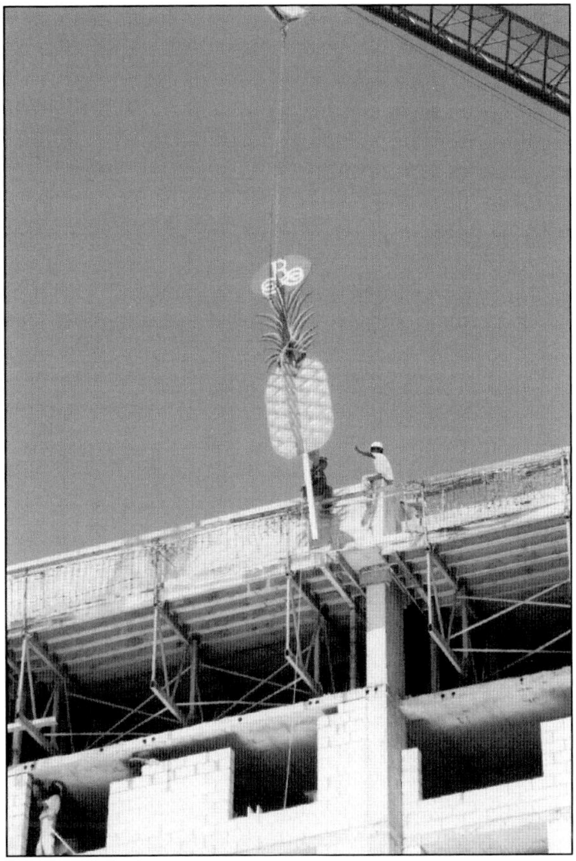

This photograph shows the hospitality pineapple on June 28, 2000. This 12-foot-tall, industrial-strength giant pineapple was designed and built by students in the industrial design department.

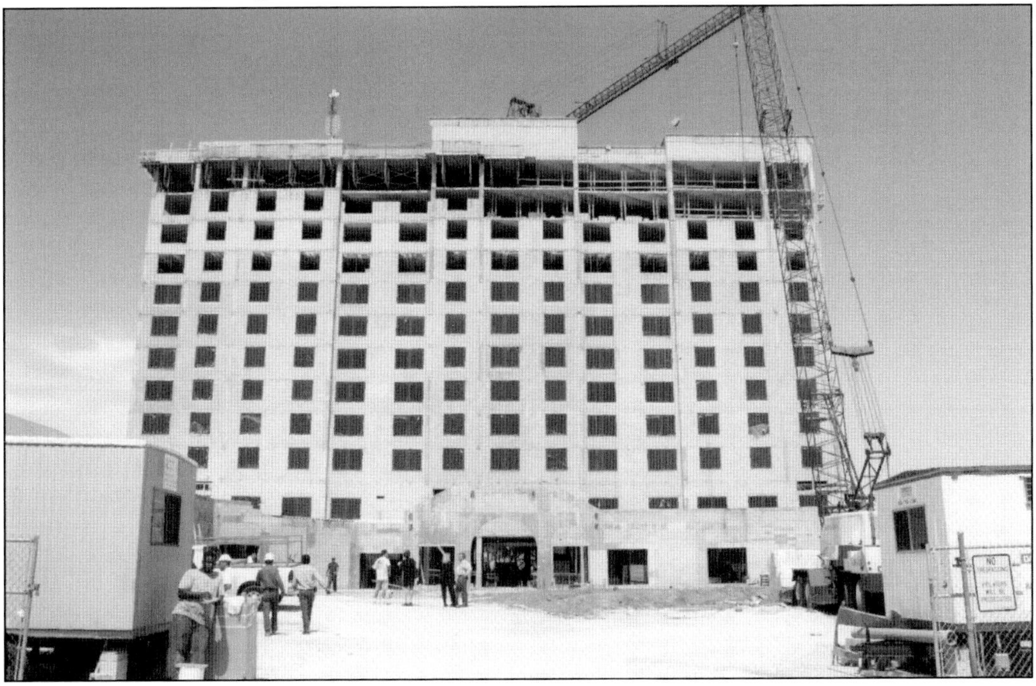

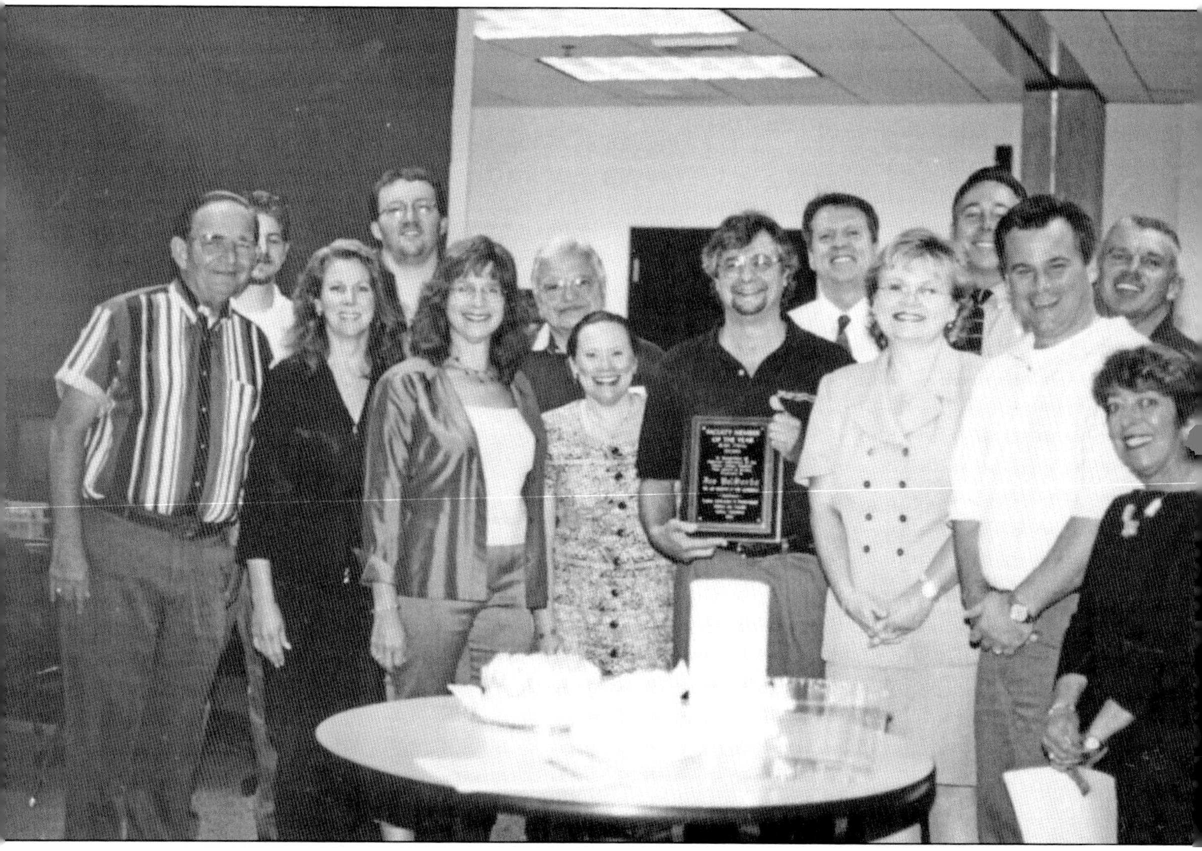

Joe Del Sordo, a faculty member of the digital filmmaking and video production department, won the "Faculty Member of the Year in Audio Visual Studies," in 2000, which was awarded by the Florida Association of Postsecondary Schools and Colleges. He is shown here surrounded by friends and colleagues. From left to right are (first row) Ed Williams, Susan Wald, Dr. Amy Phillips, LuWin Sanchez, Joe Del Sordo, Maria Barron, John Sethman, and Roni Braver; (second row) unidentified, Francisco Verela, Bill Kalaboke, Steve Schwab, Andrew Pond, and Roger Strait.

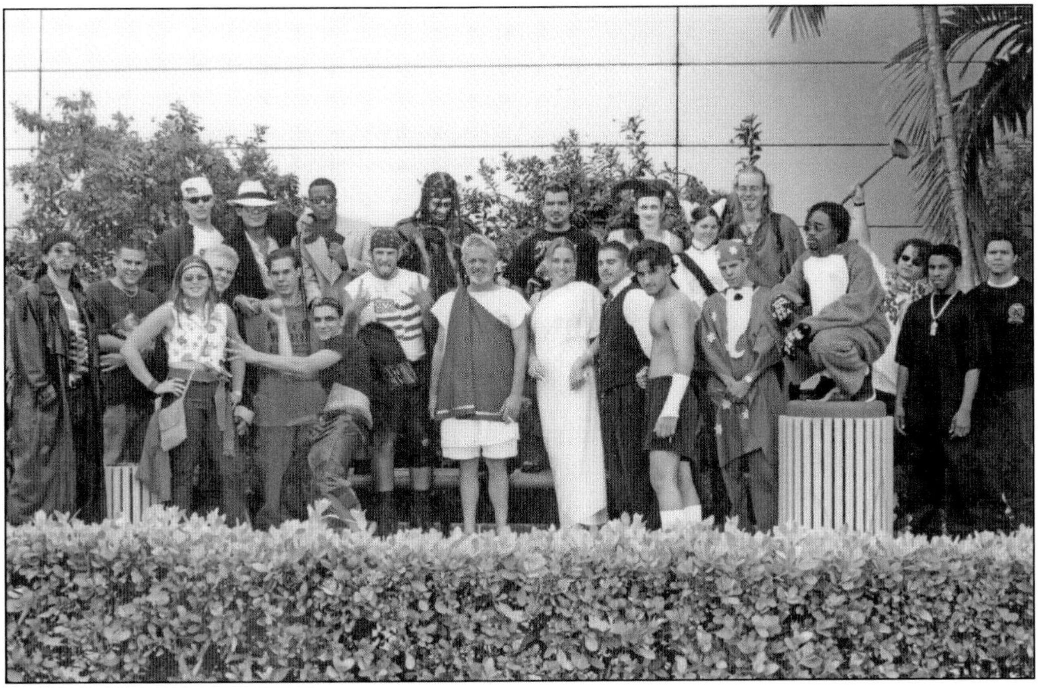

Michael Carnegie (first row, center) and students from his acting and movement class show off their costumes in November 2000.

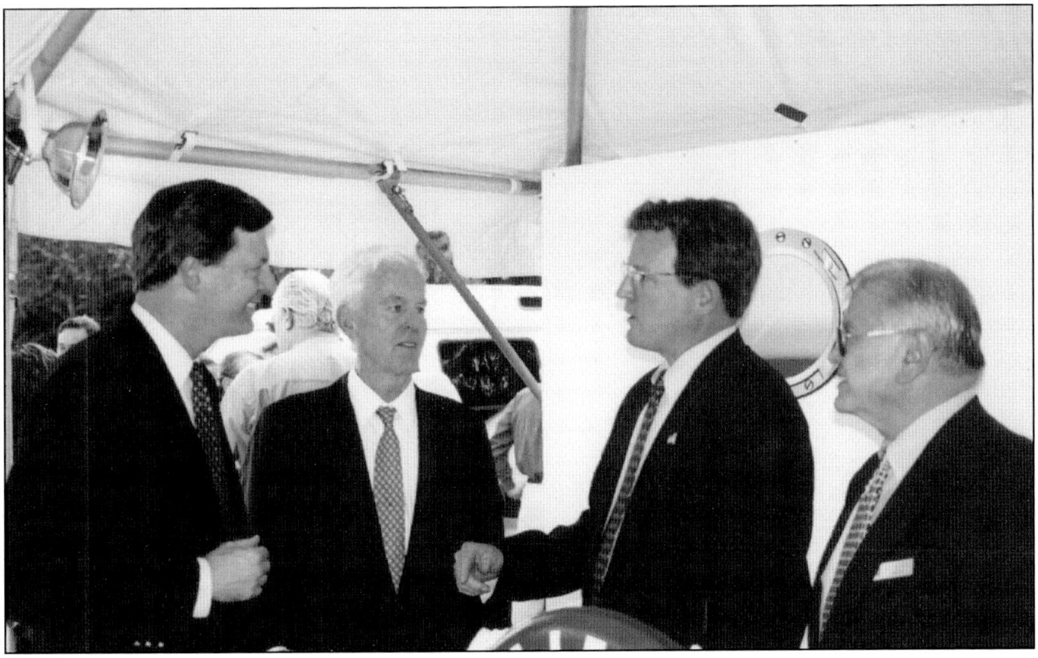

From left to right, EDMC vice chairman and chief executive officer John R. McKernan Jr., EDMC chairman Robert Knutson, Fort Lauderdale mayor Jim Naugle, and school president Bill Kalaboke celebrate the enrollment of 3,000 students on October 19, 2000.

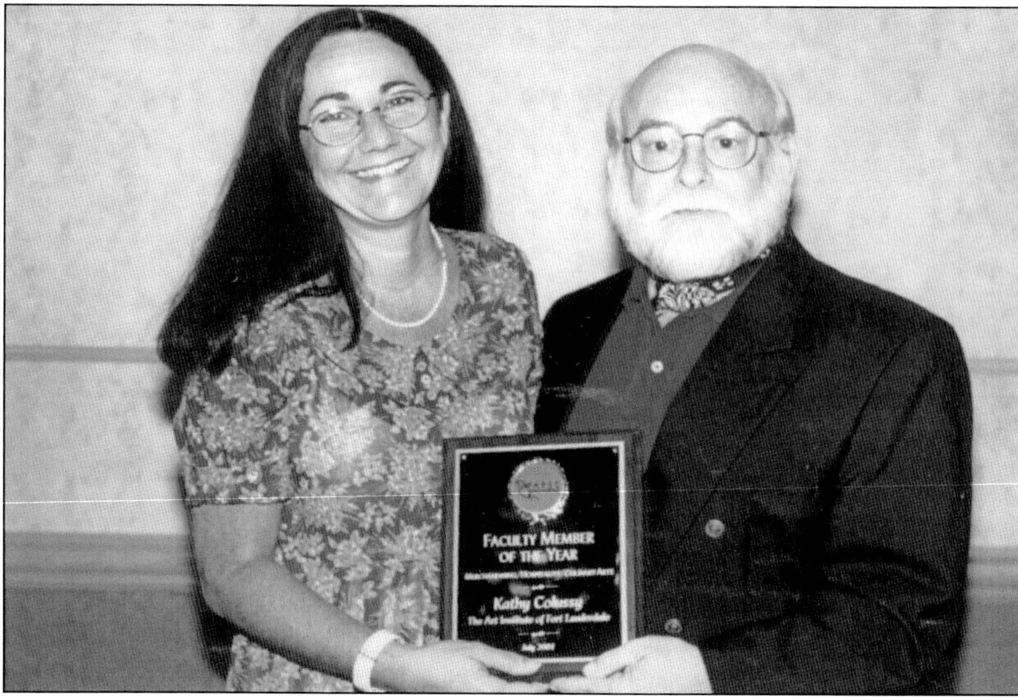

Robert Massengill, chairman of the fashion design department, presents the "Faculty Member of the Year" award to Kathy Colussy in July 2001.

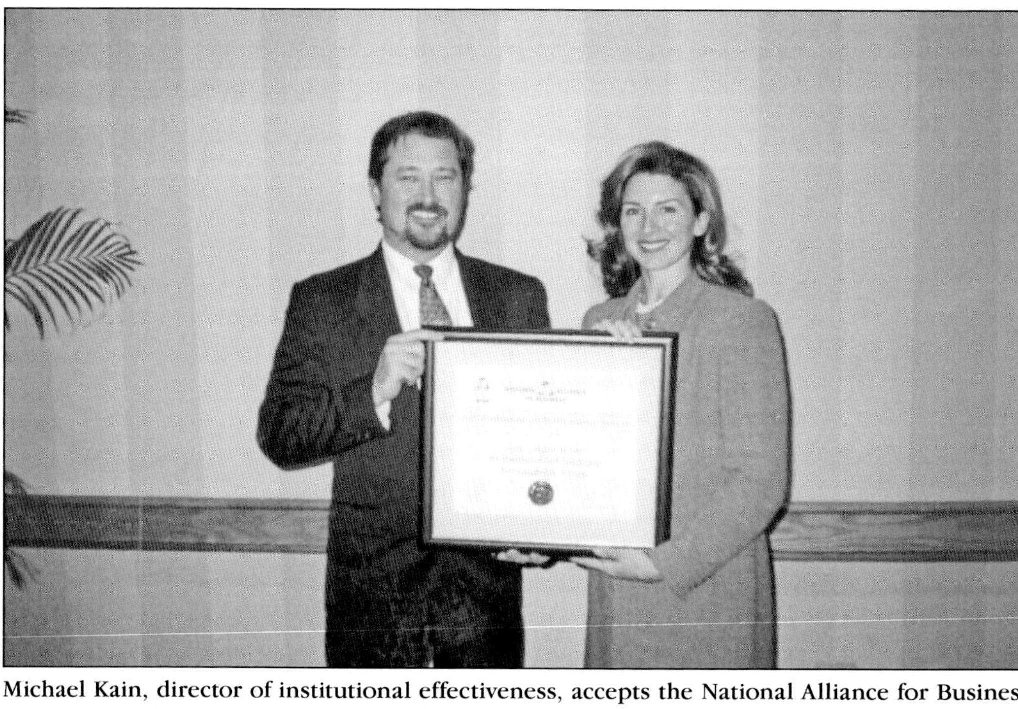

Michael Kain, director of institutional effectiveness, accepts the National Alliance for Business (NAB) award for the "Career College of the Year" in 2001.

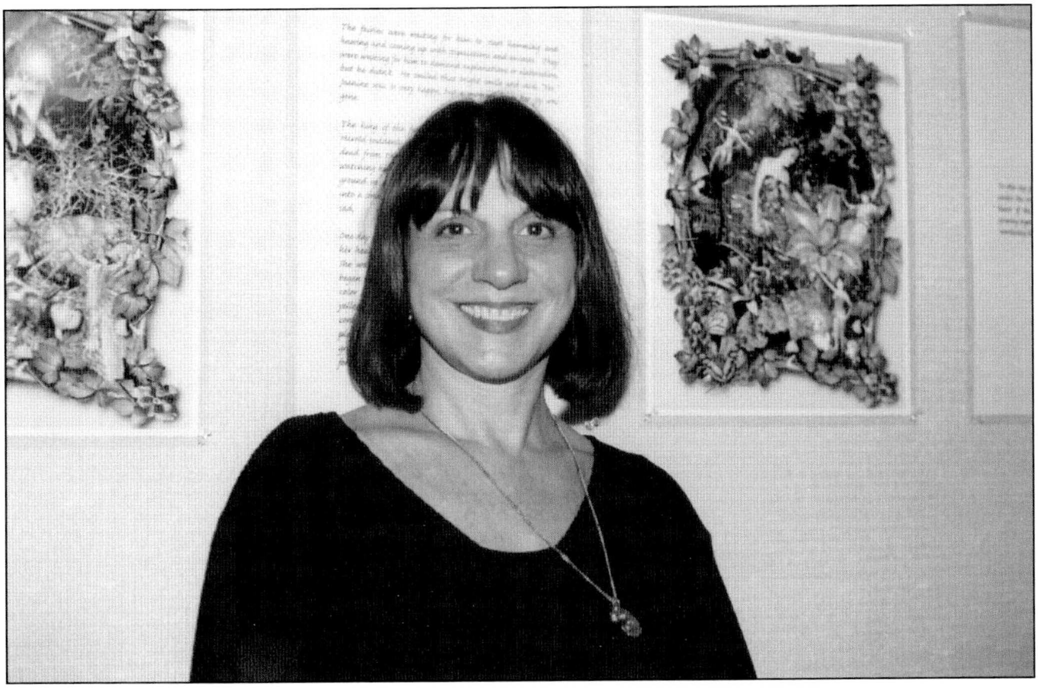
Lorna Hernandez, an animation faculty member, poses in the Wheeler gallery.

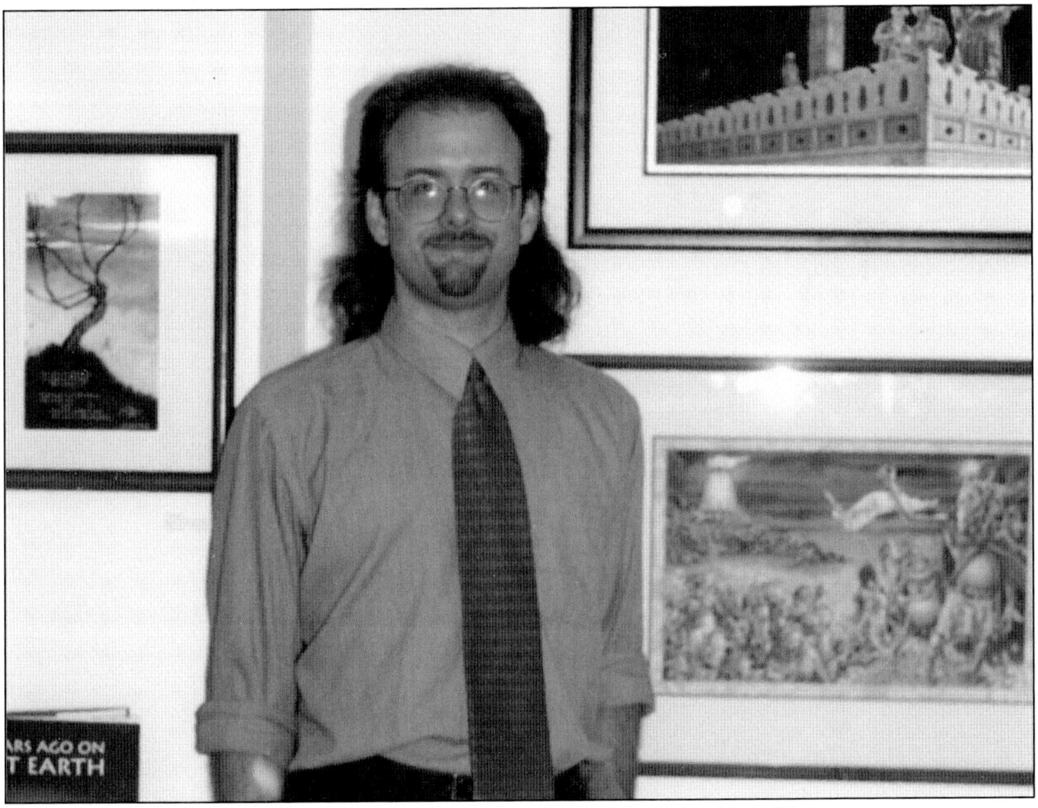

Jonathan Hunt, an illustration faculty member, poses in the Wheeler gallery.

This is a portrait of Suzanne Morrison-Williams when she joined the school in 1999 as an instructor in multimedia and web design. Today Morrison-Williams is the chairwoman of the interactive media design program, as well as the associate dean of education. (Courtesy of Suzanne Morrison-Williams.)

Below, Arlene Wites, the director of communications, poses in her office.

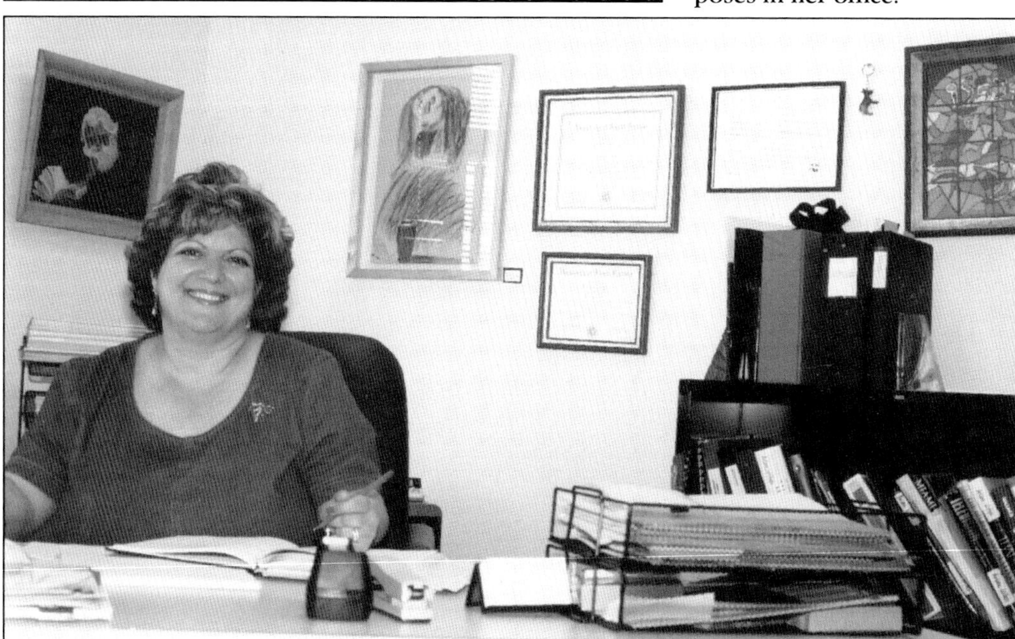

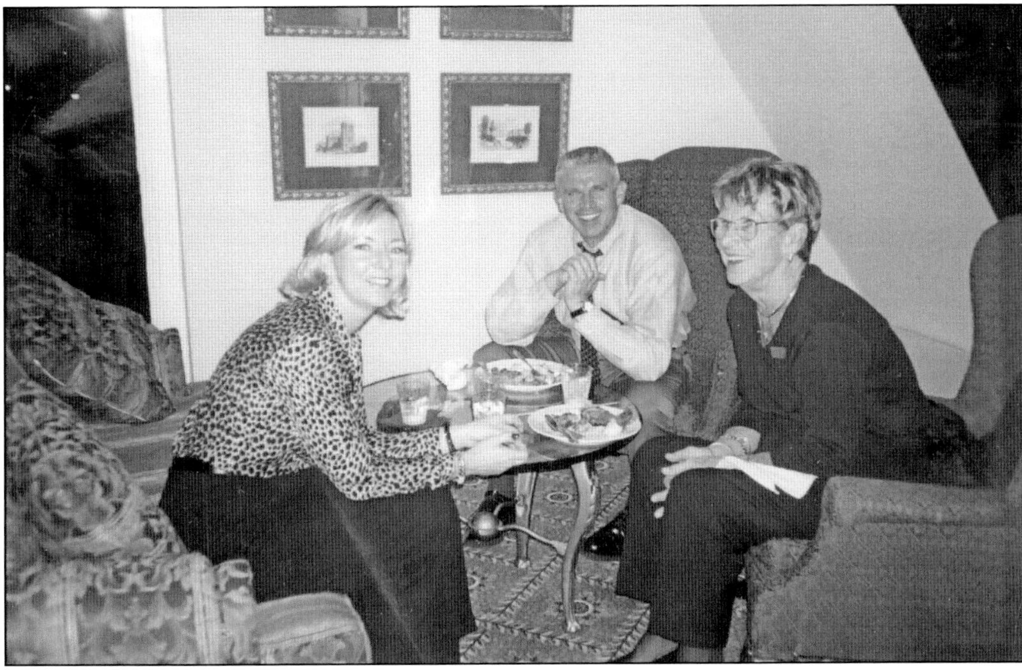

From left to right, Wendy Wagner, Roger Strait, and Dorothy Kurki celebrate the holiday season while on a cruise during the Winterfest Boat Parade.

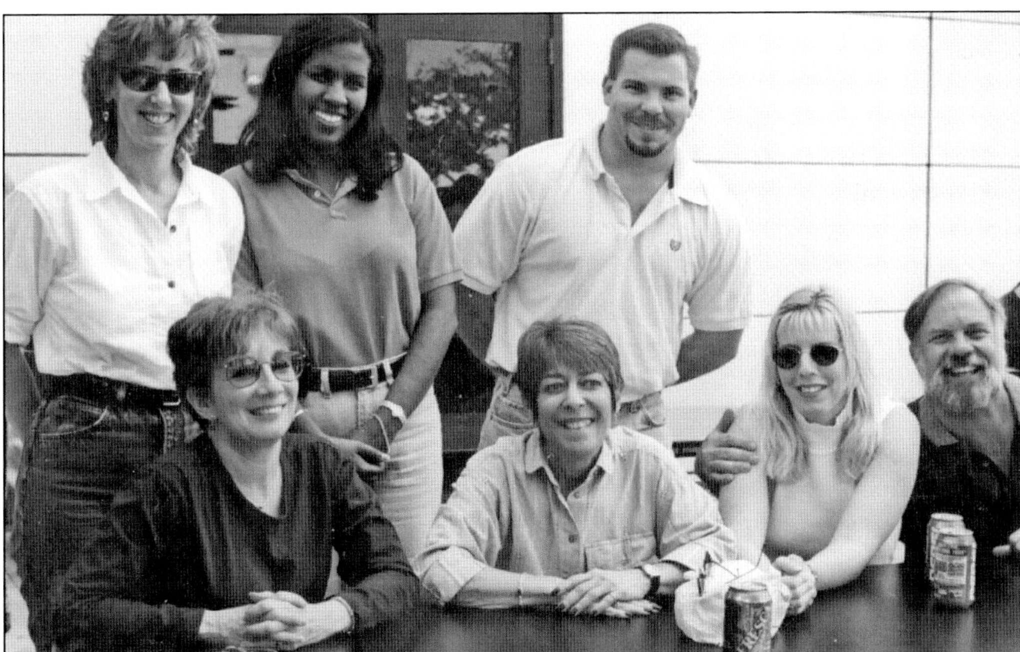

From left to right, (first row) Judy Cohen, Roni Braver, Laura Tengeres, and Michael Kraft; (second row) Kris Boatright, Beverly Johnson, and Jason Hill all enjoy a moment together on the patio behind the main building.

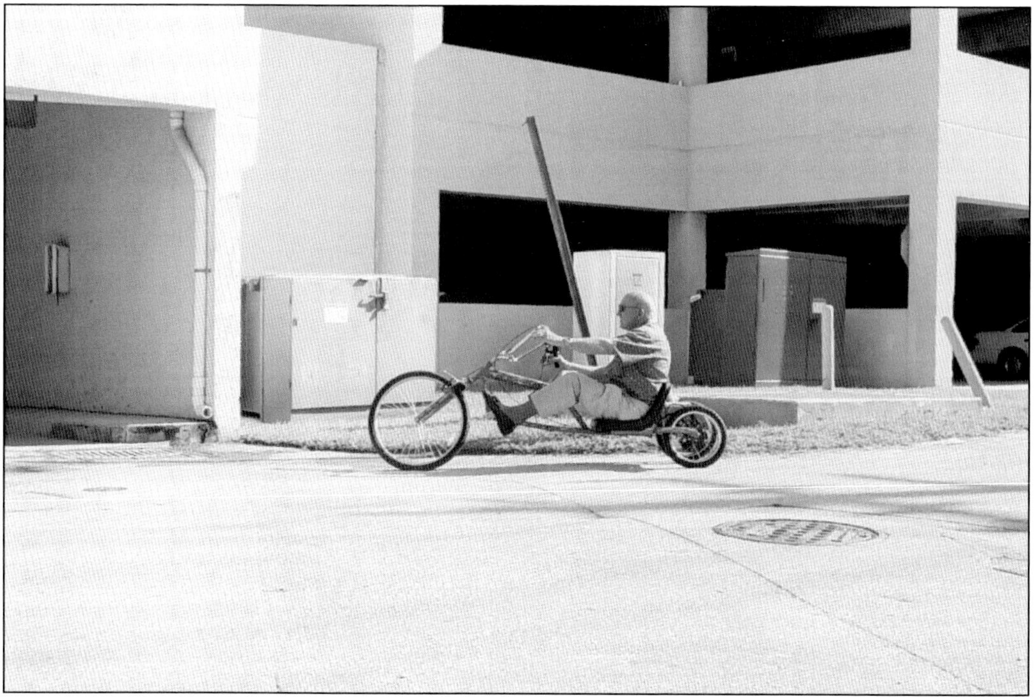

Industrial design instructor Winston Menish takes the newest tricycle for a ride. The contraption was invented by one of his students. (Courtesy of Rick Boggs.)

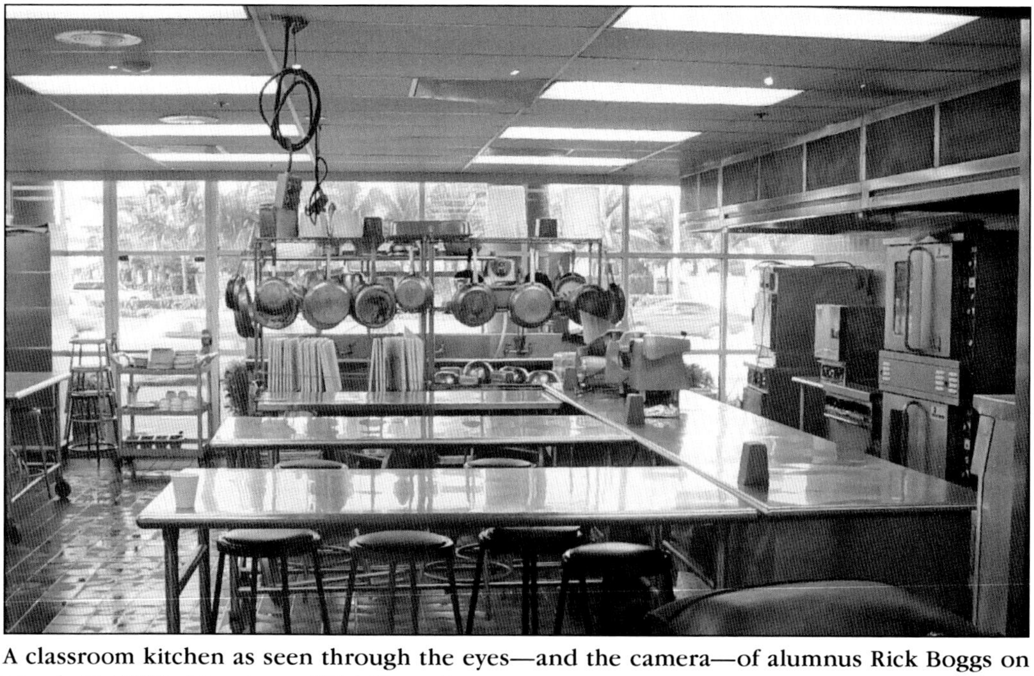

A classroom kitchen as seen through the eyes—and the camera—of alumnus Rick Boggs on March 20, 2002. (Courtesy of Rick Boggs.)

Chef Pamela Williams was awarded the American Culinary Federation Presidential Medallion in 2001 for her service to the field of culinary arts. Williams is a graduate of the Culinary Institute of America and has been with the Art Institute of Fort Lauderdale since October 1985. She was voted "Honored Faculty" in the summer of 1997.

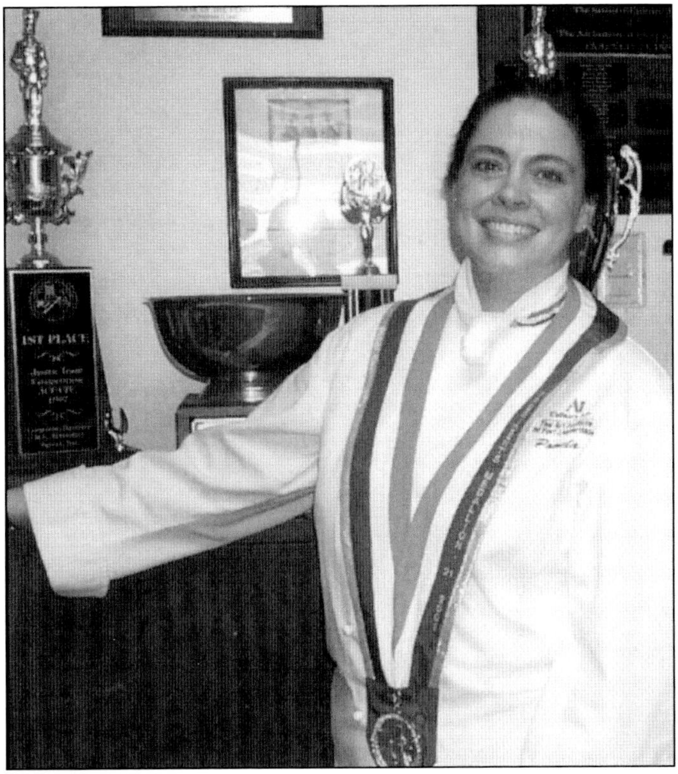

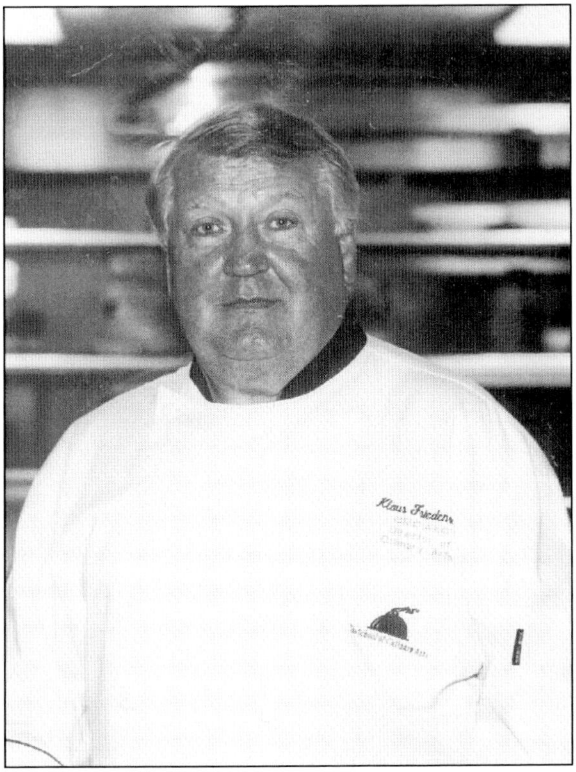

Pictured here is renowned master chef Klaus Friedenreich, the long-time director of the culinary arts department. Friedenreich retired in December 2006.

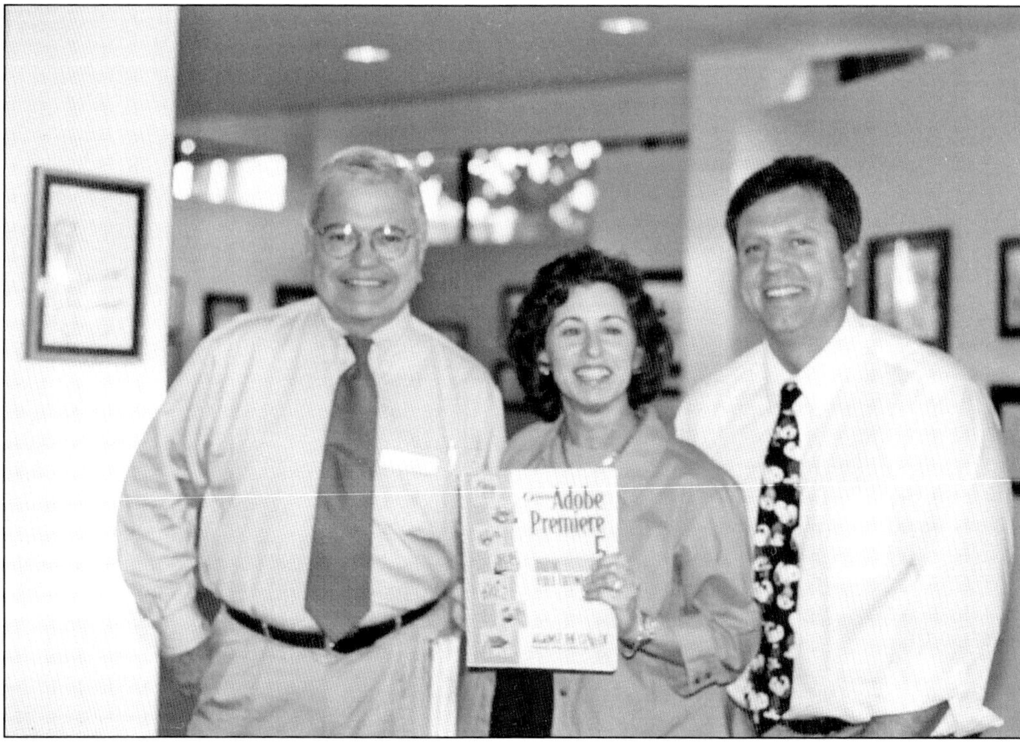

Debbie Rose Myers, a 29-year veteran faculty member at the school, is honored at a book signing in the spring of 2002, featuring *Adobe Premier 5 Digital Video Editing*, published by Prentice-Hall. Myers, who has won numerous awards for her artwork, is seen here during the reception with school president Bill Kalaboke (left) and dean Steve Schwab.

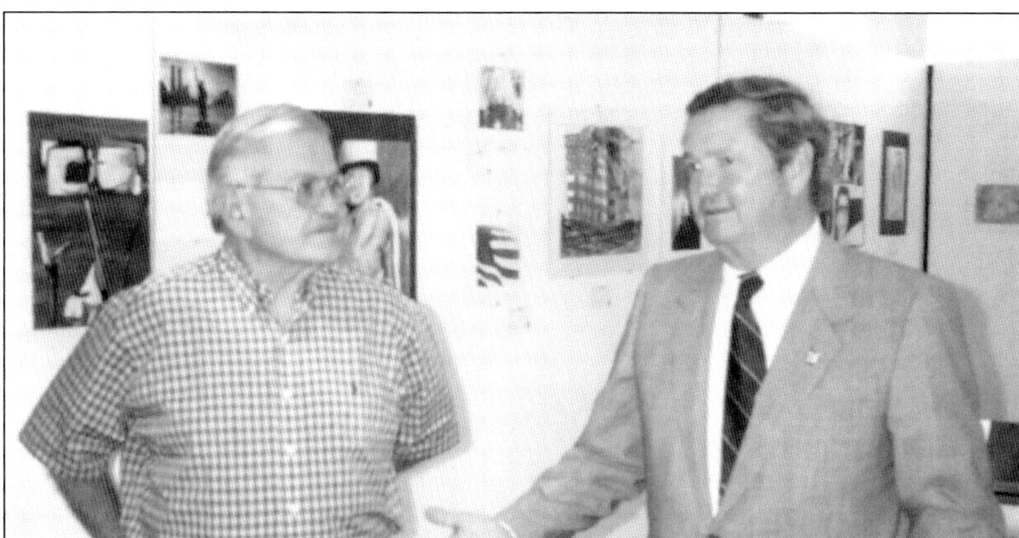

Congressman E. Clay Shaw Jr. visited the school in February 2002 to promote the Congressional Art Competition, entitled "An Artistic Discovery." Members of Congress held this nationwide art competition to encourage the development of artistic talents. School president Bill Kalaboke (left) is talking to Congressman Shaw.

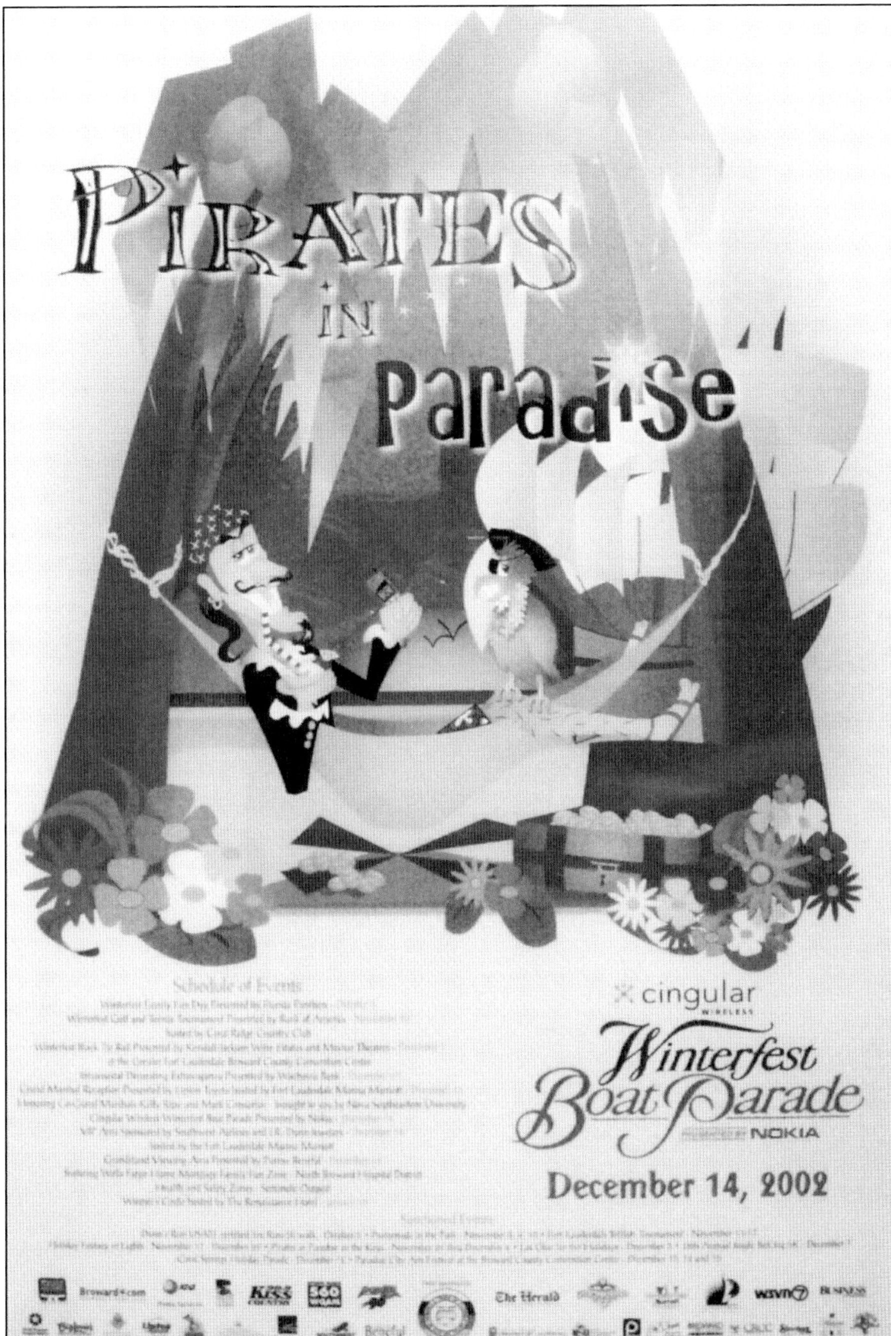

Pictured here is the 2002-winning poster for the world-famous and popular Winterfest Boat Parade, designed by Marsha Michaels with artwork by Clara Mateus. The Winterfest Boat Parade is a spectacular holiday event where hundreds of corporate and private boats are decorated around a theme, like the 2002 theme of Pirates in Paradise, for example, and then compete for awards. The boats parade through the Fort Lauderdale Intercoastal Waterway for all to enjoy. The year 2008 marks the 36th anniversary of the parade.

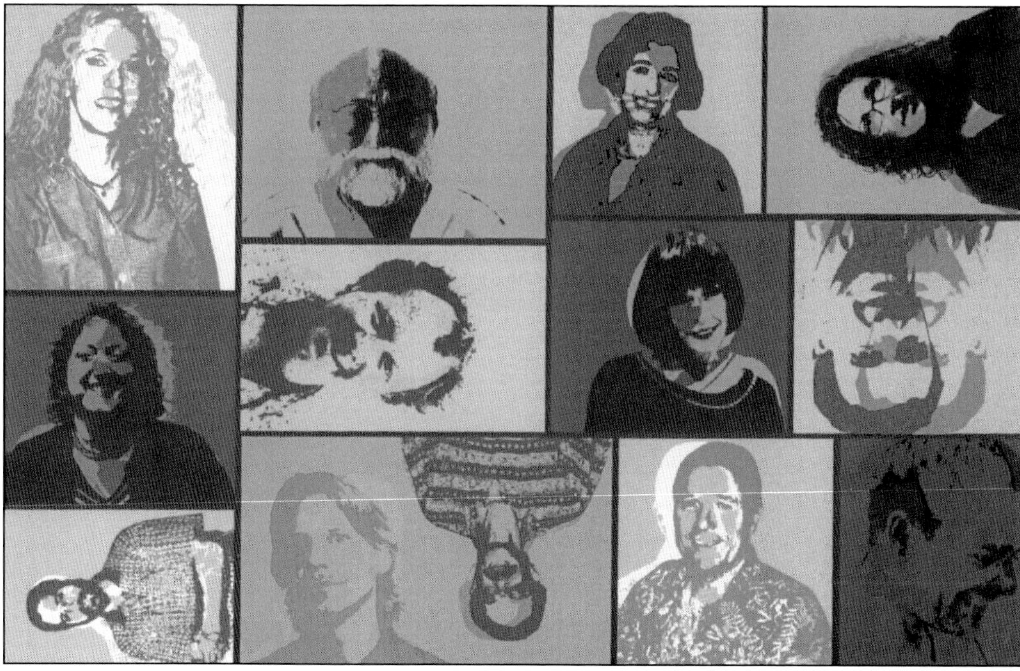

This invitation announces the 25th-annual faculty art show, which took place at the Mark K. Wheeler Gallery in 2002 from September through October. Pictured from left to right are (first row) Frank Balzano, Tim Gorski, Andy Bing, Jim Radford, and unidentified; (second row) Rosanne Gibel, unidentified, Ms. V., and Brian Wood; (third row) Linda Weeks, Robert Massengill, Debbie Rose Myers, and Janet Gold.

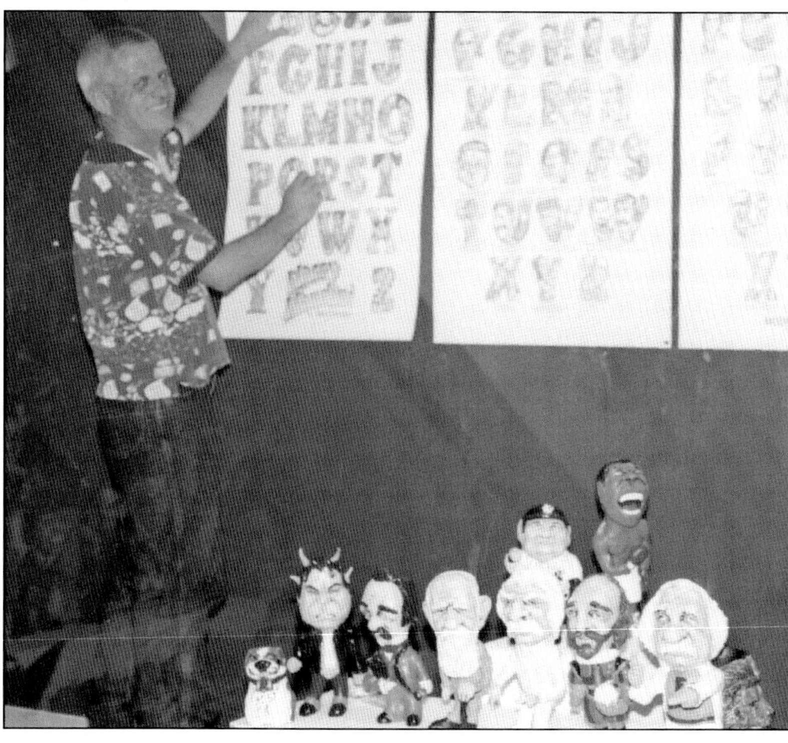

Michael Carnegie hangs his artwork, the *ABC's of the Famous and Infamous—from Elvis to Einstein, Beethoven to Bogart, and much more!*, in a display case. Carnegie has been with the school for 27 years, and was selected as "Honored Faculty" in the fall of 1998.

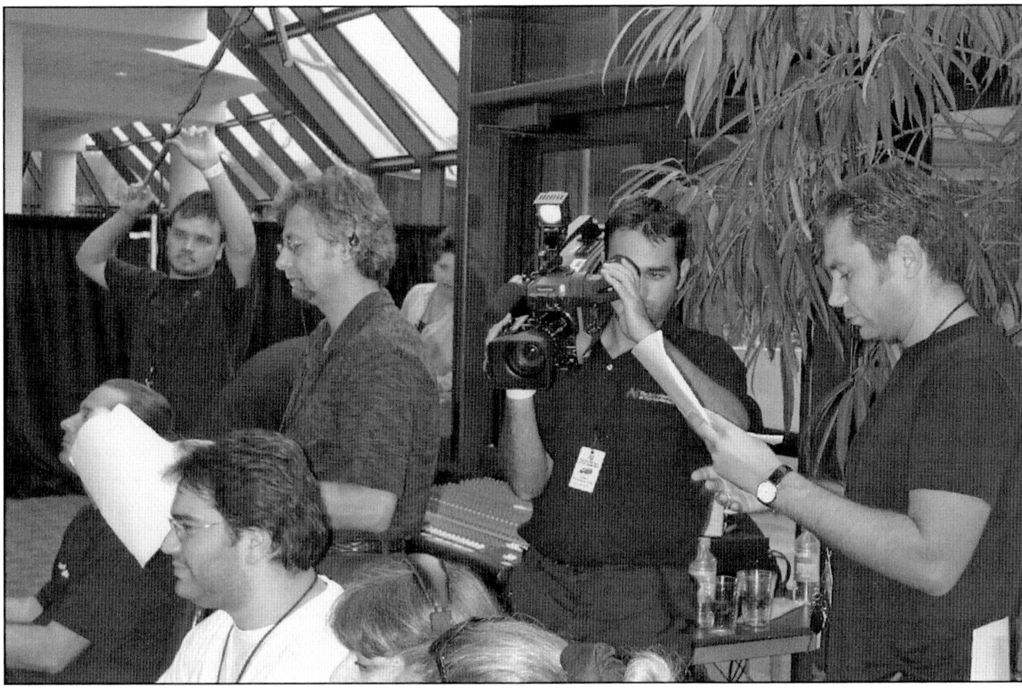

Producing and taping a fashion show is a big job. Shown above are instructor Joe Del Sordo (center left) and students who make it work. Pictured below are (from left to right) Erika Del Sordo, Stephanie Schaffeld, and Michelle Demarziano. (Both courtesy of Joe Del Sordo.)

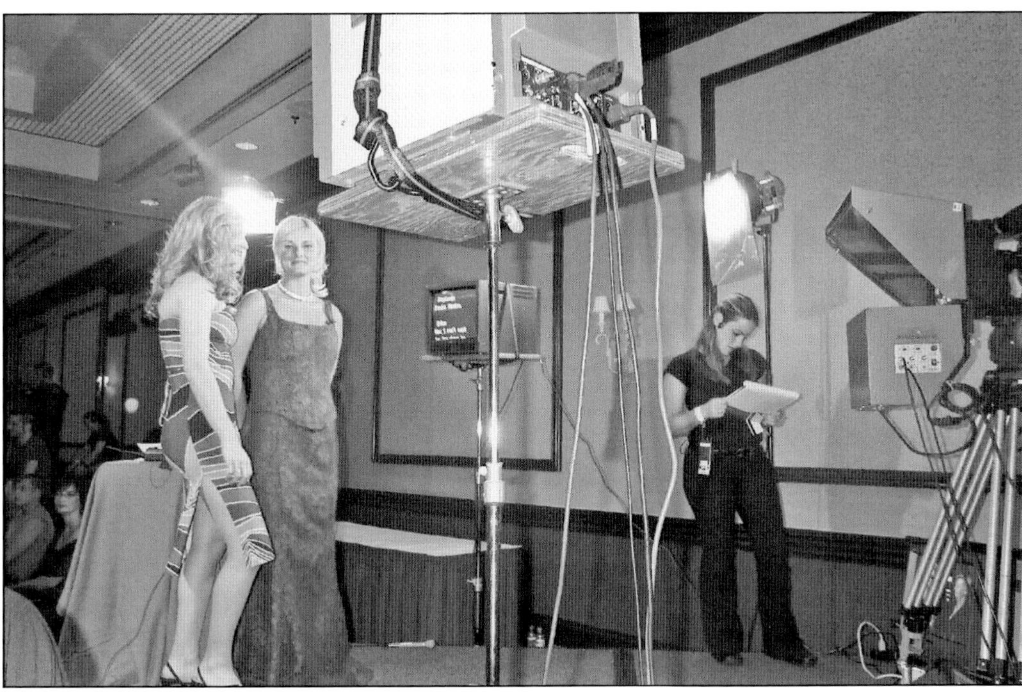

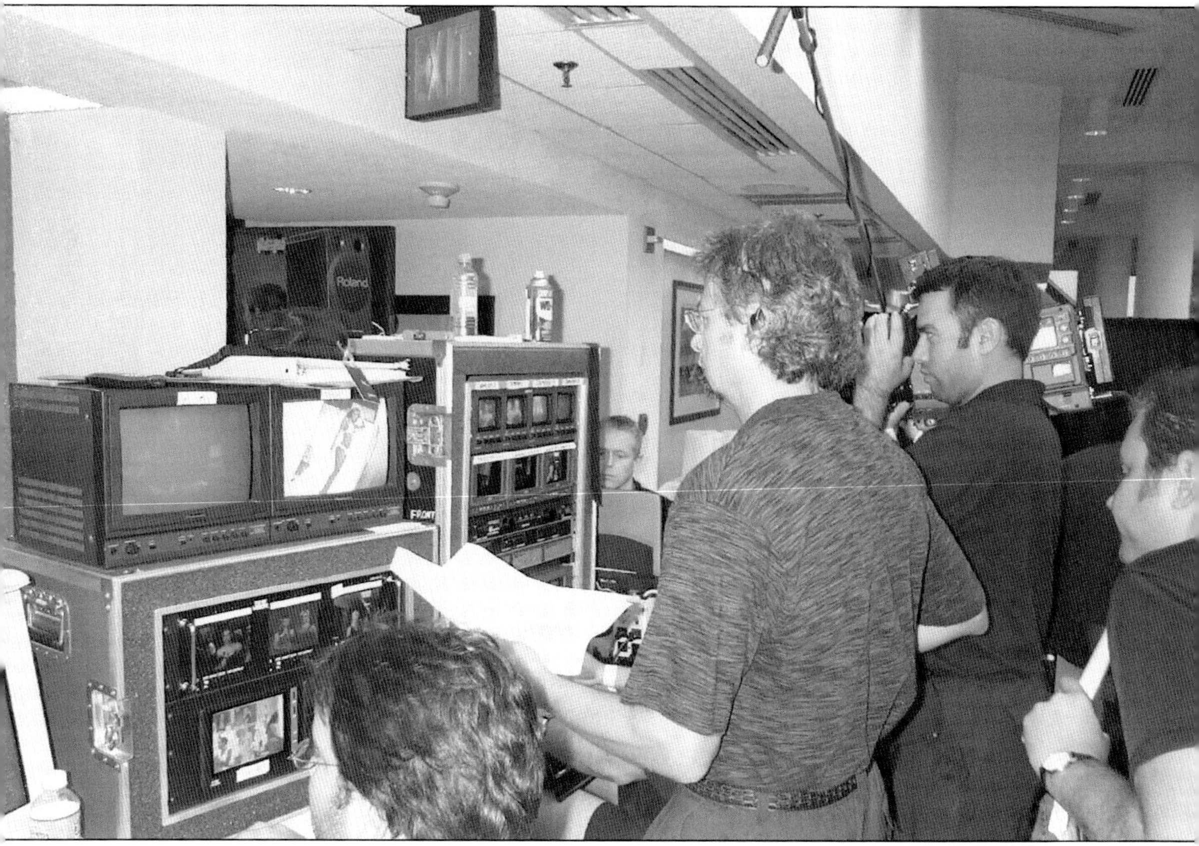

This picture of the fashion show depicts the action behind the curtain. (Courtesy of Joe Del Sordo.)

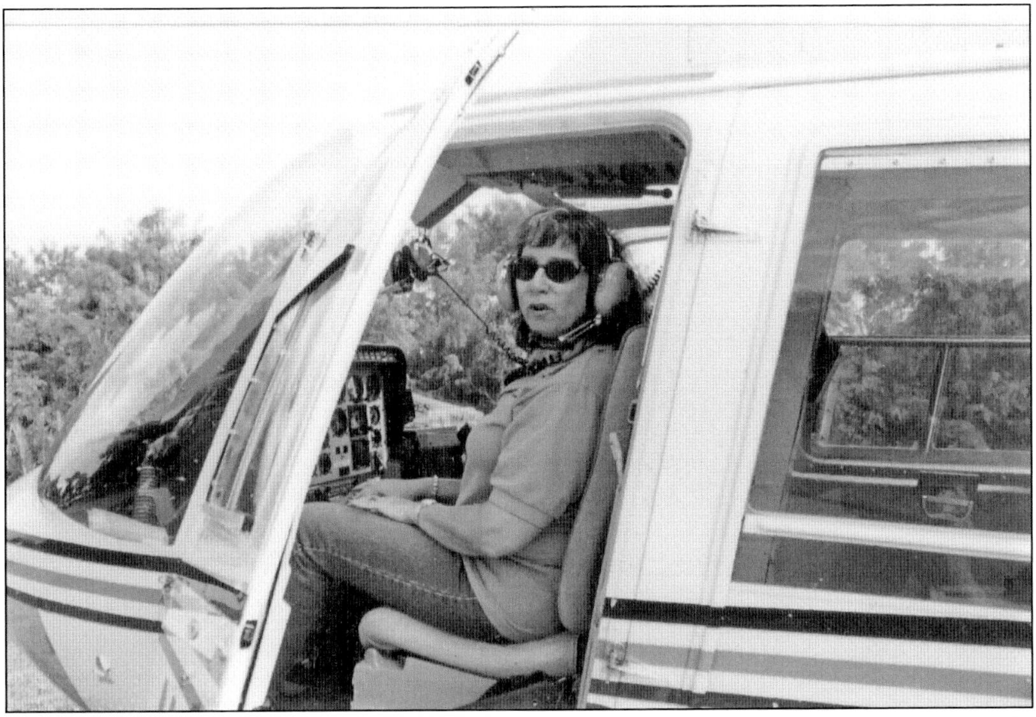

In 2003, Dr. Amy Philips, chairwoman of the communications and media production department, boarded a Broward County Environmental Services helicopter as part of the "Wave Runner" video project. Commissioned by the Fort Lauderdale–Hollywood International Airport, the 57-screen digital video production focused on the natural beauty of the Everglades, the parks, the beaches, and other Broward County scenic attractions. The Telly award–winning project was created for display in Terminal No. 2, Concourse B at the airport.

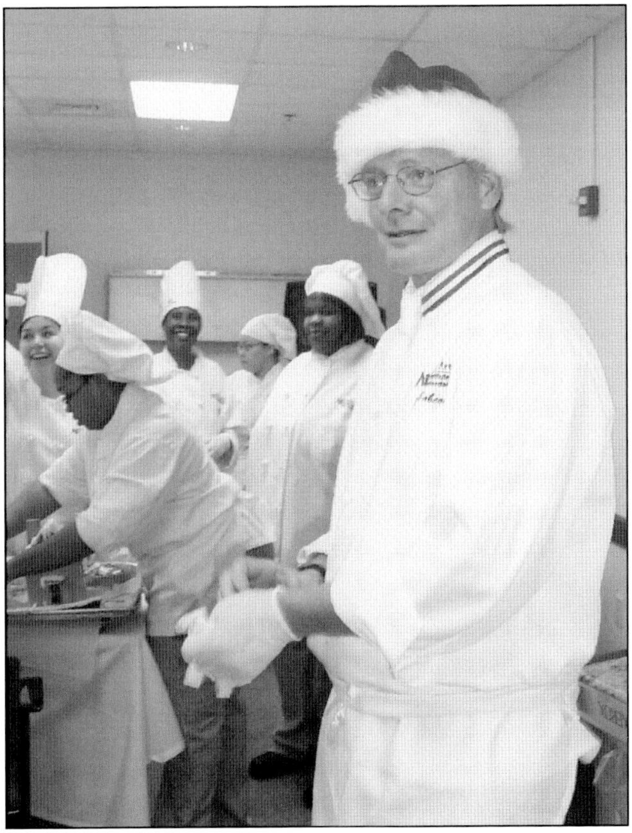

At right, chef Peter Babcock directs culinary arts students as they prepare to construct gingerbread houses for a local community event during the holiday season. (Courtesy of Peter Babcock.)

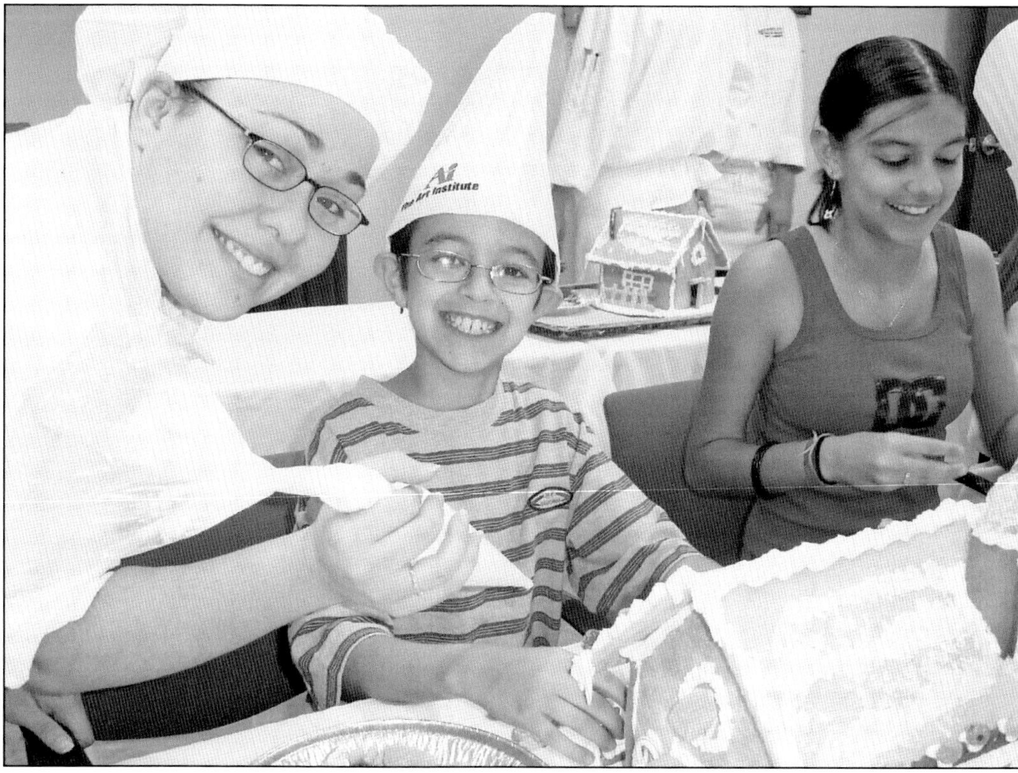

Chef Peter Babcock and his students sponsor a gingerbread house decorating party for patients of the Chris Evert Children's Hospital at Broward General Medical Center. (Courtesy of Peter Babcock.)

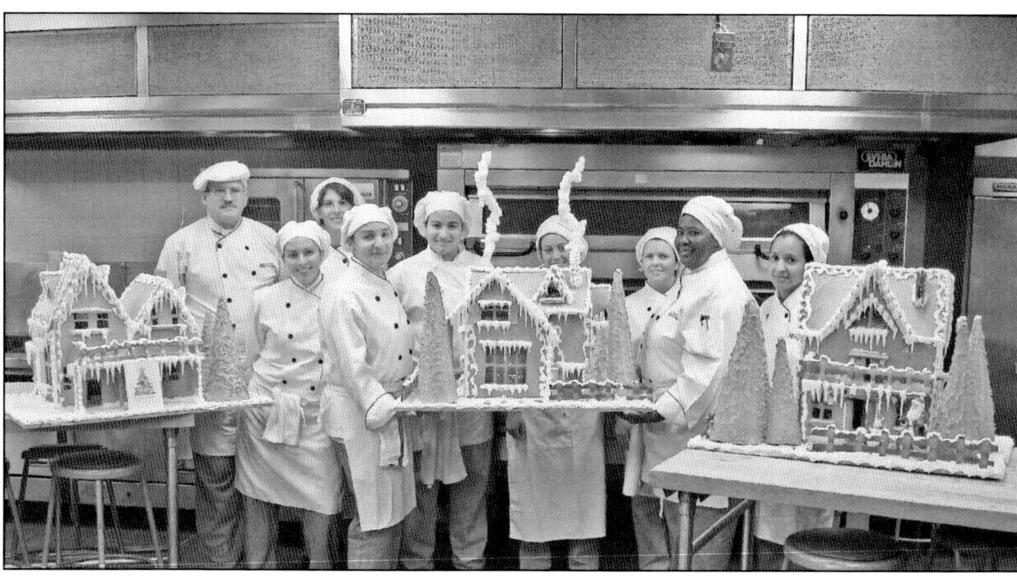

Students show off the gingerbread houses they created for a display at the Galleria Mall. The gingerbread houses were auctioned off, with the proceeds benefiting the Museum of Art in Fort Lauderdale. (Courtesy of Peter Babcock.)

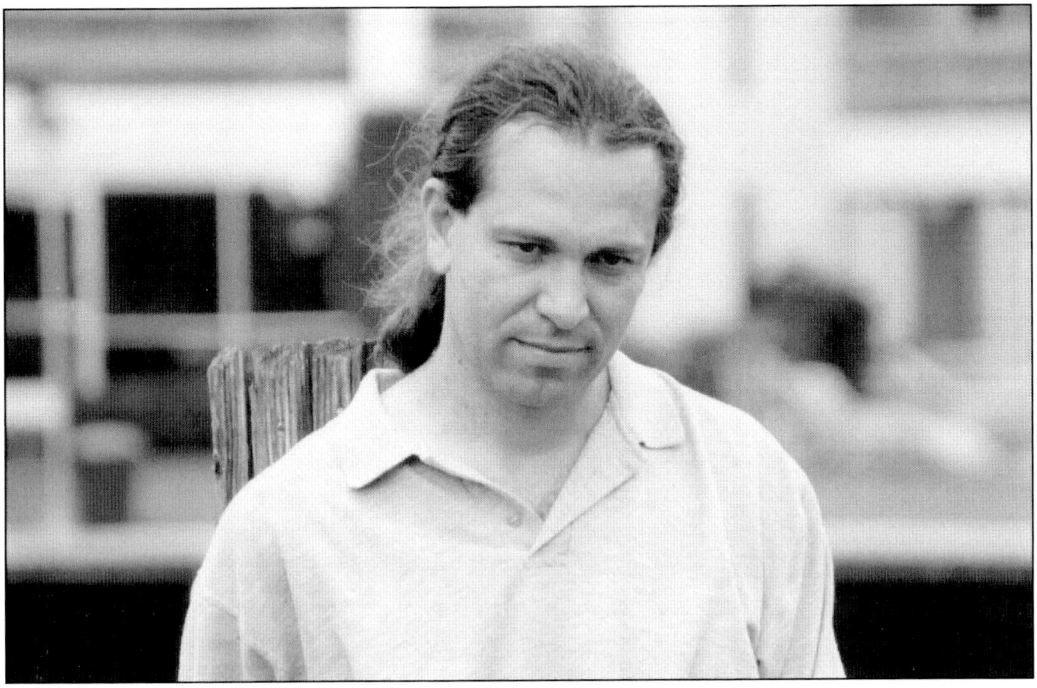

Dr. Raz Ben-Ezzer, originally from Israel, is a faculty member in the web design and interactive media department. He has been with the school since 1990.

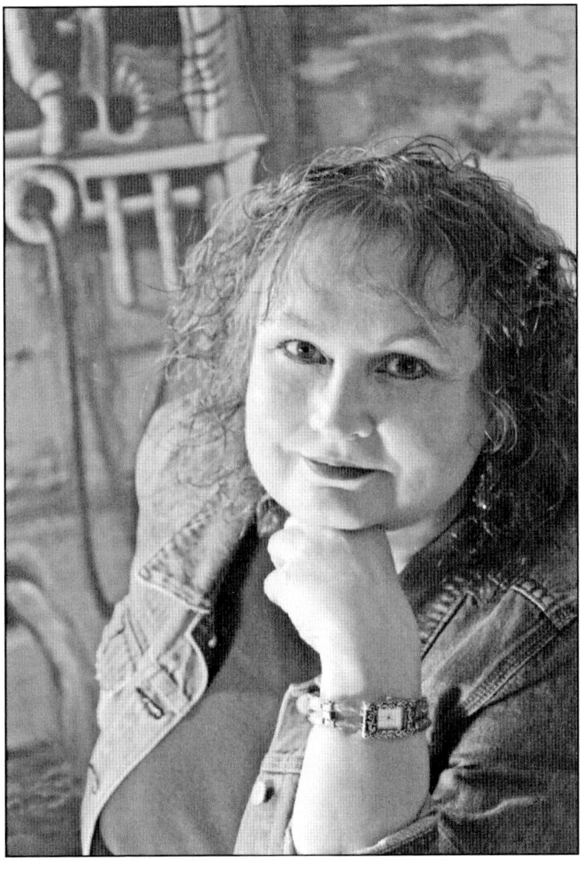

Trina Nicklas, the director of art and humanities, and chairwoman of illustration, poses in front of one of her paintings, entitled *Green Hoses.* (Courtesy of Trina Nicklas.)

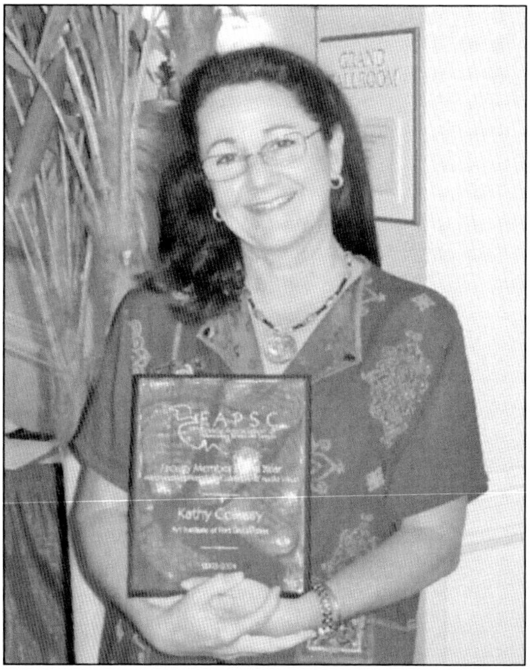

In 2004, Kathy Colussy won the "Faculty of the Year" award for the second time from the Florida Association of Postsecondary Schools and Colleges. The first time she won was in July 2001. In addition to taking students on field trips to 52 countries and 47 states, Colussy has also published four books: *Fashion Design on Computer*; *How to Research the Internet for Fashion; Rendering Fashion, Fabric, and Prints with Adobe Illustrator*; and *Rendering Fashion, Fabric, and Prints with Adobe Photoshop.* The last two titles were written with Steve Greenberg. Colussy is especially well known for her international trips. She has literally taken fashion students around the world.

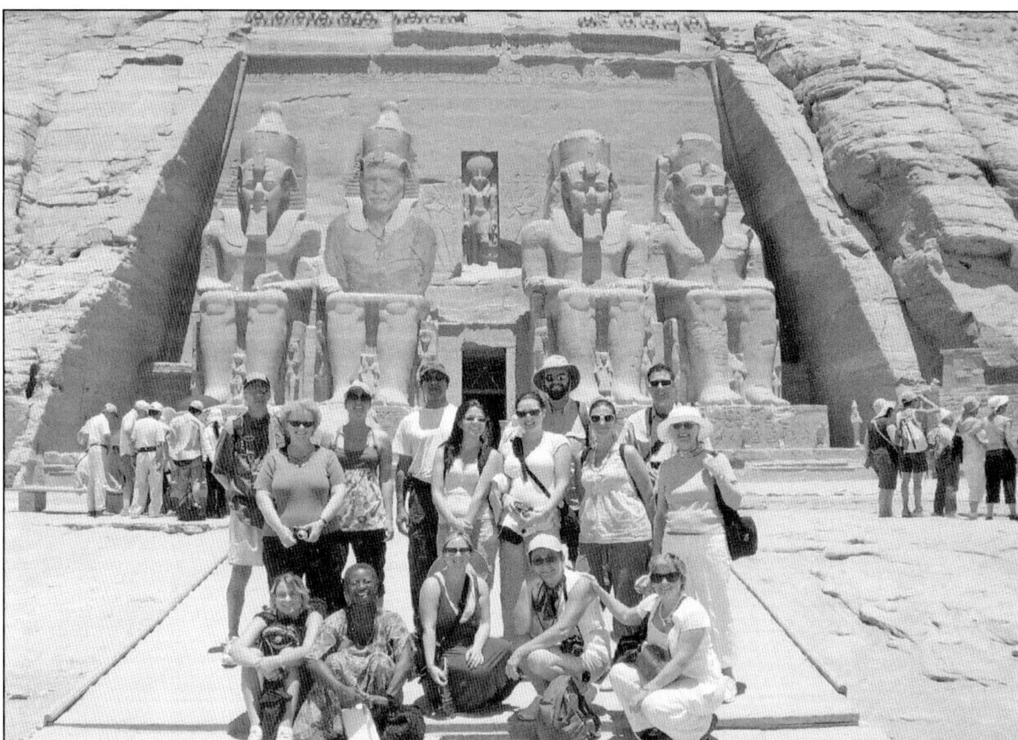

Kathy Colussy and her fashion students pose during one of their international field trips to Egypt in 2003. Long-time photography instructor Ed Williams accompanied Colussy on this trip. He is the photographer. However, because Colussy wanted Williams included in the image, she used Photoshop to replace the face of one pharaoh with his image. (Courtesy of Kathy Colussy.)

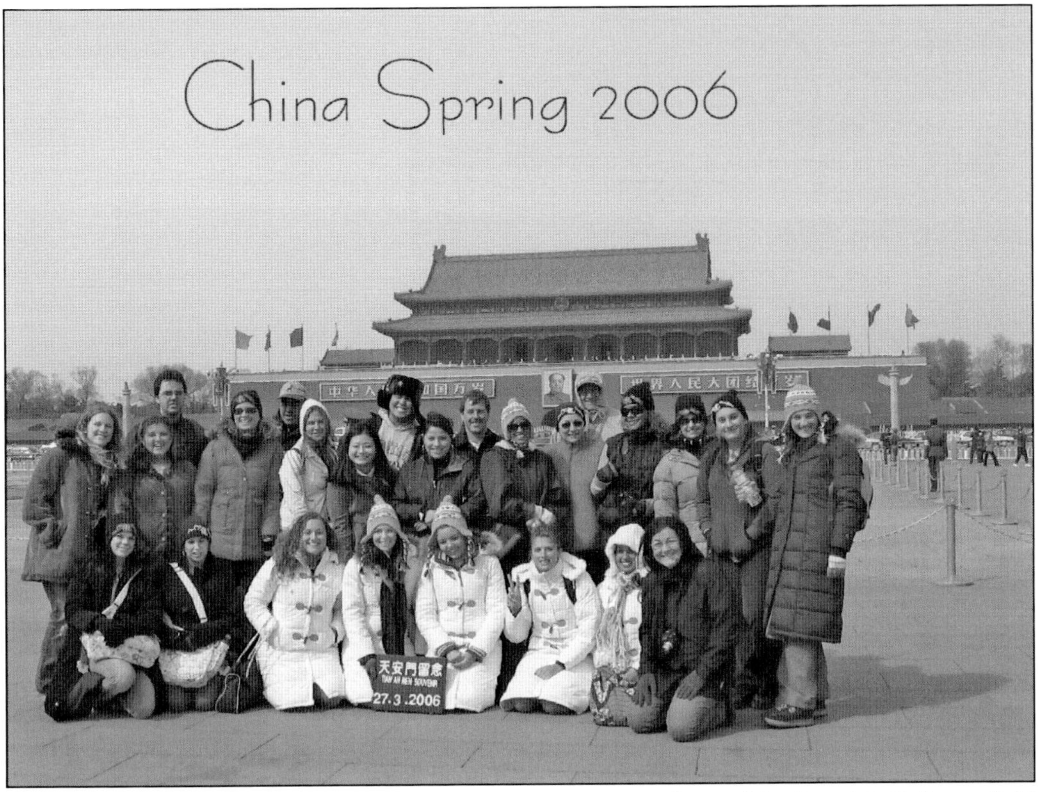

Kathy Colussy and her students pose in Tiananmen Square in front of the People's Hall on a field trip to China. (Courtesy of Kathy Colussy.)

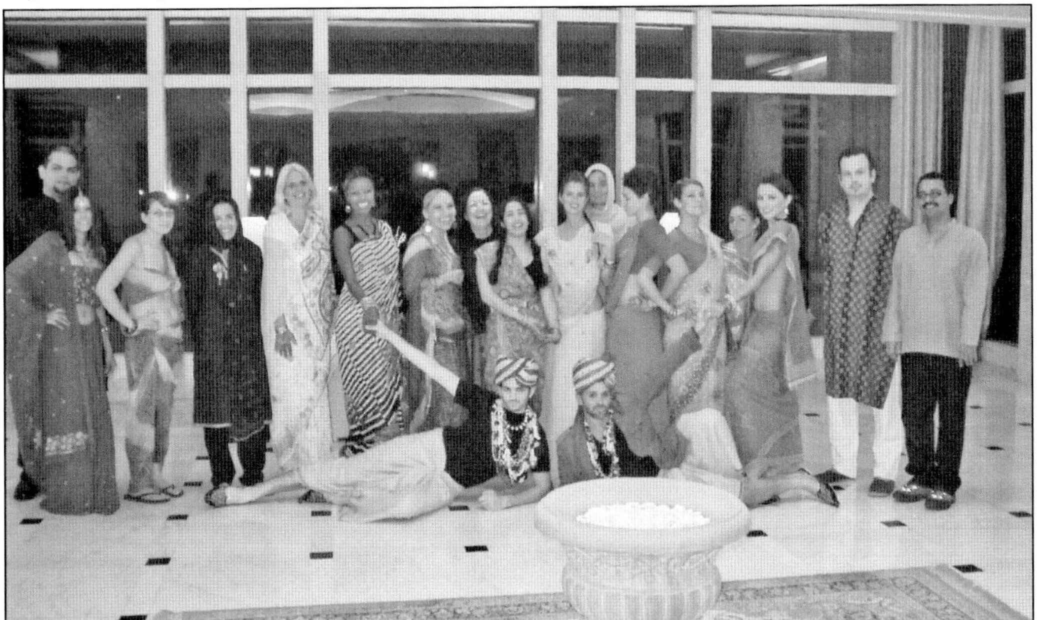

Kathy Colussy's students show off the saris they made while on a study tour to India. (Courtesy of Kathy Colussy.)

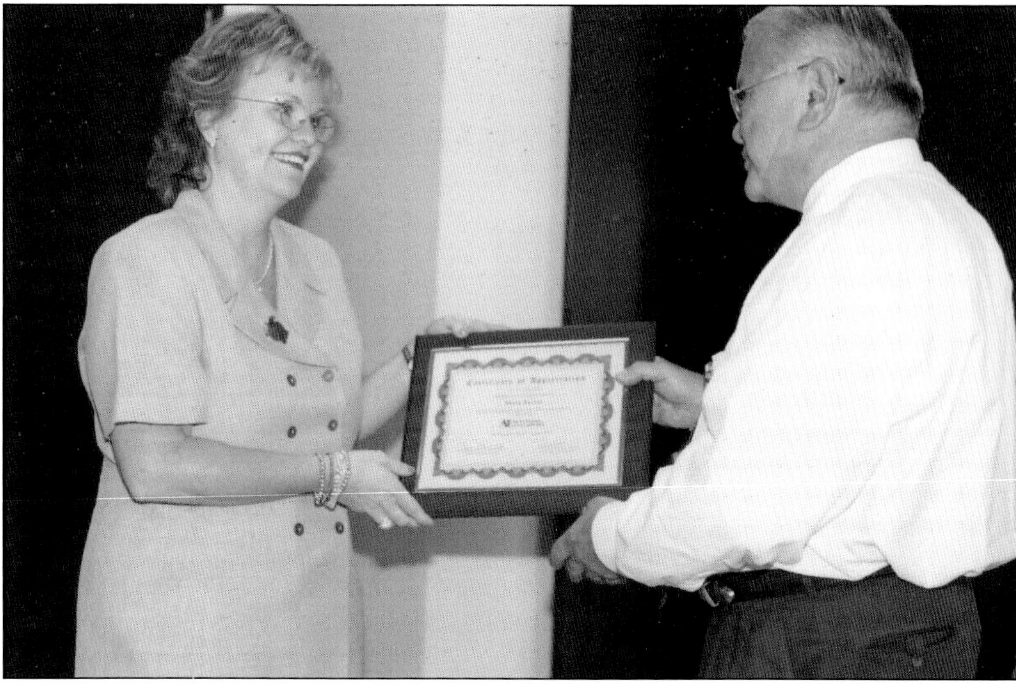

Maria Barron receives recognition from school president Bill Kalaboke in 2003 for her contributions to the PET (Productivity, Efficiency, and Training) committee.

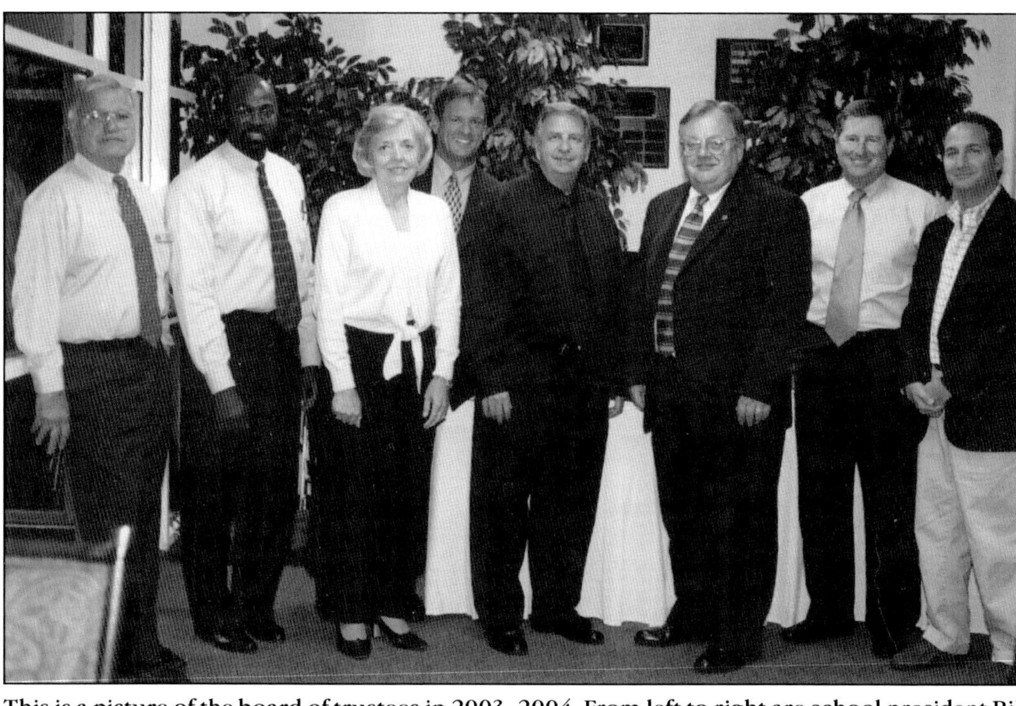

This is a picture of the board of trustees in 2003–2004. From left to right are school president Bill Kalaboke, esteemed artist Jonathan Knight, Dr. Marilyn Beck, Robert Peterson, Richard Clark, Dr. Wayne Freeberg, Robert Cypher, and Steve Leifman

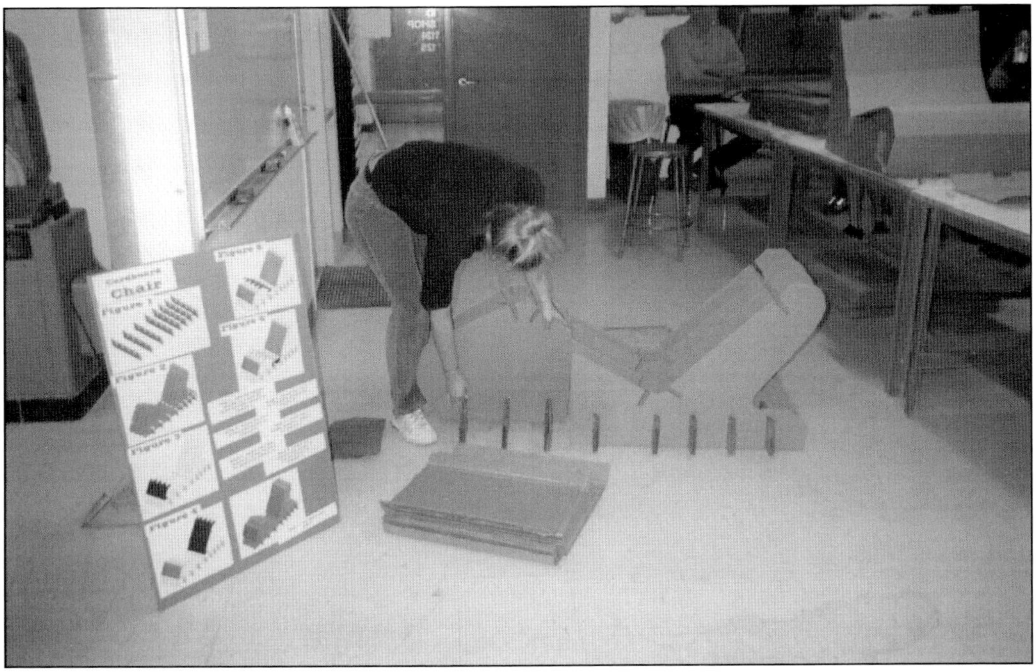

In 2004, Amanda "Mandy" Krebs, an industrial design student, built a chair in Winston Menish's structural design class. The trick was to keep the cost between $5 and $8, and design it for easy assembly and disassembly. Voila! (Both courtesy of Winston Menish.)

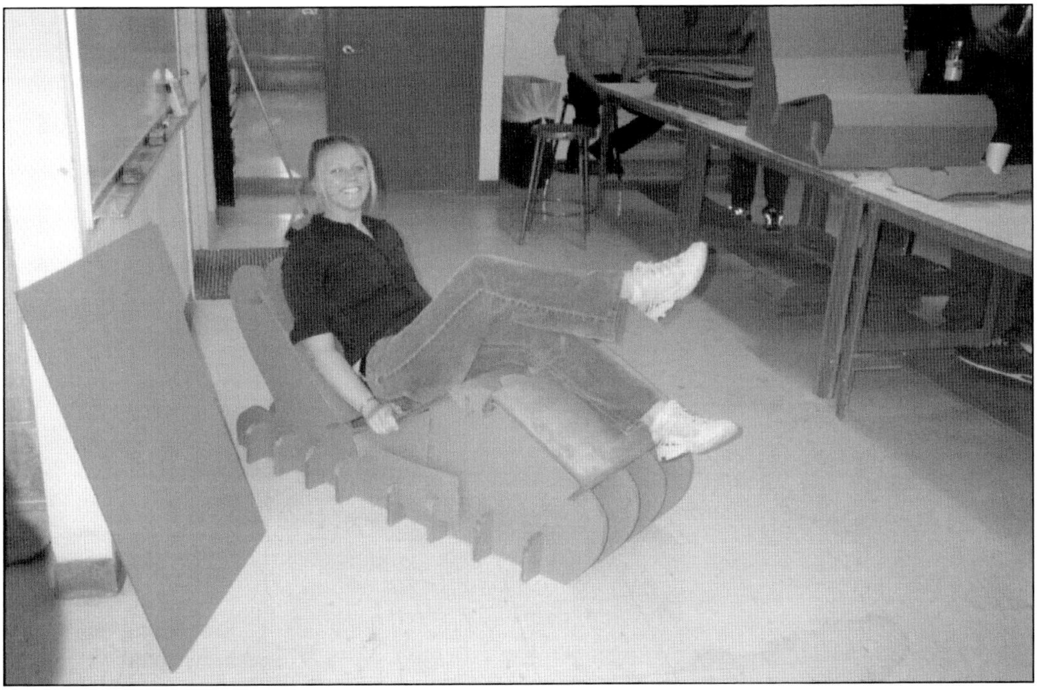

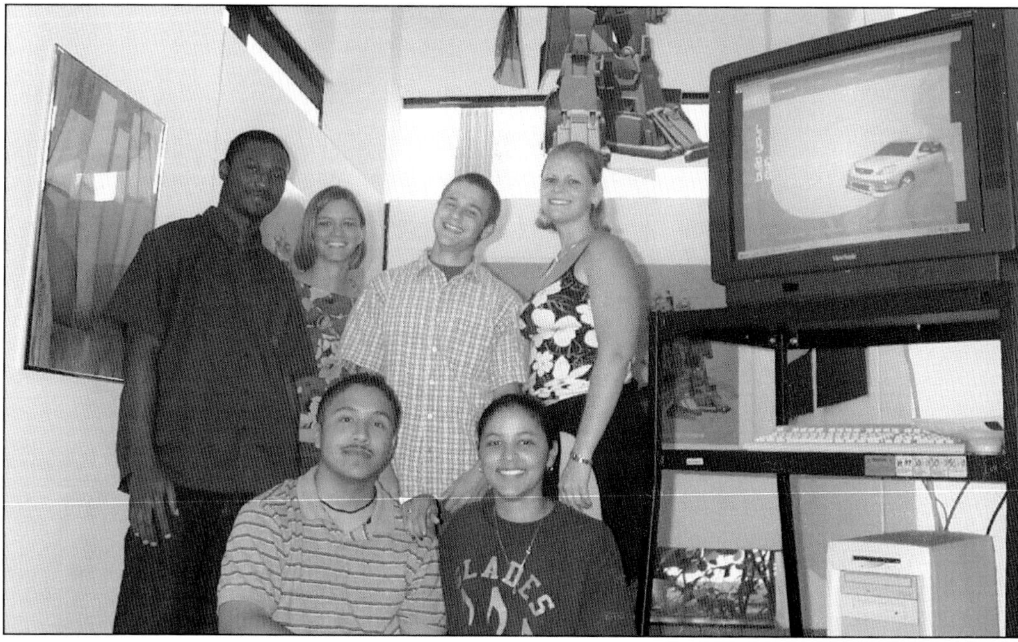

These six students were the first to enroll in the Artemis Design Honors Group. They are shown displaying their award-winning work at the 30th annual juried student art exhibit in 2004. The students entered the American Advertising Federation's college marketing and campaign competition. The client was Toyota, who chose to use the students' "transformer" concept in future commercials and advertising.

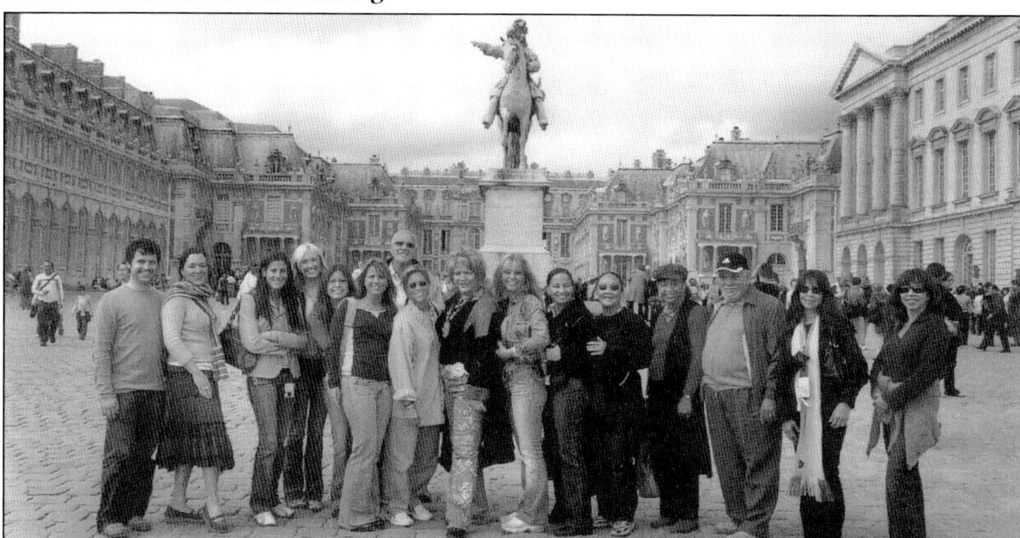

Faculty member Norma Ayee (fifth from the right) was photographed in France at the Chateau De Versailles with interior design department students. The study tour focused on French architecture, art and design, furniture, and textiles. One of the highlights of this trip was a meeting with Patrique Frey, the owner of Pierre Frey, Inc., an internationally renowned textile design and manufacturing company. Also pictured is internationally famous interior designer Perla Lichi (eighth from right), who also serves as a current member of the school's board of trustees. (Courtesy of Norma Ayee.)

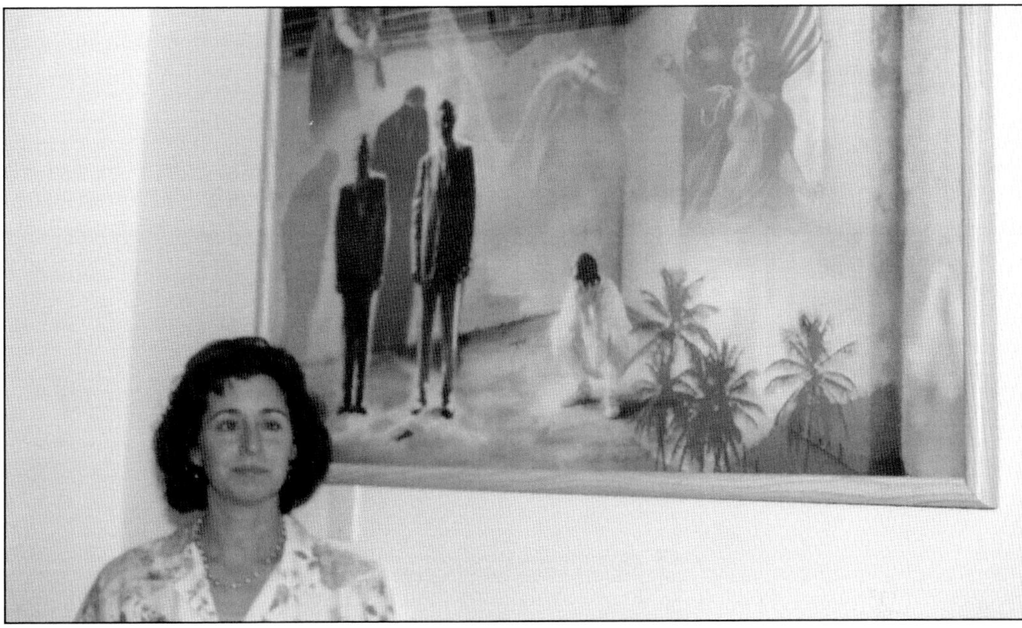

Debbie Rose Myers stands in front of one of her paintings, entitled *Judgment in the Garden*, at a three-woman show at the Wheeler gallery in 2005. When describing this painting, Myers wrote, "The nature of perception is challenged by reality. Although you were taught that there would be a happily ever after . . . life provided alternative endings."

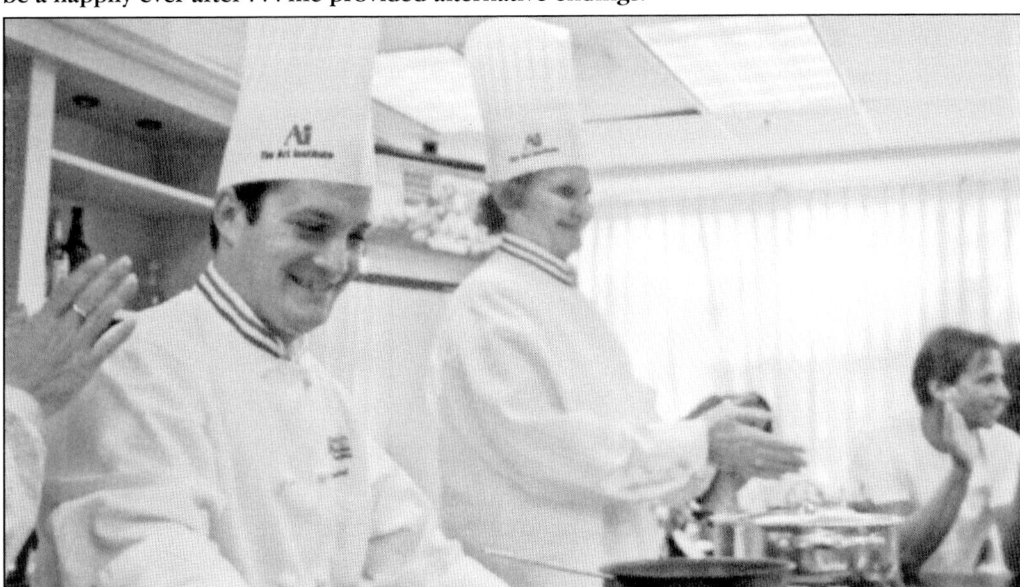

Chef Jeremy Reed and chef Lucy Doll gave an enjoyable and tasty cooking demonstration on Valentine's Day in 2005. The audience was composed of JM Family Enterprises, Inc., volunteers and Big Brothers, Big Sisters of Broward and Palm Beach Counties. Approximately 90 adults and kids prepared healthy snacks such as "ants on a log" (celery sticks stuffed with peanut butter and topped with raisins), and "Brains and Eyeballs" (turkey meatballs with olive centers and tri-colored pasta). As part of the focus on health, the participants also walked over the E. Clay Shaw Jr. Bridge that passes over the Intercoastal Waterway on Seventeenth Street.

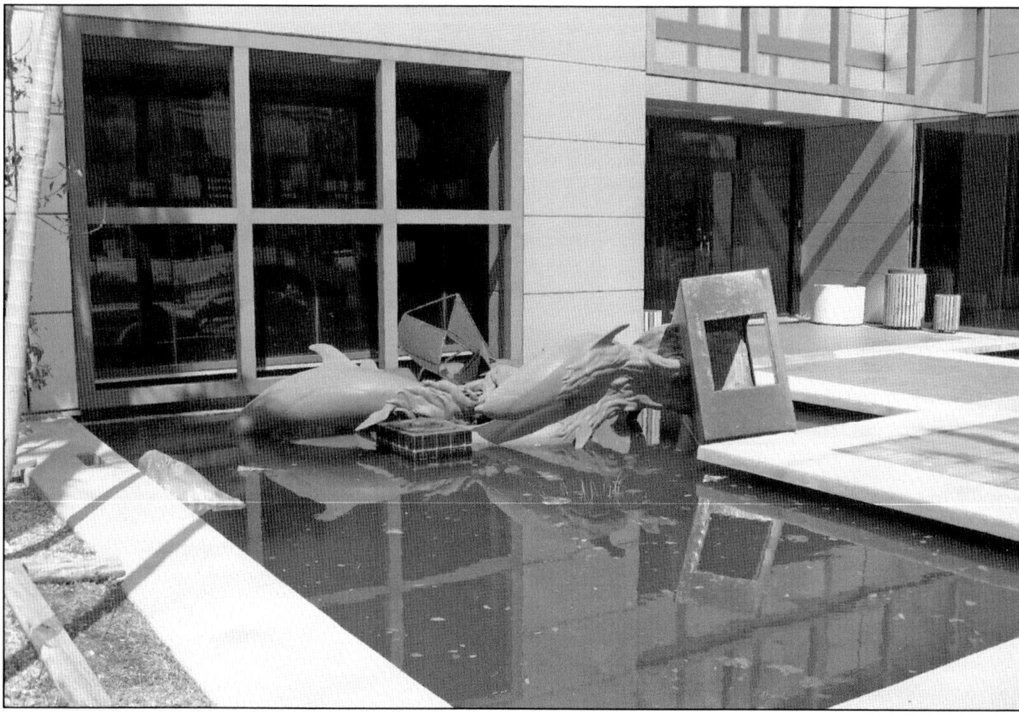

The effects of hurricane Wilma, the most intense hurricane ever recorded in the Atlantic basin, can be seen in these two photographs of the school. Wilma was the 22nd storm, 13th hurricane, 6th major hurricane, and fourth category 5 hurricane of the record-breaking 2005 season. (Both courtesy of Jane Vigna.)

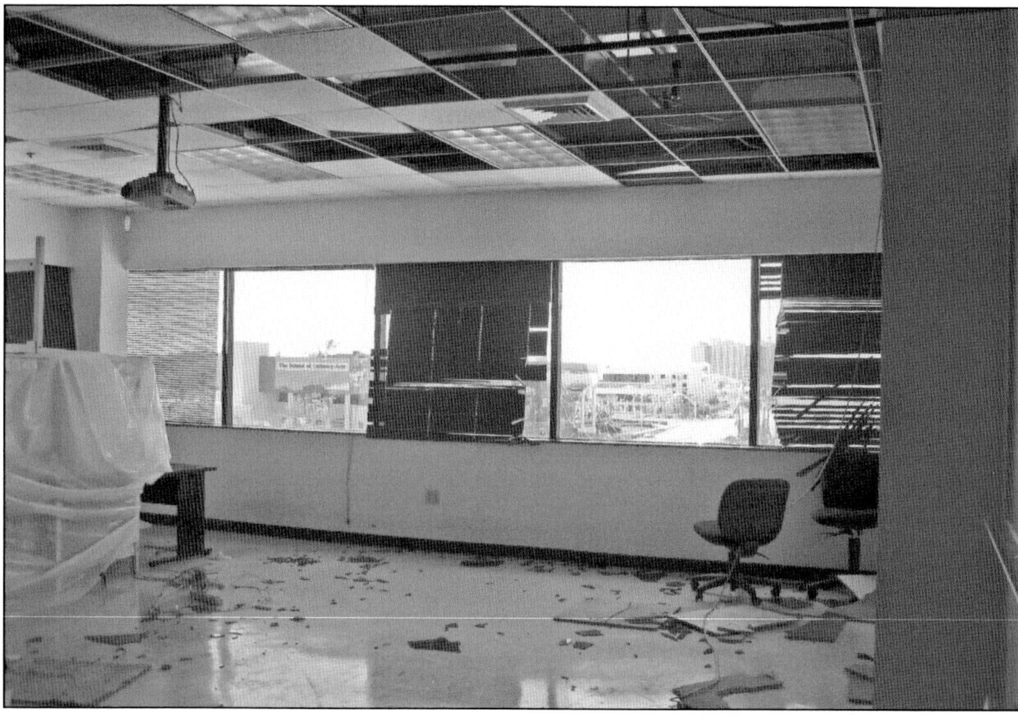

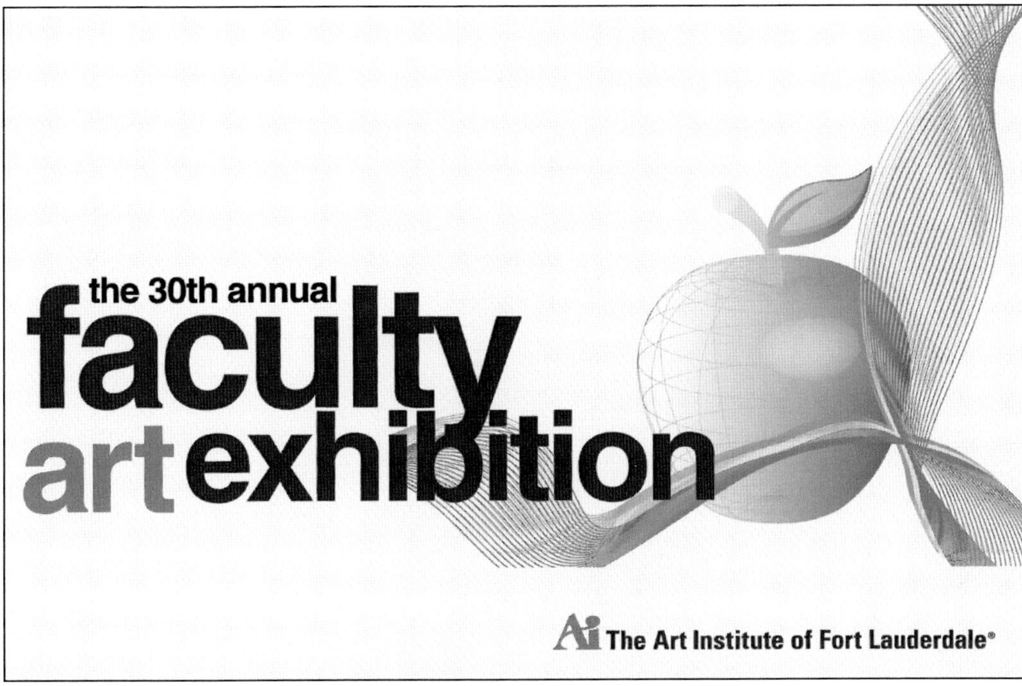

Depicted here is an invitation to the 30th-annual faculty art exhibition in 2007.

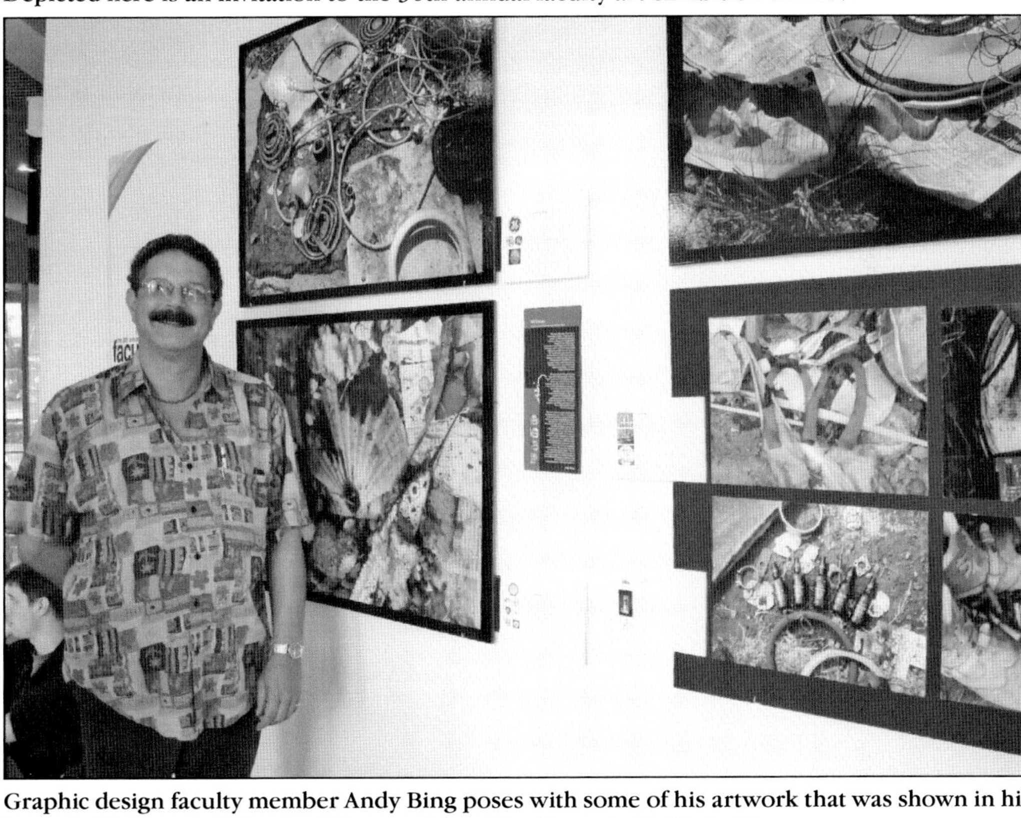

Graphic design faculty member Andy Bing poses with some of his artwork that was shown in his book *Re:Visions. A Collective History of Familiar Logos in Unlikely Places.*

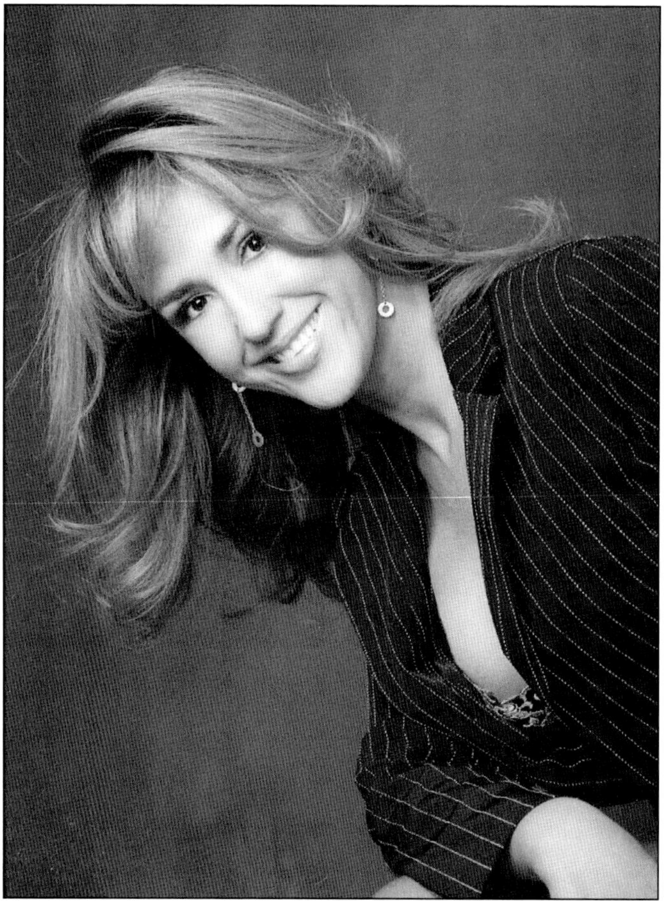

At left is a portrait of Rosita Hurtado, an internationally known fashion designer who graduated from the school. Hurtado was born in Bolivia and studied fashion around the world. She now has an atelier in Miami and is part of international fashion shows, as well as the design world surrounding Latin television productions. Below are several of her creations, worn by her daughter. (All courtesy of Rosita Hurtado.)

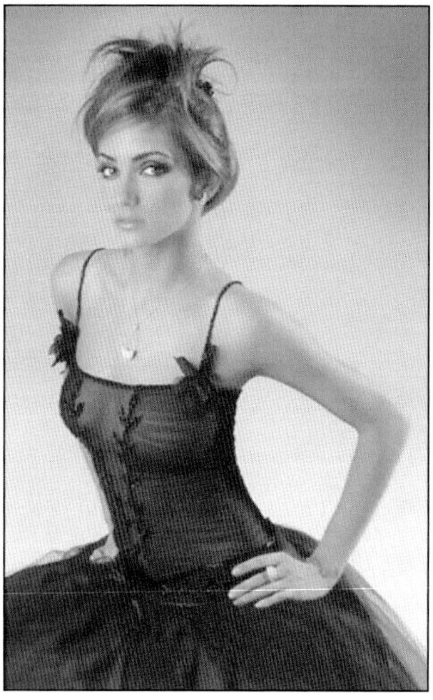

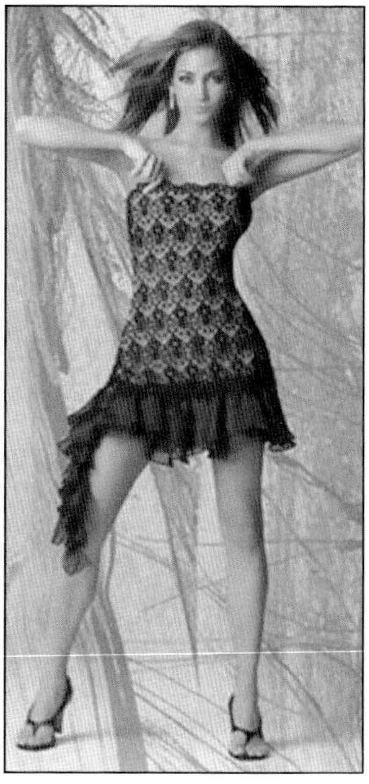

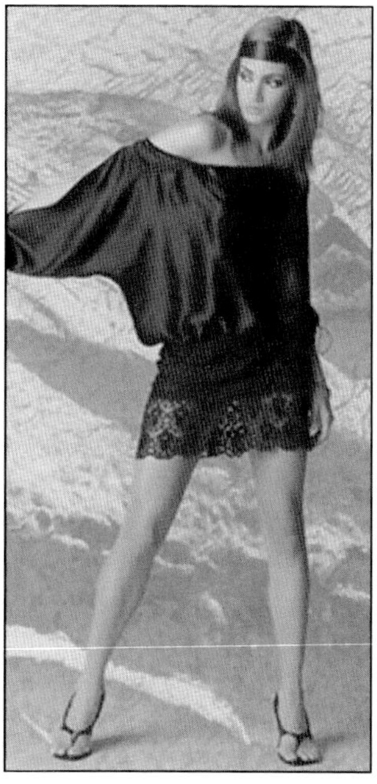

Chef Rob Sobkowski Jr. carved this giant popcorn Mickey Mouse at Disney World. This extremely complicated process was shown on the Food Network television channel in 2006.

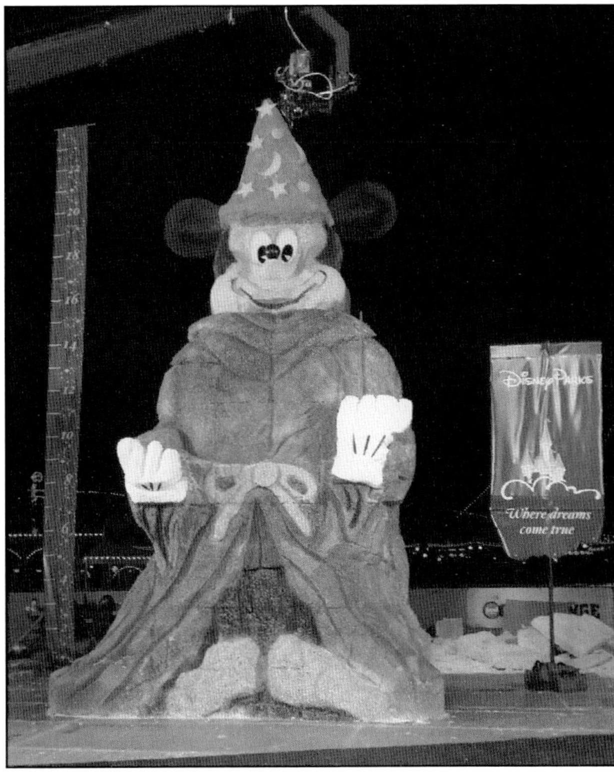

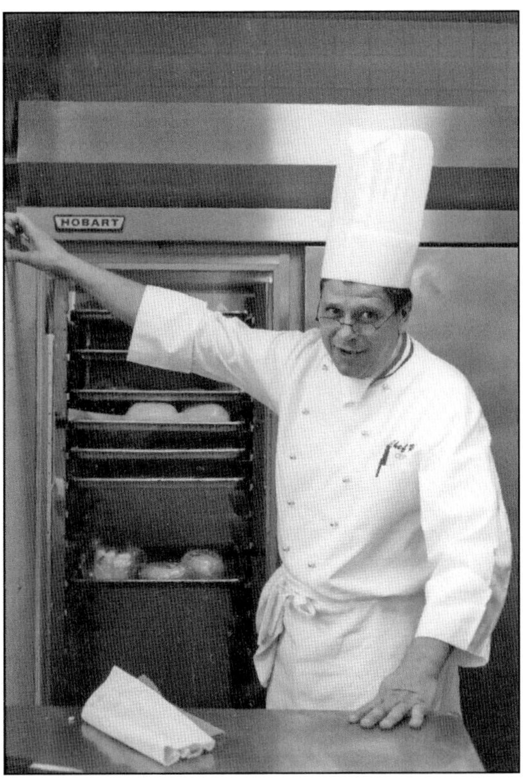

Chef Rob Sobkowski Jr., founder of the business Sensational Chocolates, enjoys a break from class.

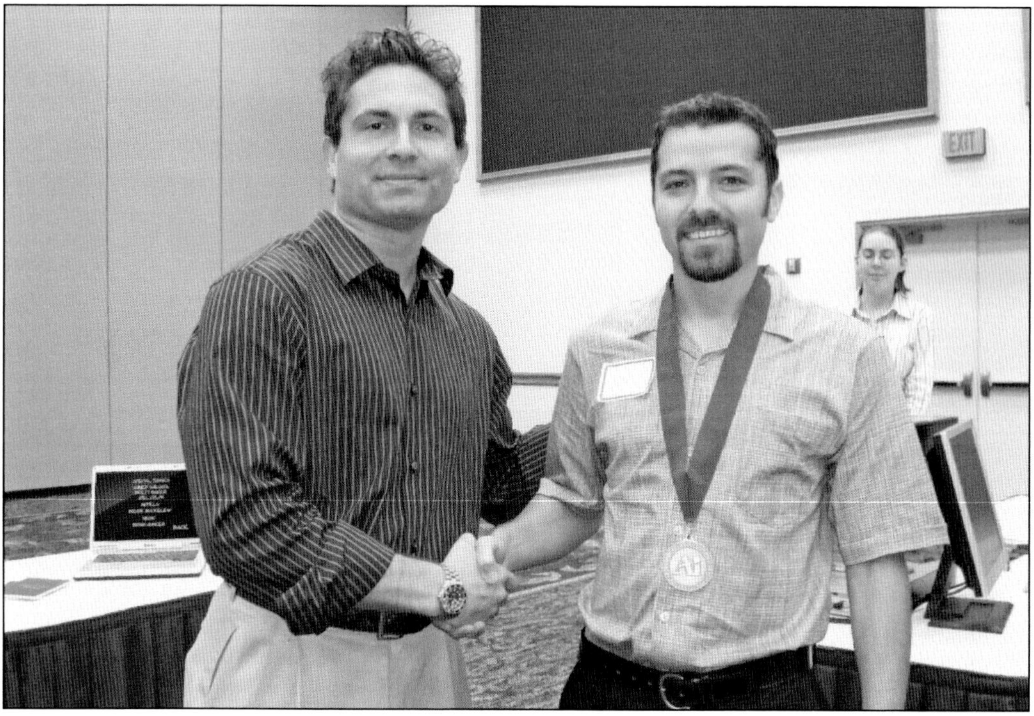

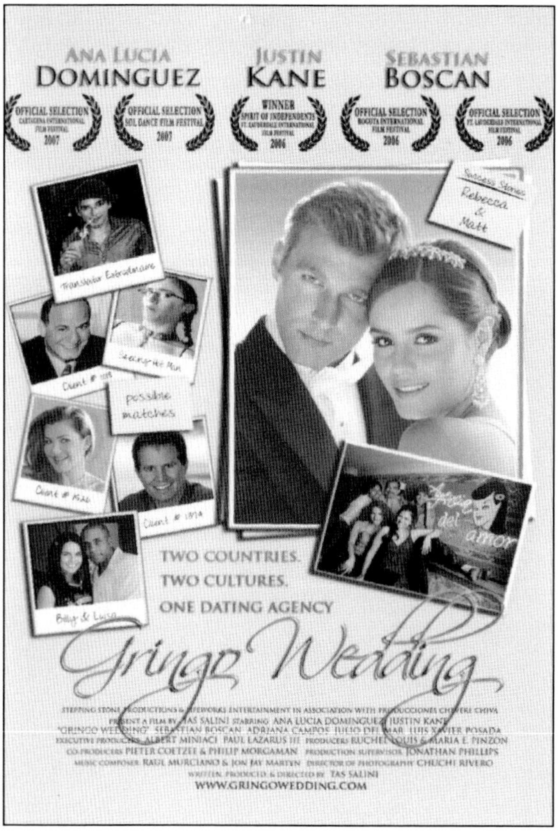

Above, Brett Baker (left), the chair of the visual effects and motion graphics; animation; and game art design department, congratulates Erik E. Echols, who was awarded best print and best digital portfolio in animation during the spring of 2007.

Written, produced, and directed by faculty member Tas Salini, *Gringo Wedding* was a major motion picture and romantic comedy about finding true love through an international dating agency. The movie was shot on locations in Colombia and South Florida. It was released in early 2007.

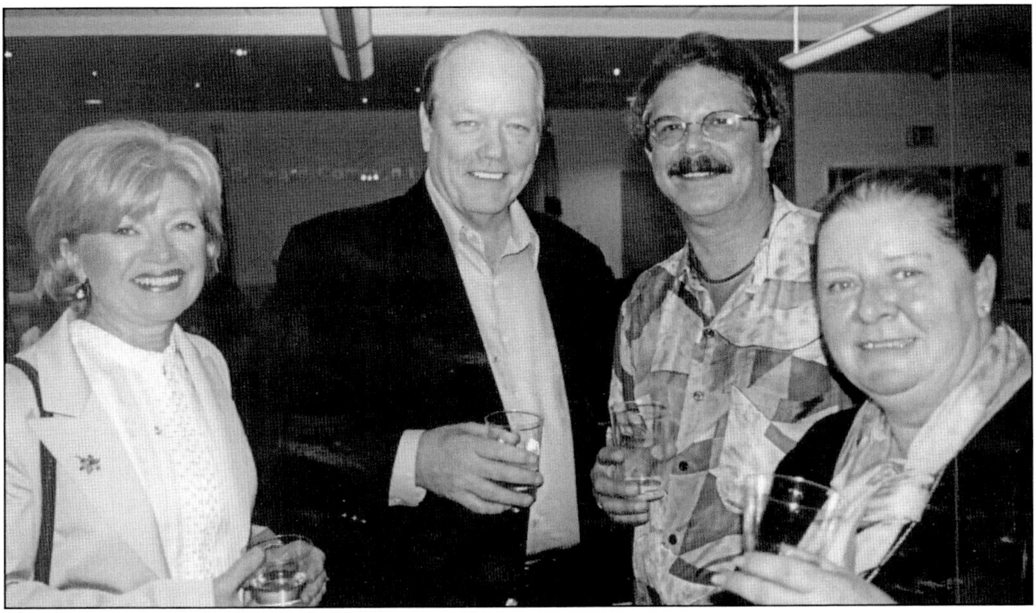

Pictured from left to right are Patricia Nagele, wife of school president Chuck Nagele, President Nagele, Andy Bing and Dr. Monika Reuter at the reception for Altered States—An Exhibit Featuring the Work of Six Extraordinary Fiber Artists, which was held at the administrative art space of the Broward Community College/Florida Atlantic University building in downtown Fort Lauderdale from March 15 through May 5, 2007. Janet Gold, a faculty member at the Art Institute of Fort Lauderdale, was the curator of the show, which featured pieces by Katherine Allen, Kathy Colussy, JoAnne OReilly, Dr. Monika Reuter, Fran Skiles, and Barbara Watler. (Photograph by David Walczak.)

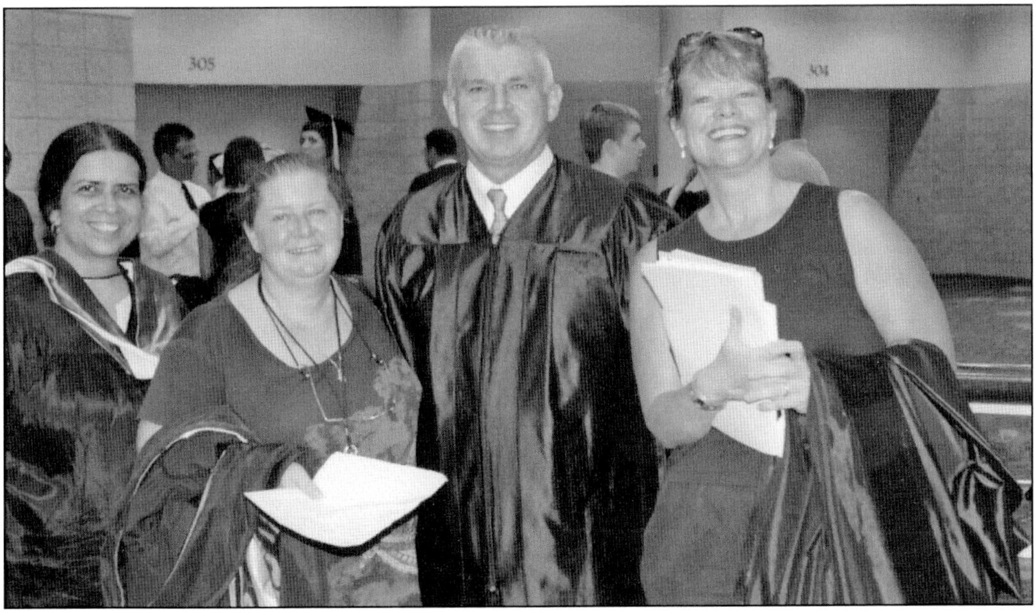

From left to right, English faculty Shefali Choksi, sociologist Dr. Monika Reuter, assistant dean Roger Strait, and English faculty and general education department assistant chair Dr. Kristin Berkey-Abbott pose during the commencement celebration on September 20, 2007. Dr. Reuter was the "Honored Faculty" of the term.

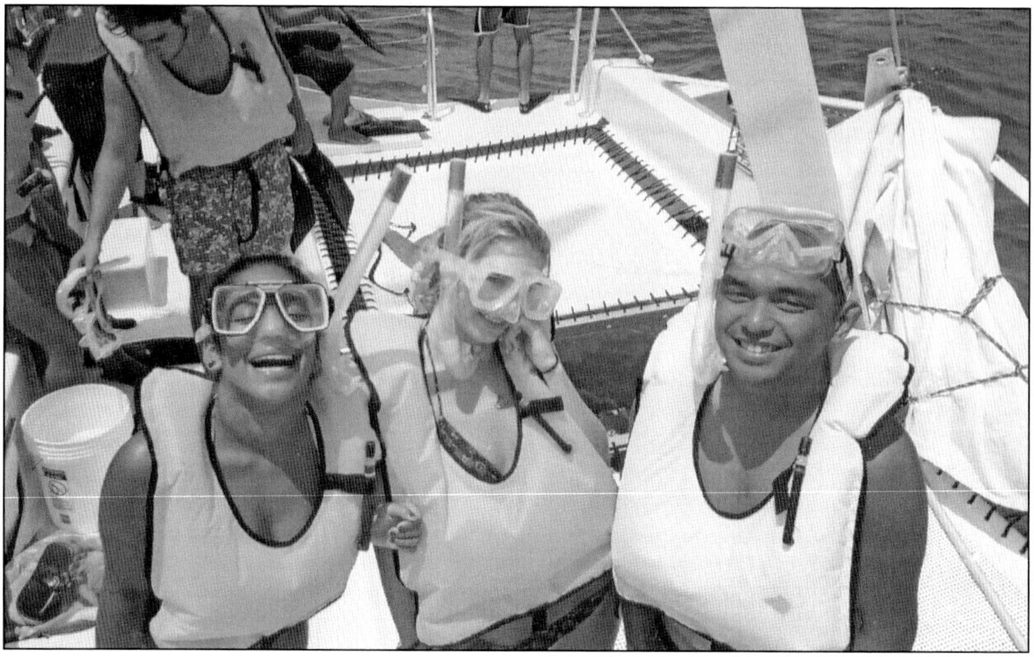

This is a photograph of some students on biologist Stacy Wolfe's quarterly snorkel trip to the National Marine Sanctuary in Key Largo in October 2007. (Courtesy of Stacy Wolfe.)

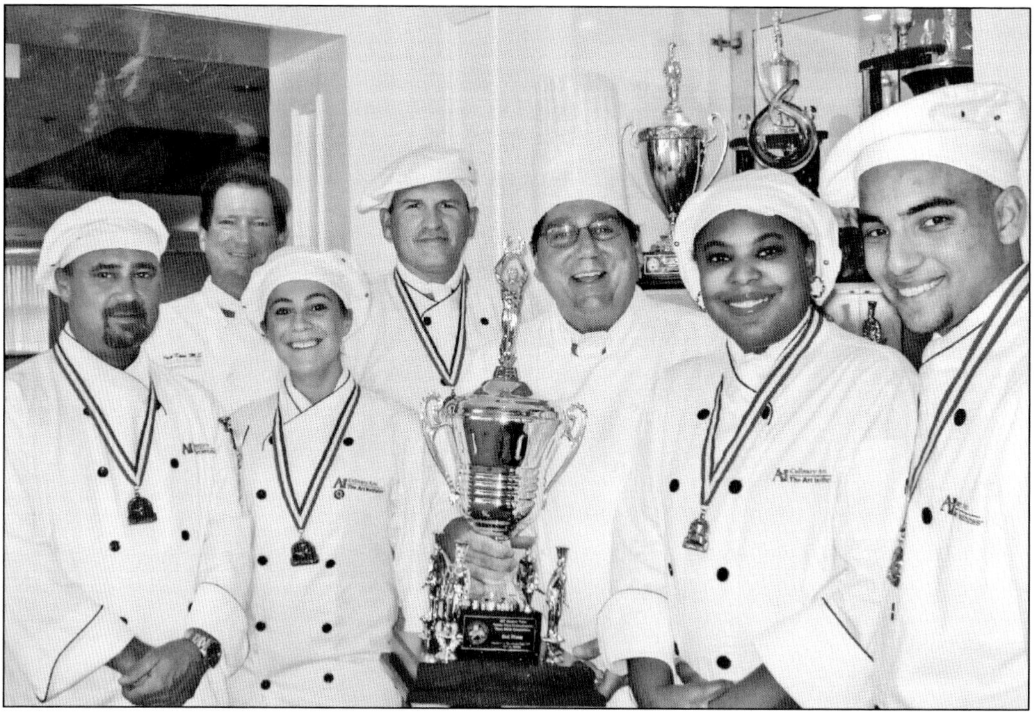

The culinary arts department's competition team won the 2007 American Culinary Federation State of Florida Student Competition in September in Orlando, Florida. Pictured from left to right are culinary arts department chair Jeffery Harmon, chef Jack Kane, Jackie Esposito, Michael Simpson, competition team instructor chef Joe Scarmuzzi, Betty Rose Pradhan, and Michael Pesce.

A bagpiper traditionally leads the president's party to the dais during the commencement ceremony. During the procession, the master of ceremonies reads, "Just as it takes many years for someone to become proficient on the bagpipes, so it takes many years for someone to develop as an artist." (Courtesy of Vicki Izlar and Gradtrak.)

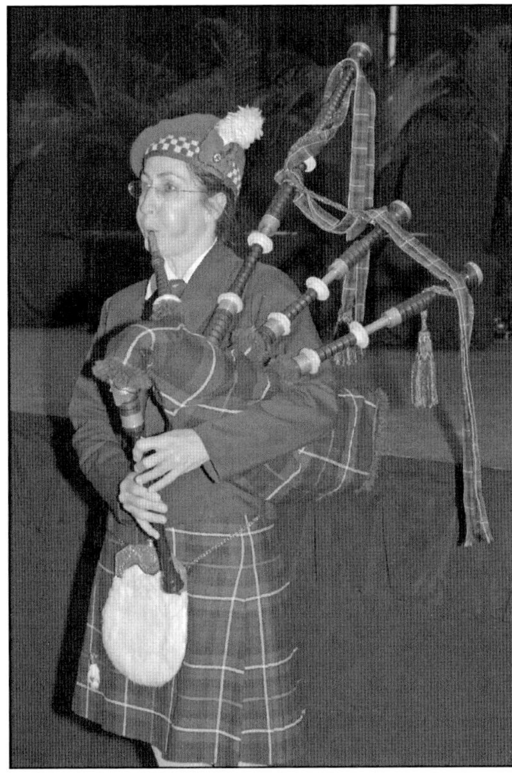

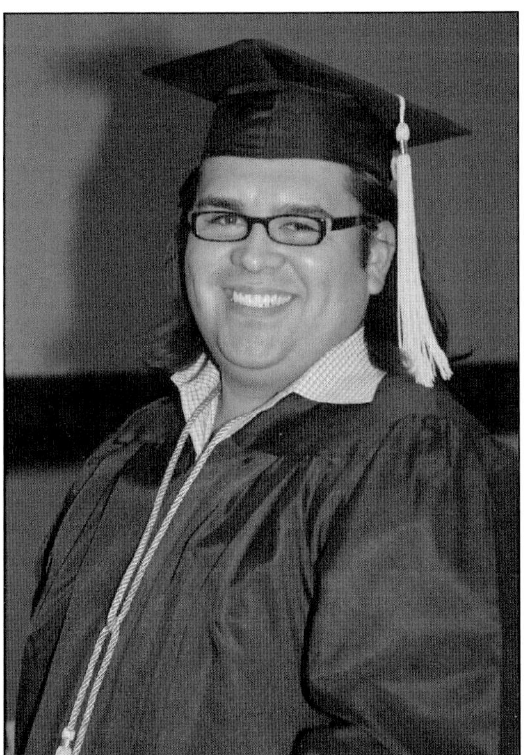

Interior design graduate Val Vigil was the student speaker during the fall of 2007 commencement ceremony. Vigil works for the Art Institute today. (Courtesy of Vicki Izlar and Gradtrak.)

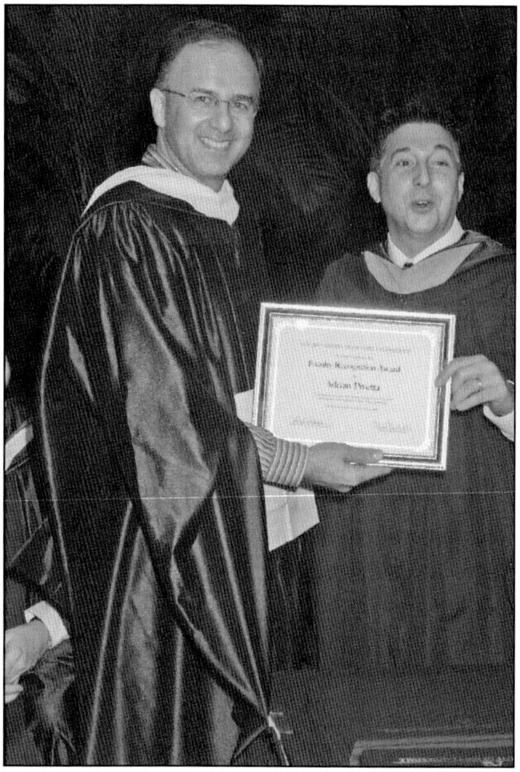

Faculty member Adrian Pivetta is pictured with dean of education Ed Galizia (right) during a graduation ceremony. Pivetta received recognition as the faculty member of the term during this occasion. (Courtesy of Vicki Izlar and Gradtrak.)

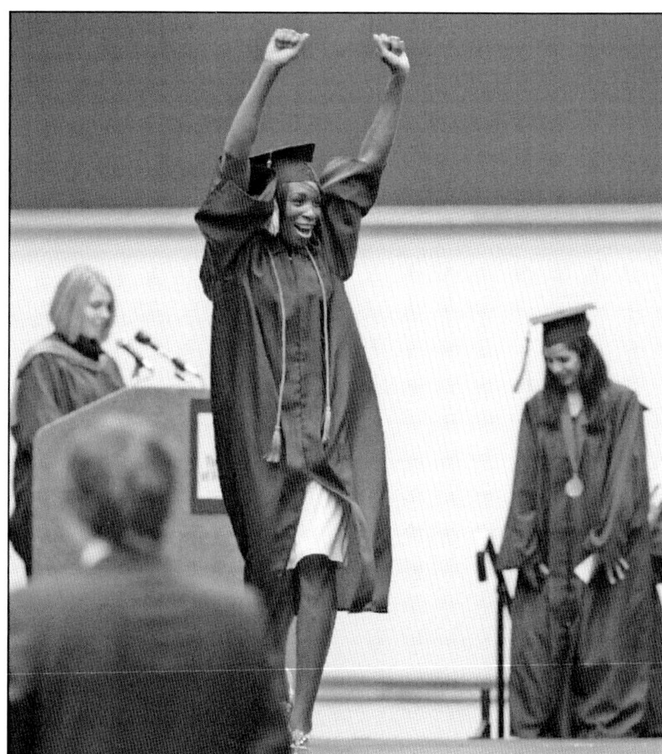

Venus Williams celebrates during the graduation ceremony in 2007. She earned an associate's degree in fashion from the Art Institute of Fort Lauderdale. (Courtesy of Vicki Izlar and Gradtrak.)

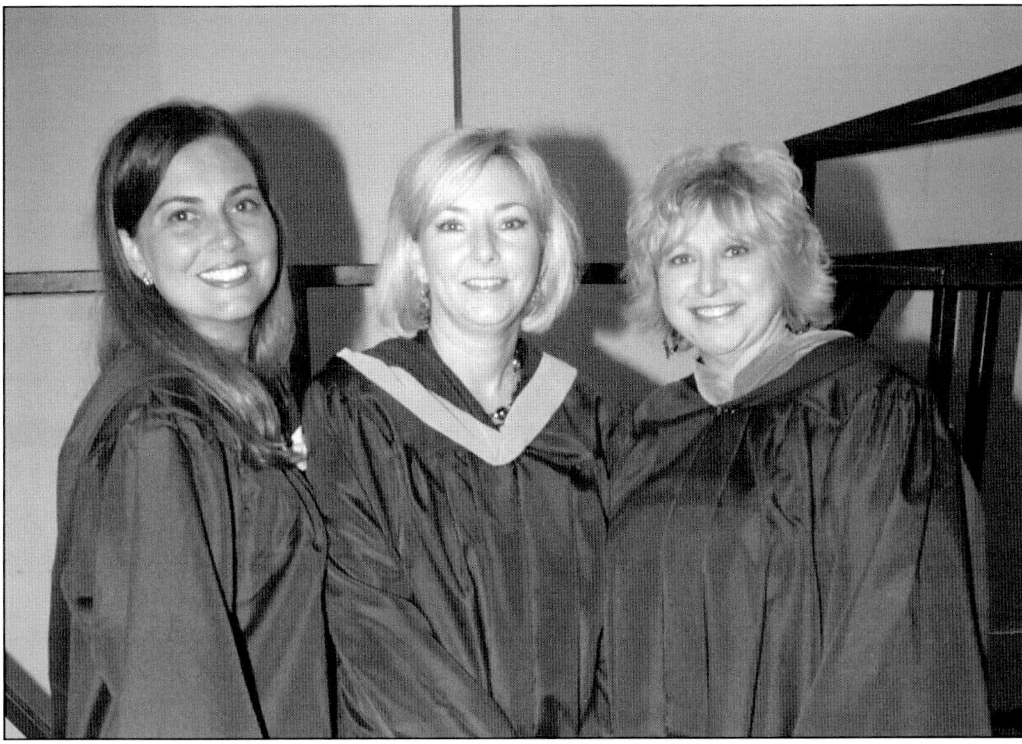

From left to right, executive committee members Lisa Whitelock (director of human resources), Wendy Wagner (director of career services), and Kathy Deaner (dean of student services) gather before commencement.

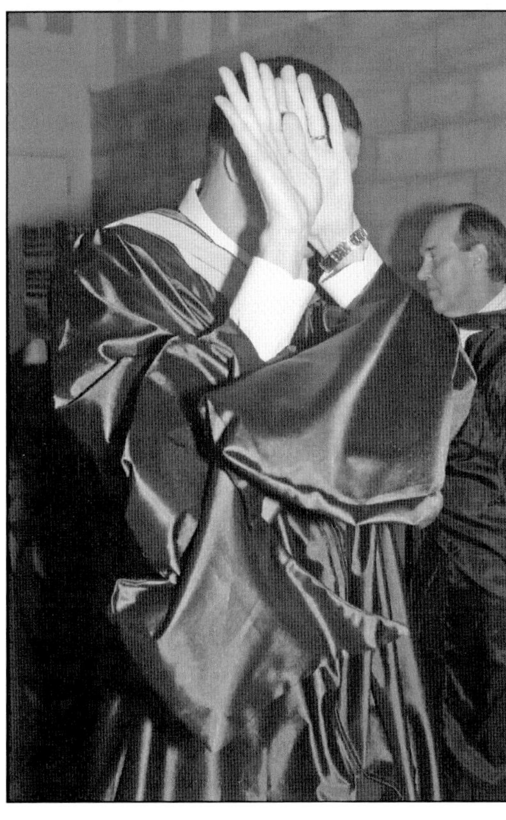

Photography department chair Will Cadieux does not want to be photographed!

1968-2008
40 YEARS
The Art Institute of Fort Lauderdale®

This is the logo, designed by instructor Andy Bing, for the school's 40th anniversary.

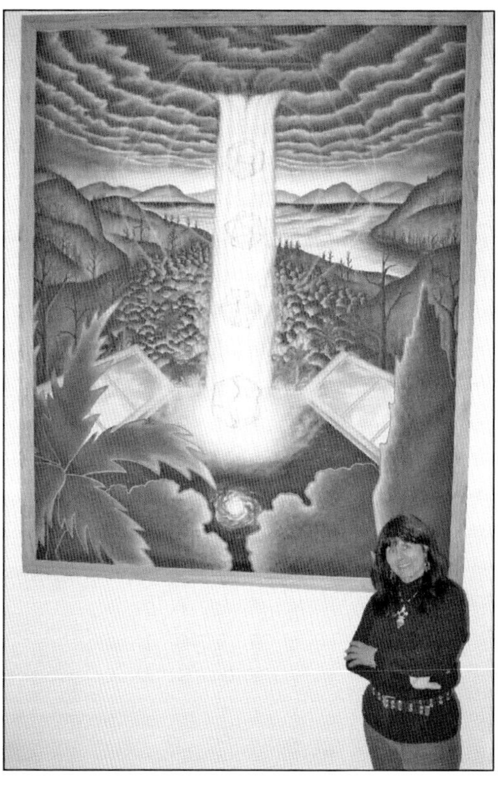

Mimi Botscheller painted *The Earth Comes Back for What It Wants.* (Photograph by Ms. V.)

At right is a portrait of Dr. Peter West, who became the dean for academic affairs in January 2008.

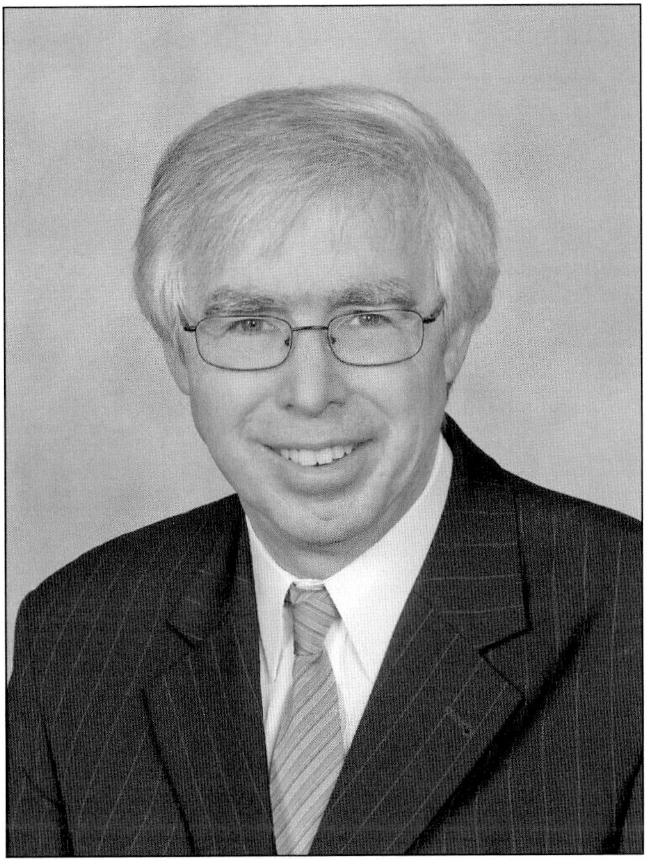

Pictured below in 2008 are animation faculty member Randy Gossman and Chriss David, chairwoman of graphic design and advertising, and director of the Artemis group.

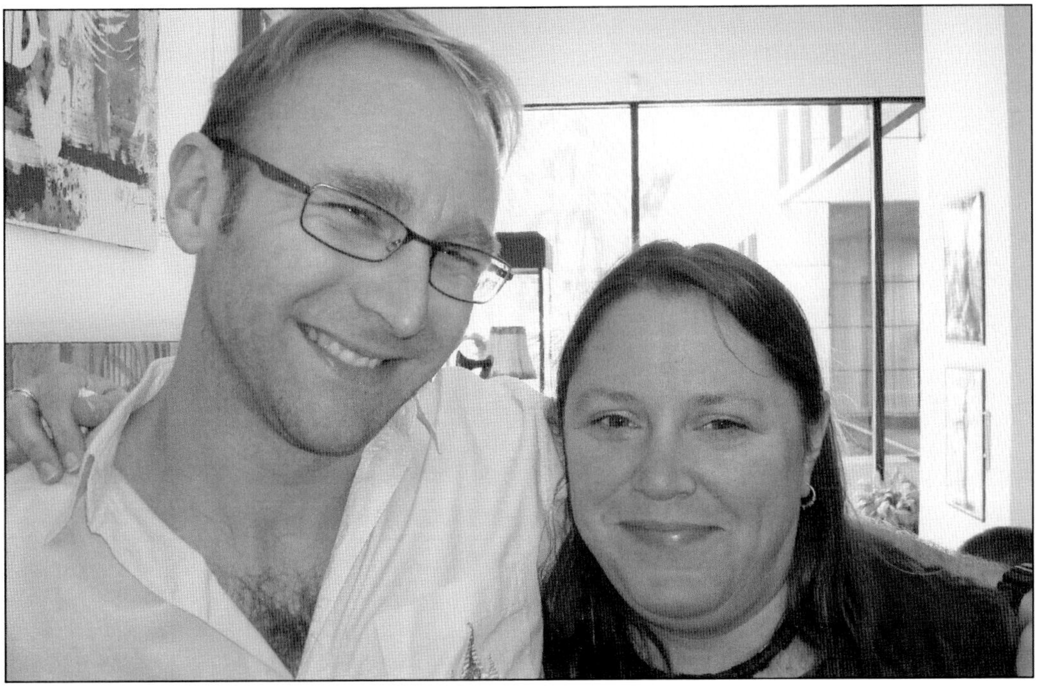

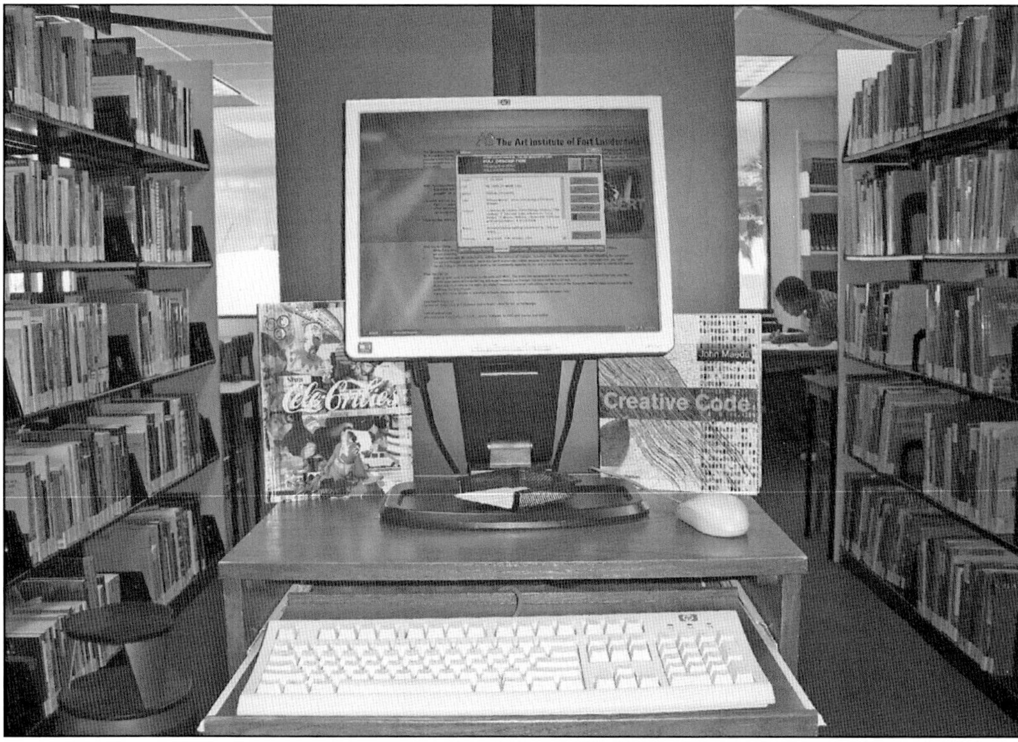

The library moved into this location in the summer of 2004 after the school acquired the third floor of the Harbor Place building, located to the west of the Harbor Walk building. Pictured here are 2008 photographs of the central reading area, including a computer station for searching the collection and the bookstand adjacent to a workstation. (Both photographs by Melanie Levi.)

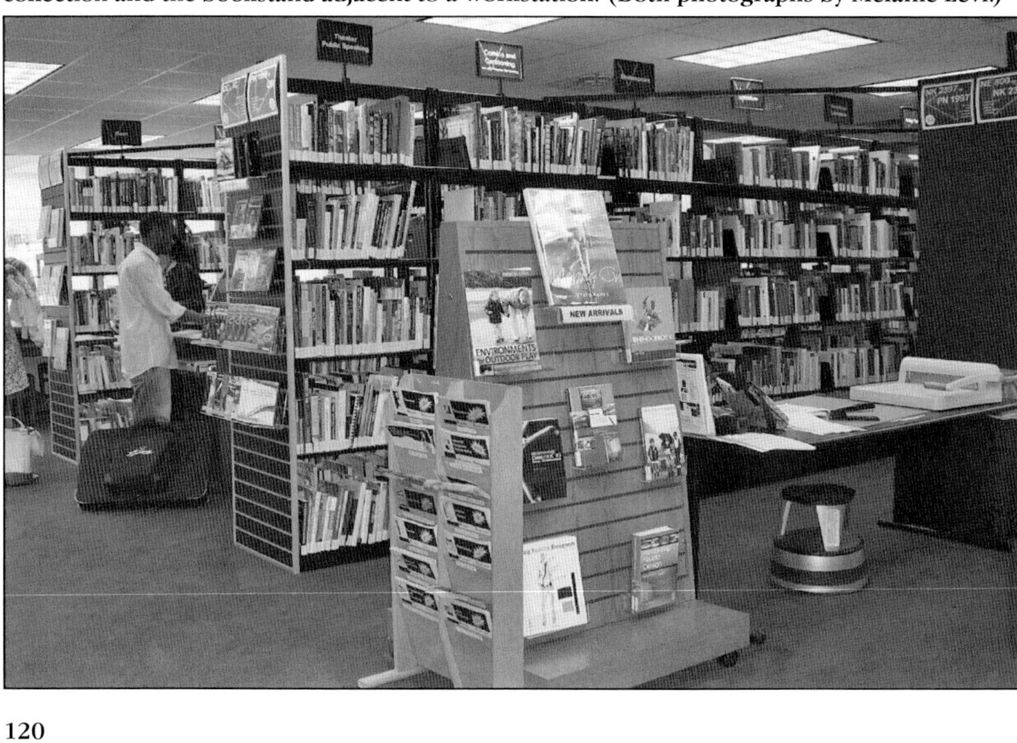

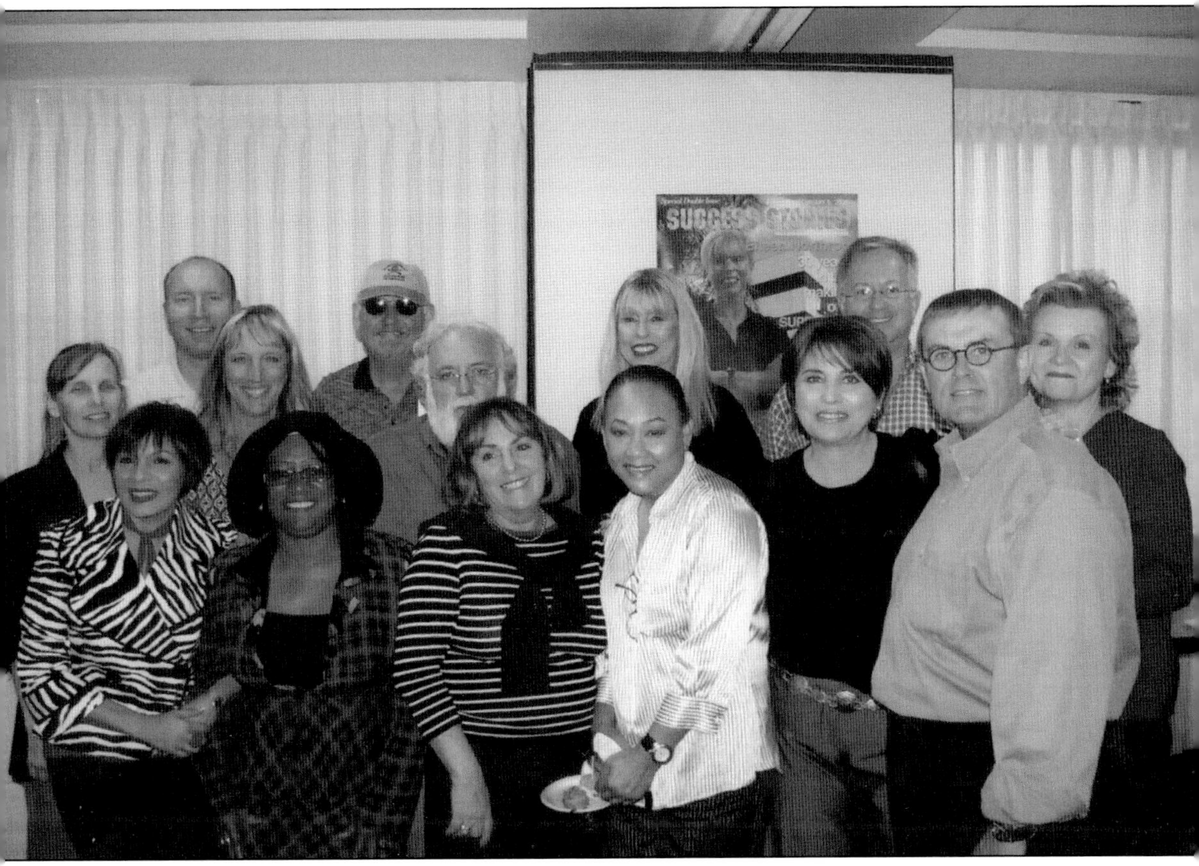

Eileen Northrop (standing in the back beside a poster depicting her photograph) retired in early 2008. She was vice president and director of admissions. Celebrating her retirement with her are, from left to right, (first row) Celeste Birger (an school veteran of 13 years), Lee Tufts (20 years), Jodi Berkshire (started in 1976 as a part-time instructor), Norma Ayee (29 years), Kim Moss (16 years), and Bill Kobrynich (31 years); (second row) Joy Cummings (18 years), Daniel Toye (18 years), Kim Farmer (18 years), Pete Hughes (24 years), Gary Tepper (28 years), Eileen Northrop, Buck Miller (29 years), and Maria Barron (25 years). (Photography by David Walczak.)

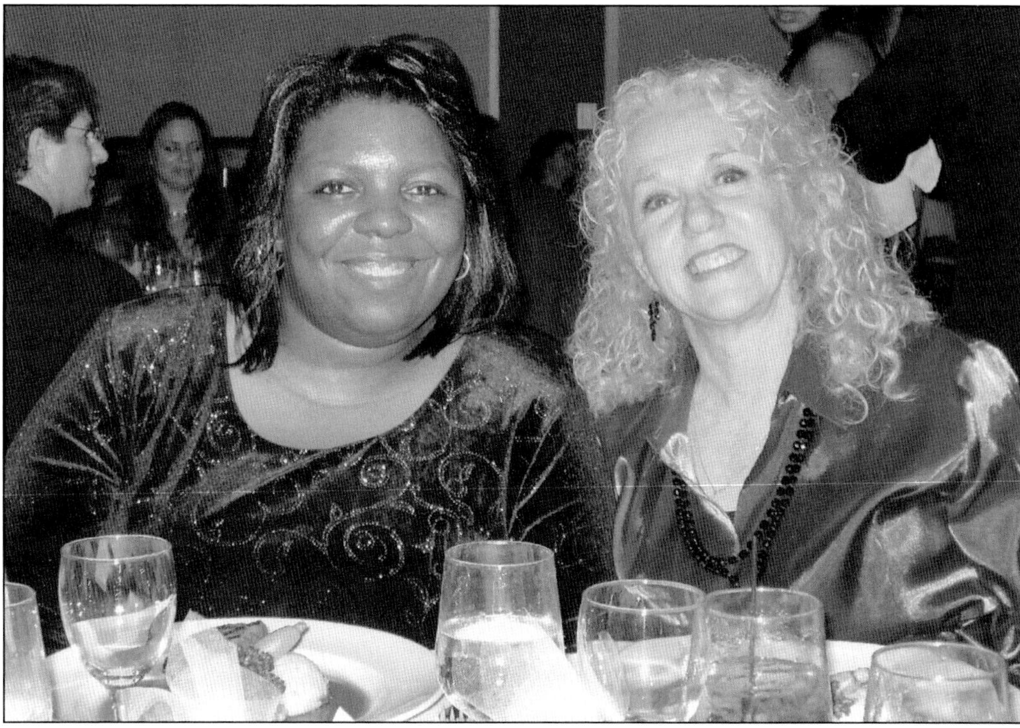

Graphic design student Kimberly Moore (left) won a Silver ADDY award in the collateral material category in the winter of 2008. Celebrating with her is Linda Weeks. Annual ADDY awards are given by the advertising federation of the greater Fort Lauderdale area to honor local businesses and agencies for advertising excellence.

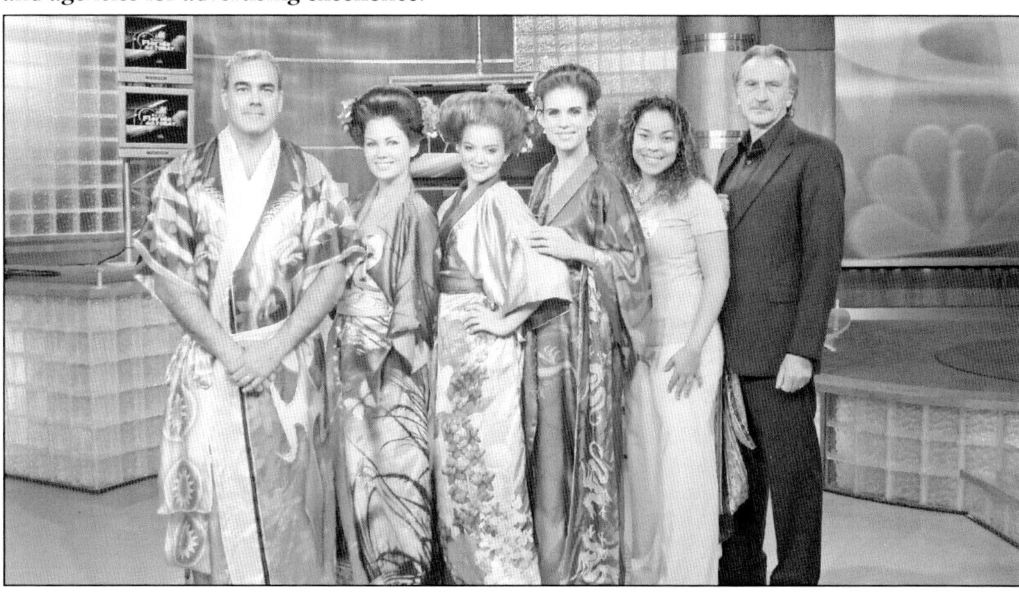

From left to right, fashion design department chairman Andre West, students Dena Venable, Fabianna Negro, Serena Foster, and Sheila Rodriquez, and graphic artist Ciro Marchetti visit the local NBC television studio to promote the Cherry Blossom Festival kimonos to benefit the Florida Opera Society.

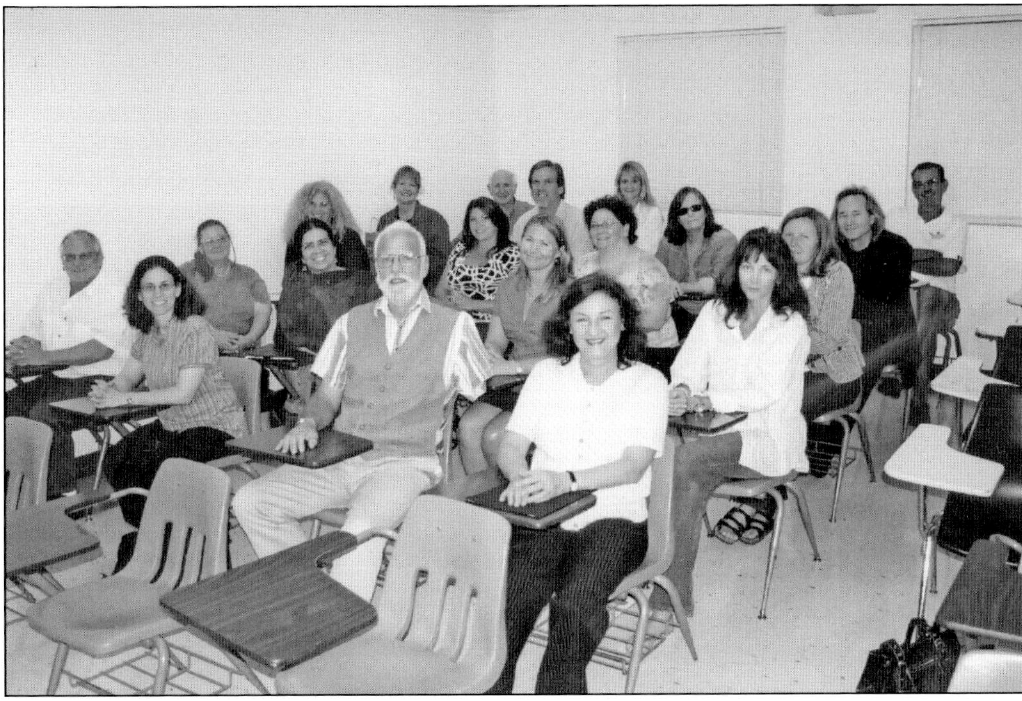

General education faculty are pictured during a March 28, 2008, faculty meeting. Starting with the row against the wall, from left to right, are (first row) Dr. David Walczak, Dr. Monika Reuter, Lori Kerrigan, Dr. Kristin Berkey-Abbott, and Sean Quilter; (second row) Deborah Posner, Shefali Choksi, Stacy Wolfe, Ben Ruby, and Kristin Stover; (third row) Dr. Victor Garlock, Melanie Neale, Annemarie Jameson, and Mary Ardiff; (fourth row) Helena Snyder, Nancy Doyle, Dr. Andrea Larson, Gary Fallon, and Gary Gilbert. (Photograph by Alicia Nestor.)

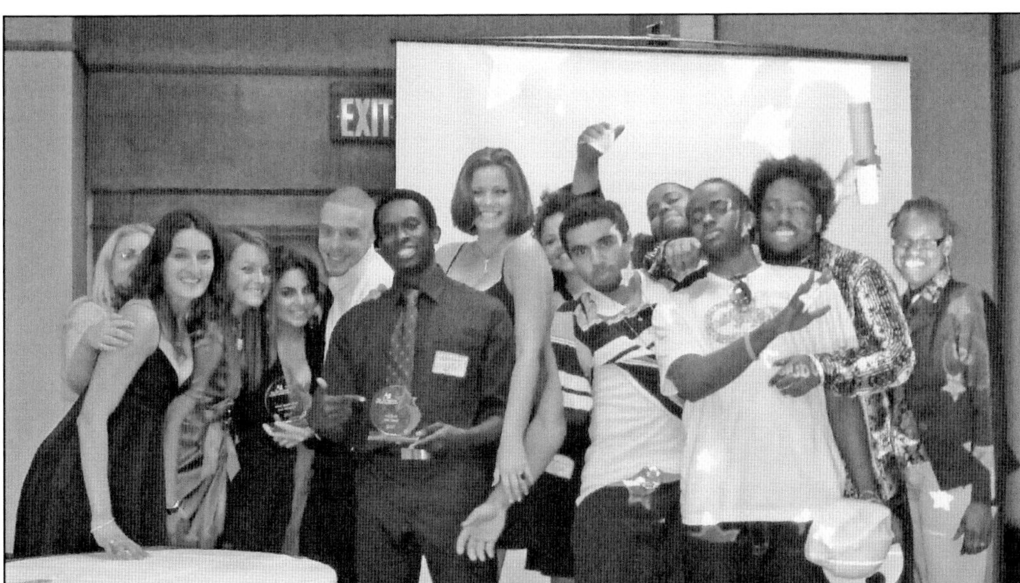

Students and staff celebrate the first annual student recognition and awards gala at the Embassy Suites hotel in 2008.

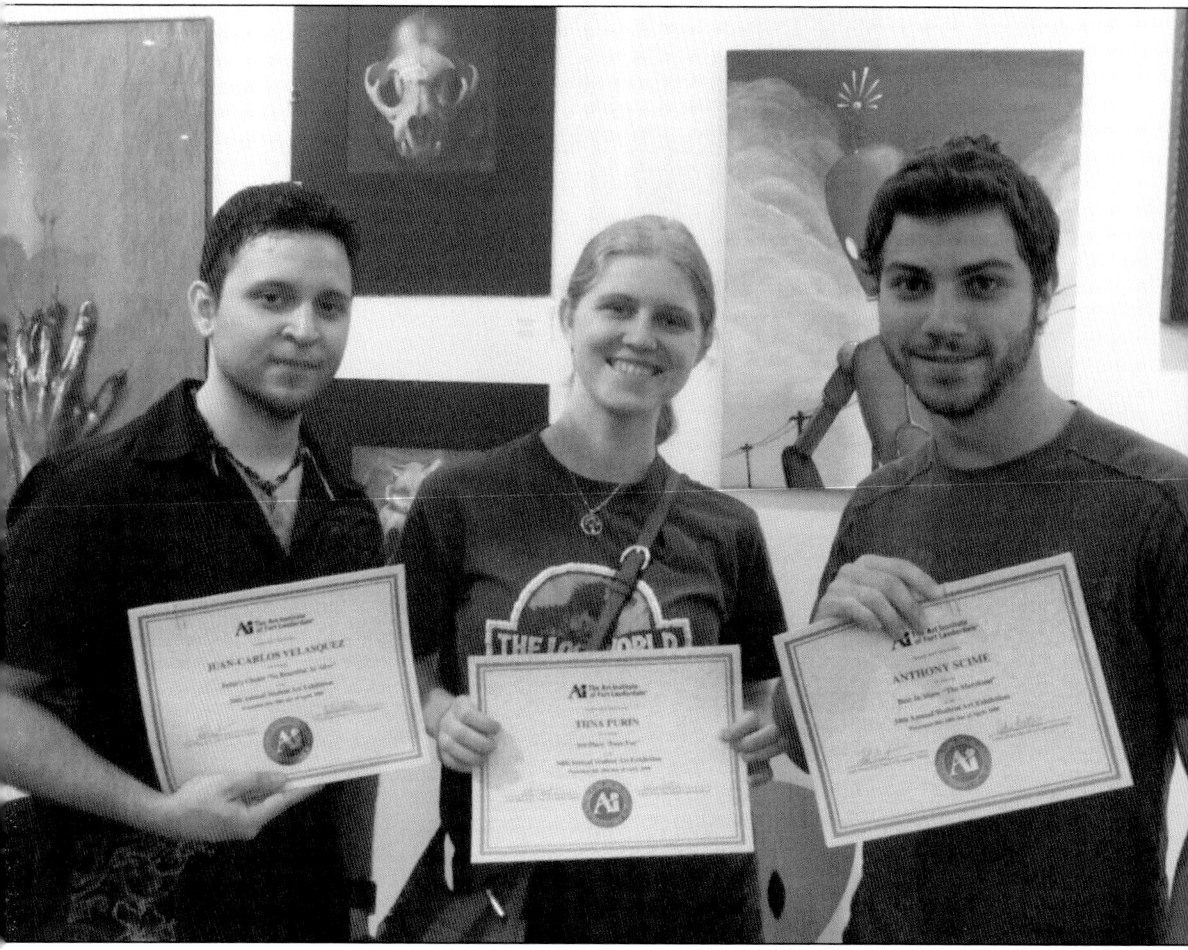

These students are among the winners of the 34th-annual juried student art exhibit. Pictured from left to right, are Juan-Carlos Velasquez, who won the judges choice award; Tiina Purin, who won third place; and Anthony Scime, who won first place and best in show.

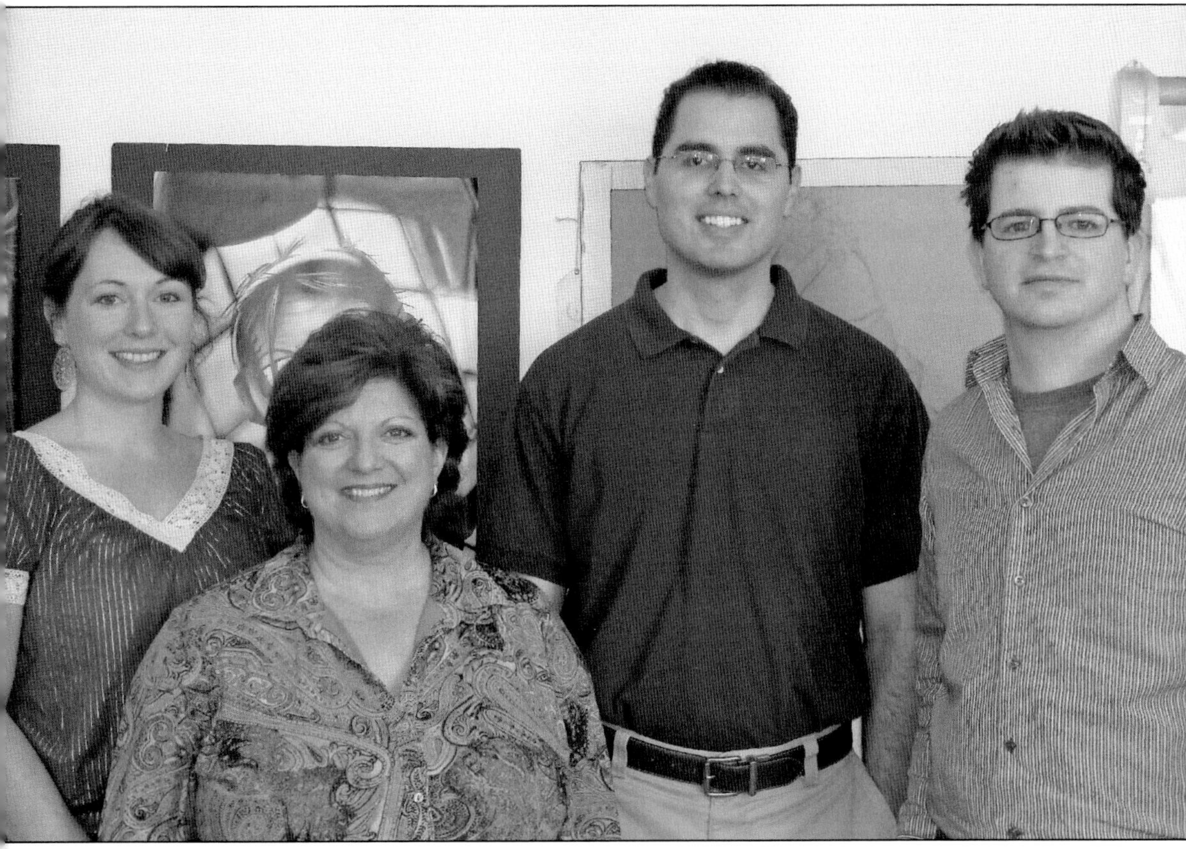

Arlene Wites, director of communication (second from left) poses with her staff: (from left to right) Melanie De Vito, assistant director of communication; Ramon Diaz, web coordinator; and Scott LeBlanc, art director.

CHARLIE CRIST
GOVERNOR

September 16, 2008

Dear Friends:

Congratulations to The Art Institute of Fort Lauderdale on celebrating your 40th Anniversary!

Art education provides many opportunities for Floridians to explore careers in the field of creative arts. Since 1968, The Art Institute of Fort Lauderdale has been instrumental in the development of professional, productive, and successful artists.

Thank you to The Art Institute of Fort Lauderdale for helping to launch many aspiring artists into their careers. Your dedication has impacted the lives of many individuals throughout the Sunshine State.

Again, congratulations on celebrating your 40th anniversary!

Sincerely,

Charlie Crist

THE CAPITOL
TALLAHASSEE, FLORIDA 32399 • (850) 488-2272 • FAX (850) 922-4292

Florida governor Charlie Crist congratulated the Art Institute of Fort Lauderdale in a letter on the occasion of its 40th anniversary.

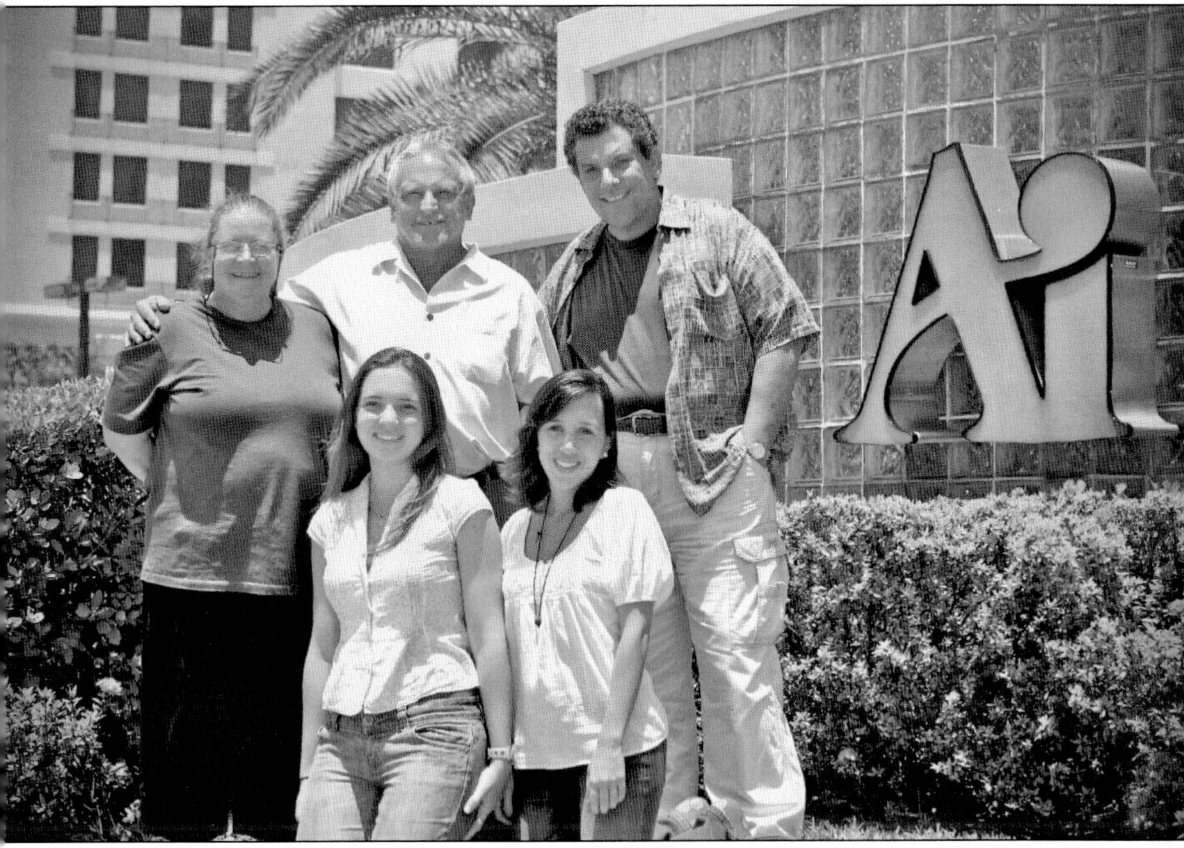

This is the Art Institute of Fort Lauderdale team that assembled this book. Pictured from left to right are (first row) Artemis students Marinés Espinoza and Daniela Stolk; (second row) coauthors Dr. Monika Reuter and Dr. David Walczak, along with Artemis Design Honors Group director and instructor Paul Kane. (Photograph by Justin Braithwaite.)

Discover Thousands of Local History Books Featuring Millions of Vintage Images

Arcadia Publishing, the leading local history publisher in the United States, is committed to making history accessible and meaningful through publishing books that celebrate and preserve the heritage of America's people and places.

Find more books like this at
www.arcadiapublishing.com

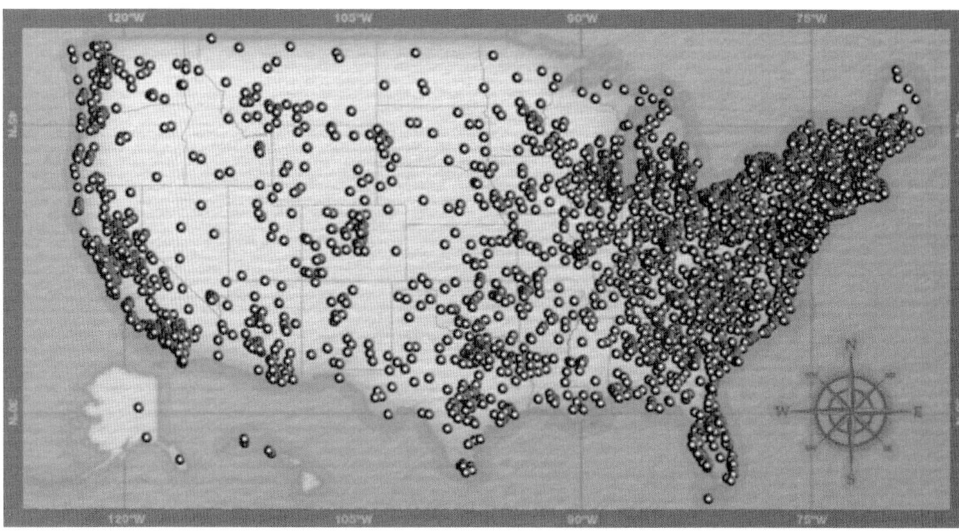

Search for your hometown history, your old stomping grounds, and even your favorite sports team.

Consistent with our mission to preserve history on a local level, this book was printed in South Carolina on American-made paper and manufactured entirely in the United States. Products carrying the accredited Forest Stewardship Council (FSC) label are printed on 100 percent FSC-certified paper.

MADE IN THE USA